I'LL TELL THE JOKES ARTHUR

ARTHUR EDWARDS
WITH
JUDY WADE

BLAKE

Published by Blake Publishing Ltd,
98–100 Great North Road, London N2 0NL, England

First published in Great Britain in 1993

ISBN 1 85782 0495

British Library Cataloguing-in-Publication Data: A catalogue
record for this book is available from the British Library.

Typeset by BMD Graphics, Hemel Hempstead

Printed by WSOY, Finland

1 3 5 7 9 10 8 6 4 2

DEDICATION

This book is dedicated to my wife Ann, for patiently
putting up with all the times I was with the Royal Family and
not my own. It is also for three fine people, my children
John, Paul and Annmarie.

Contents

ACKNOWLEDGEMENTS

In 1990 a memo was issued to everyone on the Prince and Princess of Wales's staff by Commander Richard Aylard. It warned them all not to speak to any journalists, not to acknowledge them in any way. It is my good fortune that some of them were brave enough to disregard this order from on high. If they had not, this book would not have been possible to write.

I would like to thank all of these people, many good friends of mine, who for obvious reasons cannot be named. Some just wanted to set the record straight, while others wished to help with this project. Many other generous souls contributed by giving freely of their time, experience and expert knowledge. I am grateful to Judy Wade for nagging me to get started five years ago and for her input up to the finish, to Stuart Higgins for his inspiration and amazingly helpful contacts, to Robert Jobson for providing vital information I couldn't dig up myself, to Martin Keene who encouraged me to continue, and for advising me on the illustrations in this book. Credit must also go to Tony and Hilary Scase, Fiona MacDonald-Hull, Dave Shapland, Peter Grose, and Jim Bennett. And my special thanks to Kelvin MacKenzie for bullying me into getting this book written.

CHAPTER ONE

I'm Spreading My Wings

The Princess of Wales walked in to the throne room of the British Ambassador's residence in Paris with her private secretary Patrick Jephson. Towering over everyone in her spiky high heels, she cut a dramatic figure in a slinky black velvet dress slashed with red satin down one side.

'You look stunning,' I said.

In reply, she raised her fists high and shimmied like a go-go dancer. 'Do you really think so?' she asked with a jokey attempt at coyness.

'Yes,' I said, laughing at her wiggling figure. And indicating her curly hairdo I added: 'And I love the barnet.'

The Ambassador, Sir Ewen Fergusson, who had joined us, accompanied by his wife, looked puzzled. 'What's a barnet?'

The Princess laughed. 'Oh, that's Barnet Fair – hair,' she said, explaining the Cockney rhyming slang. Flicking one blonde lock, she added: 'I think it's much better than some of those hairstyles I've had in the past.'

I had been called to the embassy to take a group picture of the Princess with her household, a copy of which would be given to each member of the party as a memento of the Paris trip. They were all gathered in the splendid throne room of the mansion in the Faubourg Saint Honoré which had once belonged to the Duke of Wellington after Waterloo. When the five-minute photo session was over I had been invited to stay for a drink.

'I'm just going to do some presentations to the embassy staff,' the Princess said as she disappeared through a door, promising to return in a few minutes.

With Geoff Crawford, the Palace press secretary for the French trip, I walked through to the drawing room and waited while the Princess thanked everyone who had worked on her three-day visit to France.

She returned just as her sister, Lady Sarah McCorquodale, who had accompanied her on the trip as lady-in-waiting, came in to ask if her dress was too long. Sarah, who is several inches shorter than her sister, was wearing a blue silk cocktail dress that I had seen the Princess wearing four years earlier in New York. The Ambassador promptly dropped on to his knees and lifted the hem of Sarah's skirt three or four inches to see what effect it would have. 'Let's get some pins and see how it looks,' he joked.

Diana examined his efforts and kicked off her high-heeled shoes. 'Here, try on my tart's trotters,' she said, shoving them towards her sister.

'They look much too big for her,' I suggested.

'Yes, I know, but they will make her legs look much nicer,' Diana giggled as she sipped a glass of champagne.

'Ooh, I couldn't wear heels this high,' Sarah groaned as she tried to stagger around in her sister's black stilettos. 'They might give me varicose veins,' she added, taking them off again.

Diana turned to the Ambassador. 'We're both worried about getting varicose veins because Mummy's got them,' she explained.

This informal, family chit-chat revealed a Princess I had never seen before. All day long she had been the concerned charity worker, visiting an AIDS information centre, watching young ballet stars perform and visiting the handicapped in Paris. Now, off-duty, she was having fun.

The happy, intimate atmosphere was infectious. Even the Ambassador joined in with the jokes. Still on his knees after altering Sarah's dress, he pretended to grovel.

'Lower, lower, your nose must touch the carpet,' the Princess teased. But her attempt to appear disdainful was ruined by a fit of giggles. She took another sip of champagne and walked over to a grand piano where Sarah had begun to play something classical. Setting her glass down, Diana joined in an impromptu duet, delighting us all with their accomplished performance. It was obvious the two sisters regularly performed together and they beamed and bowed as we applauded at the end.

She asked if I was feeling jet-lagged. We had returned from an arduous tour of Korea and Hong Kong only two days before leaving for France, and perhaps the effects were still obvious.

'I'm fine now,' I said. 'Do you suffer from jet-lag?'

Diana shook her head. 'I don't suffer jet-lag when I'm coming home east to west. But it really affects me going the other way, west to east. I was fine coming home, but on the way out to Korea I took three sleeping tablets and I still couldn't close my eyes. I was like a zombie when I arrived in Seoul,' she said. 'I was like this,' she added, tightly clenching her outstretched fists, stiffening her neck muscles and fixing her eyes in a robotic stare.

When the Prince and Princess had touched down at Seoul's military airbase after an eighteen-hour flight from London Heathrow, they had hardly looked overjoyed to be back working together. One glance at Diana's forlorn expression had convinced me that this would be their last tour together. In fact, the royal couple were on the point of announcing an official separation; it came a little more than three weeks later.

But it didn't take a Palace statement to tell all of us there what was going on. Diana's miserable face said it all. In fact, she was not only desperately unhappy, but desperately tired, too. Prince Charles, who never copes well with air travel, also admitted the following day that he was feeling weary.

The headline, 'THE GLUMS', accompanying one newspaper's story of their arrival in Seoul, accurately described the way the couple looked. The Korea trip was destined to be their last joint overseas trip, but Diana promised me in Paris that she would undertake many more.

'You'll be travelling more than ever next year,' she added, in a broad hint about her future plans. And draining her glass of champagne she went on, 'I'm going to Nepal next year with the Red Cross. I'm going to look at some of the good work they're doing there.'

'Will the Prince be going with you?' I probed.

Looking me straight in the eye, as if willing me to realize what was about to happen, Diana shook her head. 'No, it's time to spread my wings,' she said meaningfully.

Alarm bells started ringing in my newsman's brain. I knew what she meant by 'spread my wings'. She was trying to tell me what the Prime Minister, John Major, would tell the world from the Despatch Box in the House of Commons on 9 December 1992. The fairy-tale marriage that had turned into a nightmare was over.

My mind was buzzing at the implications of what she had said. 'Is this your new approach to your work?' I asked, hoping she would give me another clue to her future.

'No, it's been going on for some time. It's just that you, the media, haven't noticed,' she said, watching my reaction to see if she was getting the message across.

I had received a tip that Charles and Diana would undertake tours of Mexico and Poland in 1993, so I was puzzled. 'Are you looking forward to seeing Mexico?' I asked. Diana pretended not to hear, so I tried again: 'What about Poland?'

Instead of an answer, she looked into my eyes and smiled. I knew then that when Prince Charles set off on his next tour his wife would not be with him.

It had been only a year since Princess Diana had undertaken her first major solo tour abroad, a trip to Pakistan, originally arranged at the invitation of Prime Minister Benazir Bhutto in 1990. After she had been deposed, the tour was put on ice for a year, but when it finally went ahead in September 1991 it had been a resounding success.

Six months later, Diana had gone alone to Hungary, and soon afterwards was off again on another solo trip to Egypt. The message was unmistakable: Diana was about to cut loose from Charles and make her own royal way in the world.

A member of her staff told me: 'The Princess is going to take on more of these trips without the Prince. As long as she keeps out of Africa, which would upset Princess Anne and the Save the Children Fund, she will do many more of these jaunts overseas.'

I thought back to 29 July 1992, Diana and Charles's eleventh wedding anniversary. At the time the Prince and Princess were trying to maintain a united front, following the sensational revelations in Andrew Morton's blockbuster book *Diana, Her True Story*. When an agency reported that Prince Charles had left Sandringham that day to return to his wife's side on their anniversary, Palace minions didn't deny the story. It was exactly what they wanted the public to believe. But I learned the next day that the Prince did not go home to Kensington Palace and dine with his wife. Instead, he chose to have dinner with his grandmother, Queen Elizabeth the Queen Mother, at Sandringham House.

When I heard that, I knew there was no hope for their marriage. I should have guessed it six months earlier when I chatted to the Princess in Cairo at the end of her Egyptian tour. At a cocktail party in the garden of the British Embassy, I asked her if she was going to watch Prince Charles play polo that summer. In reply Diana rolled her eyes to heaven and gave a heavy sigh. 'No, I'm not going. I hate the game. I don't understand it and I never have. I also hate the sycophants who hang around it. So I'm not going at all this summer.' She went on: 'The boys won't be going either. They don't like it and, anyway, it's a waste of quality time.' She convinced me that she had seen her last game of polo; I told my picture desk I wouldn't bother to cover it any more.

My surprise can therefore be imagined when, three weeks later, she turned up briefly at Smith's Lawn, Windsor with Prince Harry on their way from Highgrove back to London. After that, I had to go to every match throughout the summer in case she or the young Princes turned up again. They never did. But what a summer it turned out to be!

Within a few weeks, everything had changed. It became known that she had suffered from the eating disorder bulimia, and that she was desperately unhappy in a loveless marriage. She had hidden this sadness for seven years behind a beaming smile and never let the world guess how trapped she felt behind closed palace doors. That is, until she accompanied Prince Charles on an official visit to Korea.

5

On my arrival in Paris just ten days later, I had expected to see the utterly miserable woman I had left in Seoul. Instead, she looked triumphant, as if she had just scored a great personal victory. And she was full of excitement about the new direction her life was taking.

She talked about being more than just a name on a charity's letterhead. 'From now on, it's a strictly hands-on approach. I want to become more involved with the Red Cross, for example. No more glitz. Arthur, you don't know how much I hate the glitz. I hate all those premières, but I have to do some.'

I looked at my watch. The Princess and her party should have left for a banquet at the Palais d'Orsay twenty minutes earlier. 'Are you all set to leave?' I asked.

'Oh, I've got my speech ready,' she said.

'Do you write all your speeches yourself?' I asked.

'No, I just take out all the unnecessary, flowery words – like wonderful and brilliant,' she said, making a chopping action to show she was in control. 'But I'm making a big speech next Tuesday for Europe Drug Prevention Week,' she went on. 'Virginia Bottomley asked me to get involved and, of course, I agreed.'

This invitation from the Health Secretary seemed to signal that even the government was now taking her seriously. Her long fight to emerge from the shadow of her husband was paying off. The Princess's more personal, 'hands-on' approach to her job, comforting the dying in Calcutta, lepers in Nigeria and AIDS sufferers in Brazil, first set her apart from all other members of the Royal Family. Now it had won for her international recognition as a great humanitarian.

The previous day Diana had spent more than an hour talking with Danielle Mitterrand, who has been as much of an inspiration to her as Mother Teresa, the nun renowned for her work among the dying and dispossessed in Calcutta. The French president's wife is much respected in France for her humanitarian work.

In July 1992 Madame Mitterrand narrowly escaped death in Iraq at a Kurdish refugee camp. A car bomb was detonated as she drove past in a bungled assassination attempt. It was believed to have been masterminded by Saddam Hussein, who was infuriated by her work for human rights.

Like the Princess, Danielle Mitterrand has broken out of the traditional role of official spouse to become an international figure in her own right. Diana enjoyed meeting Madame Mitterrand so much that their half-hour scheduled chat was extended to ninety minutes, during which the busy president delayed important talks to join them. For the Princess it was proof positive that she is at last being recognized as a woman of substance. Encouraged by her meeting with Mother Teresa in Rome in February 1992 and inspired by her talk with Danielle Mitterrand, the Princess told me she hoped to visit the war-torn area once known as Yugoslavia. 'I want to go there as soon as it's safe to do so,' she said.

A decade during which she had become one of the most famous women in the world had left her unfulfilled. She found the admiration was superficial, based simply on how she looked, not on what she did. Disillusioned by being regarded as a royal bimbo, she was determined to be taken seriously. Now, at thirty-one – an age when the bloom of youth starts to fade – she is entering a new phase. The world is fast forgetting Disco Di, the girl who spent her days shopping and bopping with showbiz stars like John Travolta and Michael Jackson. She much prefers these days to slip quietly into the Royal Opera House, Covent Garden, or Sadlers Wells, with a few friends, or with her sons William and Harry.

Her new maturity is even more noticeable in her official life. Her pioneering work for AIDS sufferers has raised her to the top rank of the world's celebrities. And she had to fight every inch of the way to get there because the Palace old guard were bitterly opposed to any support for HIV-infected people. One of her closest friends told me: 'They were against it from the beginning. They argued there could be a backlash from the public, who might not like the Princess helping people whose immoral lifestyle had led to their affliction. But she would not give up.'

The Princess stood firm, and told her staff: 'I must do something. No one else will.' In a very short time, her patronage of various AIDS charities did much to banish the stigma associated with the disease. The Princess's unflinching stance was summed up when she said in a speech: 'Give them a hug – heaven knows they need it.' And she practised what she preached all over the world, cuddling AIDS babies in São Paulo, holding a doomed tot on her lap as they drove through Washington DC, and sitting for days by the bedside of her dying friend Adrian Ward-Jackson.

These simple acts of love did more to break down barriers of fear and ignorance than any television campaign or newspaper advertising could possibly do. And her achievement far surpasses anything any other member of the Windsor family has ever done.

While Anne, the Princess Royal, richly deserves credit for more than twenty years of fund-raising work in the Third World, even her fantastic efforts cannot equal what Diana has accomplished. I once toured Malawi, Swaziland, Zimbabwe and Kenya with Princess Anne and was so affected by what I saw that I sponsored a little girl in Lesotho. Although the Princess selflessly shared the privations of the aid workers, camping out in remote refugee camps, she lacked the obvious compassion Princess Diana never fails to show. I never once saw Anne cuddle a sick baby or even comfort a troubled mother.

At a mass vaccination in the hills of Swaziland in 1982 I saw Princess Anne stand watching as 5,000 crying babies in the arms of their fearful mothers were inoculated against the usual childhood illnesses. Not a flicker of feeling passed over her face. Trained, like the rest of her relatives, never to show her emotions, the Princess Royal failed to reveal what was obviously in her heart. Of course, her work with the Save the Children Fund speaks for itself. But with Anne it's always a case of 'hands off', while Diana just can't stop herself from getting involved.

On her visit to Pakistan in September 1991, Princess Diana was scheduled to visit a medical centre to hear about its work with refugees from Afghanistan. Unfortunately, the ragged refugees had all been sent back to their makeshift camps before the Princess arrived; local officials thought their scruffy state might offend the royal visitor. When the press party arrived we quickly informed the centre's doctor that the Princess did not mind how they looked, that she would love to meet them. Sure enough, while touring the medical annex she spotted a group of refugees waiting for treatment outside in the blazing sun and walked out to chat to them. A sad group of women were holding tiny babies, many of whom were suffering from skin and eye diseases. Unfussed by their unappealing appearance, she walked among them, holding the babies and comforting the mothers through an interpreter.

It was the same in Calcutta, when she tended to dying men in a hospice run by Mother Teresa. Most of the fifty patients were so close to death that they could no longer take any sustenance. Only something sweet tempted their waning appetites. And the Princess did not hesitate. She walked around the stiflingly hot, dusty room slipping a sweet into the mouth of each man. Without any regard for her pink designer dress, which was covered in dirt and chalk marks from the bare walls, she carried on until she had visited every single one. No one who did not genuinely care could do such heart-rending work with society's rejects.

Out of the public eye Diana likes to have fun with her friends or family, as she did at our impromptu get-together in Paris. She likes a laugh and loves taking the mickey. But more than a decade spent visiting people less privileged than herself has had a dramatic effect on the woman within. When she saw how Nepalese mountain villagers survive on the poverty line, she walked out of a mud hut and sighed: 'I'll never complain again.'

The Princess's new persona was demonstrated by her getting rid of her flash red Mercedes sports car. Like most women her age, she had long dreamed of owning one of the world's top sports cars and flying down the M4 motorway out of London on a sunny day with the top down. But the first time she went out in a Ford Cabriolet with the hood down she almost caused a fifty-car pile-up. Every motorist who spotted her took his eyes off the road to stare as she whizzed past. She learned then that a Princess may be able to get almost anything she wants, but that it may have unexpected consequences.

To most people Princess Diana was the woman who really did have everything. But, as we now know, she was bitterly unhappy. All her tiaras, designer gowns, palaces and private jets were no compensation for her loss of privacy.

She wanted a Mercedes 500 SL and she got it. She enjoyed it for a while, but soon realized it looked dreadfully extravagant in an era of austerity and high unemployment. 'I'm glad I've got rid of it, Arthur,' she told me. 'It was like a red beacon, standing out in the traffic. It was nice while I had it, but I don't miss it one bit.'

Instead of her £80,000 dream car she now uses a dark-blue Jaguar. She turned up in it at the Portuguese embassy in London in April 1993 for a formal dinner. The Queen, Prince Charles and a horde of other Royals were drawing up in their Rolls-Royces and Bentleys. By comparison with these limousines, Diana's sleek little saloon looked rather out of place.

I am sure the Royal Family would not have been displeased if the Princess of Wales had not shown up that night. It must have taken considerable courage to join them for dinner, knowing how they feel about her now. But by accepting the invitation she was showing them all that she intends to retain her royal status. She is not going to fade away quietly, as they might wish. When she stepped from her modest car there was no doubt who the waiting crowd wanted to see. And it was equally obvious who was the most regal of them all. Diana looked more dazzling than ever.

She could have arrived with Princess Margaret, her next-door neighbour, or for the sake of appearances, hitched a ride with Prince Charles. But she came alone. That's the way it is going to be from now on.

CHAPTER TWO

From East to West

The first time I set eyes on a member of the Royal Family was a big disappointment. With two hundred other boys from Saint Bernard's Roman Catholic Secondary School, I waited for two hours on a sweltering summer afternoon in east London to watch the Queen drive along the Mile End Road.

We were lined up along the edge of the pavement when the Queen flashed past us in her big limousine. Like any thirteen-year-old, I had been bored stiff waiting for the big moment to arrive. It was great cricket weather and hanging about on a hot street for a glimpse of a lady in a flowery hat did not thrill me at all. As soon as her Rolls-Royce had vanished down the road I shot off home as fast as I could.

I never found out where the Queen was going the day she drove past our school in 1953. The family who lived in the mansion at the end of the Mall, up the West End, did not interest us East Enders very much. We got fairly excited about the Queen's Coronation in 1953, but my family didn't have a television set, so I went next door to watch the ceremony at a neighbour's house. We also had a street party to celebrate the big day. But after that I never ever heard my mum and dad discuss the Baked Bean, as she is known in Cockney rhyming slang. (East London newspaper editors joke that they have the perfect headline prepared for Her Majesty's demise: in huge print the front pages will read simply: 'BAKED BEAN BROWN BREAD'.)

As I slowly roasted on that east London pavement, waiting for the woman who waved from her car, I had no inkling that

11

I would spend most of my life waiting for her and her family. Following the Windsors as they travelled at home and abroad would become my profession, and one or two of them would become my friends.

No one would have guessed when I was born on 12 August 1940 that a lorry driver's son like me would end up hanging about polo fields, palaces and presidential mansions. I should have arrived within the sound of Bow Bells like a true Cockney kid. But the Blitz was reducing London's East End to rubble, so I started life in Epping at Hill Hall Women's Prison, which had been turned into a maternity home in 1940.

I was named Arthur because that was my father's name, and my grandfather's too. I was informed that the eldest son in every generation as long as anyone could remember had been baptized Arthur. But family history did not impress me and I always hated having such an old-fashioned label.

Not long after my mum took me home to the East India Dock Road we were bombed out of our house, and we all ended up living with my father's mother. I had respiratory-tract illnesses right from the start, which later developed into asthma. When air raids came, as they did most nights, my poor mother had to drag me from my warm bed and rush out into the cold to get to an air-raid shelter. She was so worried about taking a small, sickly baby out in freezing weather that she reluctantly agreed I should be evacuated. The thick, fuggy atmosphere of the crowded shelter was not doing much for my congested lungs. And she had constant rows with other women who objected that my rasping cries, as I struggled to breathe, kept them all awake.

So I was packed off to Bideford in Devon in 1942, when I was two years old. My baby brother David, who had barely been weaned, was for some inexplicable reason sent to Sherborne in Dorset. I didn't see my mother again until 1945. While the war raged on she simply had no way to travel to the West Country to see me. But my dad managed to visit me twice in that time when he was delivering lorry-loads of goods in the area. I remember one occasion when he brought me a little wooden lorry just like his, which he had made himself. I was thrilled with it. He worked for a small haulage company with Ministry of Defence contracts. Doing this essential war work prevented him from being drafted into the armed services.

Sending children far from their parents now seems unthinkable, but the separation was a necessity then. People were killed every night during the raids on London, and the East End suffered the highest casualties as German bombers repeatedly hit the Docklands.

All I can remember of my years in Devon is sleeping in a dormitory with dozens of other children. I don't remember what the place was called or any of the staff. I barely recognized my father when the Women's Voluntary Service brought me back by train to London when the war ended. My dad had a little car that came with his job, and he picked me up at Paddington Station. My mum, Dolly, was waiting at home for me. Somehow, against all the odds, I knew her at once. I remember she had a new baby in her arms. My little sister Patricia had been born a few months earlier.

I wasn't at home long before I was sent away again. After years in the Devonshire countryside the congestion in my lungs was aggravated by my return to the grimy East End. For the sake of my health, my parents decided I should go to live with my father's brother, John, and his wife at Bexhill-on-Sea, Sussex.

I stayed there for a year, after which my Aunt Violet wanted to adopt me. I had become very fond of her and my uncle, and their daughter June, who was four years older than me. But my mother flatly refused to consider the idea, so I went back to dirty, dusty London and started school in Stepney.

I had barely settled in with my real family when a new misfortune hit us. My baby sister suddenly died of pneumonia, and losing her almost destroyed my mother. My brother David and I were told only that she was very ill and had gone to hospital. I remember my brother asked my mother: 'Will I be your baby boy now?' Our mum was so distraught we suspected the worst, but we did not dare to ask questions. Many months later I asked my dad if she had died, and he told me the truth. By then David and I no longer missed her in our midst and simply accepted it.

That was the way we did things in those days. Children were shielded from grief, and it seems a kind method of dealing with such problems. My mother did not really recover from losing her little girl until my sister Pamela was born three years later.

I was sent to the local Catholic primary school, Our Lady Immaculate in Stepney. It was there I learned to seize every opportunity that comes my way. My mother had always taught me that when I went to children's parties I should eat the sandwiches first and the cake later. At my First Communion breakfast following the church service, I sat down with all my school pals in front of a table piled with boring sandwiches and delicious iced cakes. Remembering my mother's warning, I politely picked up one of the cheese and pickle concoctions as my mates dived on the wonderful cake. In an instant every slice had disappeared and there was none left for me. Ever since that day I have tried to avoid ending up with second best.

Growing up in east London was a wonderful experience. Looking back now, I wouldn't change a single day. I learned to swim in the Regent's Canal, and risked my neck hitching lifts by jumping on the tail-end of lorries. My brother and I used to build go-carts and race them down the footpath in the Rother-hithe Tunnel under the Thames. The pavement was barely three feet wide, and one day a huge lorry clipped the side of my cart and almost killed me. My creation of pram wheels and an old fruit box shattered beneath me. Undeterred, I built another racing cart and was soon whizzing down the tunnel again. When I drive through there now I shudder at the dangers I risked daily.

I was a little horror, nicking fruit off costermongers' barrows and smashing streetlights with my catapult. We used to dream up all sorts of schemes to make money. I collected waste paper from people's homes to sell, and gathered wood from bombed houses to flog as kindling.

Discipline was not a dirty word in those days. I was whacked with a cane almost every day by my teachers. When I went on to St Bernard's Secondary School I would be caned for the slightest infringement of the rules. If I forgot to wear my navy-blue cap the teacher would raise red welts on my hand. But it didn't seem to do me any harm; I quickly learned not to break the rules. And the strict regime of those early days is, I believe, the reason I find self-discipline easier than many other people.

My one regret is I did not pay attention in school or absorb much of what my wonderful schoolmasters tried to instil in me. I left St Bernard's when I was fifteen with no real qualifications, but got a job easily. My father simply told me to sort out something before the summer holidays began. In that era of full employment I simply looked in the *Evening News* and saw a job vacancy for a boy in a photographer's darkroom in Portman Square.

That was how I stumbled on to the best training I could possibly have had for my future career. John Lee, one of London's top food photographers, hired me as his assistant. He taught me everything I know, and we remain great friends to this day. In fact, my son Paul trained as a photographer with John and he could not have had a better start.

By that time my father, who was a chain-smoker all his life, was seriously ill with lung cancer. He was only fifty, but he had been in bed for months and I didn't realize that he was becoming steadily worse. One night I decided to go to the local cinema with a mate straight after work. I was queueing up at the box office when my Uncle Harry came looking for me. 'Don't you know your dad's dead?' he told me bluntly.

Until my father's death we had a very comfortable life. A spacious, four-bedroom Victorian house came with his job. When he was gone, we had to move out of that lovely house and into two rooms in Poplar. I lived there until I got married five years later.

I met Ann, a lovely Irish girl, when I was nineteen and I saved enough money to plan a future with her by working weekends photographing weddings. Life got even better when I got married in 1961 and we had a family, two sons, John and Paul, and later a daughter called Annmarie. By this time I was working for the great fashion photographer John French. He

15

worked with all the top models of the sixties, like Jean Shrimpton and Celia Hammond, and his pictures appeared in all the glossy magazines like *Vogue* and *Vanity Fair*. John French was a real gentleman, and I had moved into a very glamorous world.

All the great faces of that era were lovely girls, but the one I liked best was Tania Mallet, who later starred in a James Bond movie. If John French had finished photographing her before her time was up, she would pose for me. This boosted my confidence tremendously, and it was a great kindness to a lad just starting out in the tough fashion-photography game.

Despite the lure of meeting so many gorgeous girls, though, I preferred football to fashion. The false world I worked in, where everyone called everyone else 'Darling', even if they hated their guts, was not for me. I spent every available opportunity watching West Ham, and photographing my idols in the claret-and-blue shirts seemed a good deal to me. That's how I ended up working for an East London photographic agency. Soon my football photographs were appearing in the *Stratford Express*, the *Newham Recorder* and the *Sun*. And what pleased me even more was that I got free passes to all the First Division games.

The boxing world fascinated me too, and I was soon out covering bouts almost every night. I sold so many pictures to different newspapers that I decided to start my own agency with a great friend, Bill Storey. But I worked so frequently for Rupert Murdoch's revamped tabloid the *Sun* that eventually the Picture Editor, Tom Petrie, asked me to do some shifts.

I started by doing football stories, but quickly moved on to hard news. As I had worked on a local paper doing eight stories a day, I found covering one for the *Sun* was a piece of cake. Fleet Street was Easy Street to me. The transition turned out to be beneficial for us both. I joined the staff of the *Sun* in 1974.

A year later my mother was admitted to hospital with lung disease. I knew she was gravely ill and went to visit her in the London hospital before driving up to Leicester for a football match. I checked with her nurse who told me she was on the mend. As I left my mum said: 'I'm OK, son,' and gave me her wonderful smile. It lit up her face and was my last memory of her. She died a few hours later.

Strangely, whenever I see the Queen I think of my mother. She has a smile exactly the same and it reminds me so much of Dolly. She would have loved to see her family do so well. My brother became a company secretary, my sister got a degree in sociology from London University, and my cousin Bill became a doctor in Colchester.

I was so happy at the *Sun*, dashing out on a sports story, then switching to a big siege or a murder case. Occasionally I was sent abroad on a soft feature story and thought life was so great it couldn't have been better if I had won the Pools.

Then one day I was asked to cover a royal story for the paper and it changed my life.

CHAPTER THREE

Mr Windsor

Prince Charles was clearly annoyed about something as he finished a game of polo at Smith's Lawn, Windsor. Cantering back to the pony lines to dismount, he suddenly stopped as he passed the spot where I was standing with a group of other photographers. 'Are you the man who took that picture of my bald spot?' he asked, glaring down at me.

'Yes, sir, I am,' I replied, wondering if I was about to get a bollocking. I had been warned earlier by the Prince's policeman, John MacLean, that he wanted to have a word with me. I knew he was unhappy about a picture I had taken a few days earlier.

I had got it as the Prince was zooming away from the polo ground at Cirencester in his Aston Martin sports car. He was in such a hurry to get back to Buckingham Palace and change for a state dinner that he hadn't bothered to comb his hair. And at the back of his head I was surprised to notice a very large bald spot. I took two frames of the back of his bonce and also a side-view of his head to prove it really was him.

I didn't immediately give the picture to the paper because I couldn't quite believe what I had seen. I decided to process it and take another look at it next morning. The Picture Editor at that time, Tom Petrie, loved it, and the following day it was on the front page of the *Sun* under the headline: 'OOPS, CHARLES, THERE'S A PATCH IN YOUR THATCH!'

I had been very nervous about having a byline on the picture because I knew the Prince wouldn't like being caught off-guard. But a reporter called Iain Walker, who wrote the splash story which accompanied the picture, convinced me it was a good idea. Iain, who tragically died in a climbing accident in 1992,

19

said to me: 'You're crazy. Everybody will be talking about this. You should have a byline.'

He was right, because about three days later the Prince tackled me about it. It wasn't the most flattering picture I had taken of the heir to the throne since I had begun covering his activities nine months earlier, so I wasn't surprised that he didn't like it. From the look on his face as he discussed it I knew I had scored a direct hit on his vanity. 'Well, anyway, not many people saw it,' he snapped, as if that was the end of the matter.

I had to grin and enlighten him. 'Only about twelve million, sir.'

Charles looked amazed to learn that the newspaper had so many readers, so I asked: 'Have you been getting some stick about it?'

With a sheepish look he admitted: 'Well, not really, but everywhere I go people are creeping up behind me to photograph the back of my head.' And trying to even the score he added: 'You can talk about me going bald, but you've not got much on top yourself.'

I had to agree. 'Yeah, you're right,' I said, 'but I'm eight years older than you. Wait until you're as old as me!'

It was my first conversation with the Prince of Wales. And, as I learned in dozens of other discussions with him afterwards, he is a good-natured bloke who never stays in a bad mood long.

Luckily, one of my mates, Tim Graham, who was then working for the *Daily Mail*, banged off a shot of the Prince chatting to me.

The *Sun* paid him the going rate for a freelance picture, then ten quid. But because I was waggling my finger at the Prince as we talked, everyone who saw it thought I was giving the Prince a dressing-down, not the other way around. And so this incident with Tim's picture provided another story for the *Sun*.

The revelation that Charles was thinning on top obviously rankled with him, because it stayed in his mind for weeks. The following month, when he was playing polo for the Royal Navy at Tidworth, in Wiltshire, he mentioned it to his Uncle Dickie, better known as Lord Mountbatten. He was having a glass of beer after the game when Earl Mountbatten came up and put his arm around him affectionately. It made a really intimate picture which has been used many times since in books and magazines. The Prince said to his great-uncle: 'There's the man who let twelve million people know that I am going thin on top with just one picture.'

Mountbatten said: 'Oh, is it?' Then he started to ruffle the Prince's hair, pretending to search for the bald spot.

I sent a picture of them together to Lord Mountbatten and he sent me a lovely letter of thanks. In the last paragraph he said: 'These very valuable pictures will be placed among my archives, and I think they are excellent.'

The Patch-in-the-Thatch picture was very special for two reasons. First, it knocked out of the paper a picture of the Queen on her 1977 Jubilee walkabout through London. This convinced me that sticking with the Action Man heir to the throne was more productive than the stuffy royal jobs that the Queen carried out. The really exciting pictures were not of the official engagements, but the candid snaps when the Royals were off-duty.

Second, this hurriedly snatched photo revealed to the world that the Prince was going prematurely bald – the first sign that the years were swiftly passing by. Yet he had still not found a wife. The whole country, not to mention his family, thought it was high time he settled down and started giving himself heirs.

A few months earlier my editor, Larry Lamb (later Sir Larry), had decided to get his staff working on this story. Who would be the next Queen of England? He wanted the *Sun* to be first to reveal the name of the very special girl Charles would choose. He sent me up to Harwich, where Charles was serving on HMS *Bronington*.

I spent six miserable days on my own, hanging about. I didn't think covering Royals was such a great idea. I wasn't to know then that in the years to come it would take me around the world ten times over. It would be not so much hanging about in Harwich but following him to more exotic spots like Houston, Hong Kong and Honolulu.

But in Harwich the Prince rarely left the ship, so I didn't get any pictures at all. At that time he was romancing the gorgeous blonde Davina Sheffield, but photographers were rarely able to catch them together. She was an outdoor girl who enjoyed the same sports as the Prince. She loved fishing, stalking and horse-riding. But delicious Davina had lived with a former boyfriend, James Beard, in a rose-covered cottage in the country, and when he revealed all about their cosy life together to a Sunday newspaper, any hope Davina had of marrying Charles disappeared.

It must have been painful at the time for them both when the Prince decided to stop seeing her. As his late valet Stephen Barry revealed: 'The romance did not end immediately. It went on for some months after James Beard had printed his story. To me this seemed to mean that the Prince was finding it hard to part with Davina.'

But I don't think that Davina would have passed the supreme test for a would-be Princess. She did not seem able to handle the publicity that went with being the Prince's sweetheart. Once when she landed at Heathrow on her way home from a visit to Balmoral, she got petrified when she spotted cameramen and locked herself in the ladies' loo to escape.

Another gorgeous blonde who came close to snaring the play-boy Prince was Anna Wallace, the daughter of a Scottish land-owner. She was nicknamed 'Whiplash' Wallace for her love of hunting, a passion Prince Charles shared. He dated her for almost a year, until they had a row when he escorted her to a ball held in June 1980, to celebrate the Queen Mother's eightieth birthday. While Charles circulated among the many distinguished guests, Anna decided she was being ignored when he failed to return to her side. Finally, she stormed out after telling the Prince in a loud voice: 'I've never been so badly treated before in my life.' As he tried to splutter an explanation Anna lashed out again. 'No one treats me like that – not even you.'

They patched up their differences after this tiff. Then the next time they were seen out together again, Charles offended her in exactly the same way. They were attending a polo ball held by Lord Vestey at Stowell Park. Instead of whirling around the floor with the beautiful but demanding Anna, the Prince danced again and again with his old friend Camilla Parker Bowles.

He had dated her in his early twenties until his duties with the Royal Navy intervened. She had then married an Army officer, Andrew Parker Bowles, but Camilla and the Prince had remained close friends.

Looking back now, it is surprising that no one realized the significance of this incident at Stowell Park. Apparently, Anna Wallace was shrewd enough to recognize that the Prince was happier with Camilla than with her. Refusing to be used by any man, even the Prince of Wales, she walked out on him. Halfway through the polo ball, she borrowed Lady Vestey's car and drove herself home, never to be seen with Prince Charles again.

Soon afterwards, Charles left the Royal Navy and following his new career as a full-time Royal became a full-time job for me.

Up until 1977, there was no such thing as a royal specialist in Fleet Street. News Editors and Picture Editors handed the royal jobs out like treats to favoured staffmen. But I had realized that, when I went to cover the Prince of Wales playing polo on my weekends off, on most days I got cracking pictures. And if I persevered when everyone else had given up, I often got a great exclusive.

On one occasion at Cowdray Park in Sussex, when it was so late it was almost dark, and all the other photographers had gone home, Charles flicked some water at one of the girl grooms. She was a good-natured, busty blonde named June. Charles had just won the game, and whenever he wins he is always very happy and pleased with himself. To get back at him the groom impulsively grabbed some ice out of a bucket and put it down the back of his polo shirt. The Prince quickly evened the score by shoving some down her front. She squealed, and he grabbed some more ice and put it down her back.

I rushed back to the office with the pictures and processed them in time for the last edition. Next morning my picture of the Prince's horseplay with the groom made the front page.

A few days later he stopped and spoke to me about my scoop. 'I see you made the last edition,' he said. 'And I'm glad you did the decent thing,' he added, referring to the fact that the published picture was not a saucy shot of him shoving ice down the groom's front, but down her back. What neither Prince Charles nor my editor knew was that the more suggestive picture had not been sharp enough to publish.

I gradually became so involved in photographing the Prince and his girlfriends that I began working every weekend, when the best pictures seemed to happen. When the Royal Family moved to Balmoral in August, I went too. Even during an air strike in 1977 I managed to get up there by catching the overnight train on a Saturday just to cover the hour-long Sunday-morning church service at Crathie near the Queen's Highland home.

These long weekends proved rewarding. One of the best that I remember happened in 1978 when Charles was interested in a dark-haired beauty called Angelica Lazansky. The Prince had invited several Fleet Street photographers to Balmoral that weekend to take official pictures to be released on his thirtieth birthday a few months later. As usual, the royal rota system was operating. This involved drawing the name of one newspaper photographer, and one agency photographer from all the organizations who applied for passes. Monty Fresco of the *Daily Mail* and the Press Association's Ron Bell were the lucky men, and they were accompanied by a government cameraman from the Central Office of Information.

I had a tip that Charles's guest that weekend would be Angelica, whom I had spotted the previous summer with him at a polo tournament in Deauville, France. When I turned up at the Sunday service there she was. And I got some exclusive pictures. But, later that day when I was flying back to London, she arrived at Aberdeen Airport to catch the same flight. I was worried that Monty Fresco, who was leaving with me, would snap her, but she got out of the royal car with Prince Charles's press officer, John Dauth, and Monty presumed she was his secretary, so he didn't bother to take any pictures. The result was another scoop for the *Sun*.

That was the last time Angelica was ever seen with the Prince of Wales. I should have realized she wasn't a serious girlfriend. She was not only Catholic, but a brunette, and Charles always had a weakness for leggy blondes.

Susan George, the film actress, was briefly linked with the Prince, when she was invited as a special guest to his thirtieth-birthday party at Windsor. He had met her at a film première a few months earlier. For a while she used to visit him secretly at Windsor, but the Prince and the Showgirl were obviously destined never to marry.

The heiress Sabrina Guinness fascinated him for several months. But the romance didn't last because she was a real townie, who had worked in Hollywood, and he was basically a country person.

Few of these girls were ever invited to meet the Queen. But one who often did was Lady Jane Wellesley. In the late seventies she was the top tip to become Princess of Wales, simply because she seemed so suitable. The daughter of the Duke of Wellington, Jane was slim and attractive, with a bubby personality.

Unfortunately, the Prince never fell in love with her and she was only ever a friend of the family. But in 1978 press interest in the Duke's lovely daughter was at its height. I remember once, when I was covering a royal pheasant shoot at Sandringham, Jane and the Queen joined Prince Charles, Prince Philip and the Duke of Kent when they stopped for lunch at a village hall in Shernborne, Norfolk. When photographers began blazing away at the Prince and Lady Jane the Queen came to her rescue. She had her car waiting at the door so Charles's girlfriend could make a fast exit. 'Quick, Jane, quick!' she called. 'Get in.' And they both sped off together in a Land Rover.

The minute photographers spotted the Prince of Wales with any female they would close in like sharks in a feeding frenzy. Once, in Rheims while Charles was touring the Champagne region of France, their eagerness to snap him with a lovely blonde almost led to a riot. Photographers were falling over themselves, pushing and shoving to get pictures of them together at a formal dinner. In the mad scramble to get close-ups of Charles and his companion his uncle, seventy-nine-year-old Earl Mountbatten, was shoved against a wall and almost knocked to the ground. The Prince shouted: 'This is madness.'

But the elegant woman dining with the Prince was, in fact, Madame Marie Hélène Giscard d'Estaing, sister-in-law of the French president. The photographers were all thrown out of the dinner and vented their anger on the royal visitor next day by whistling and booing when he appeared. White-faced with anger, Prince Charles barked: 'No one whistles at me.'

Then he walked over to me and asked: 'Can't you do anything about this situation? Can't you reason with them?' I explained that I had tried and that they wouldn't listen. The local police were finally called to deal with the frenzied Frenchmen and the Prince gave up and left them still arguing.

Whenever I saw Charles with a new girl, I used to ask his Scotland Yard protection officer John MacLean: 'Is this girl *the* one?' He always gave me the same reply: 'She could be the one. You can never tell. A friendship can turn into a romance, and a romance into marriage. How do you or I know?'

Finding the girl Charles would marry became something of an obsession with me. For two years I worked on this story non-stop. I used to stay up at Balmoral and Sandringham for weeks at a stretch and very rarely took a day off. Finally, Tom Petrie said: 'Why don't you take a break?' But I just couldn't. Too many great pictures were happening all the time.

The Prince of Wales was a young, good-looking man, the world's most eligible bachelor. He enjoyed being seen with pretty girls. He liked having fun and he didn't mind who knew it. While some of his family wanted to be photographed only while they were on duty, Prince Charles was different. He knew you had a job to do and provided you played the game, and didn't get too pushy, he did his best to co-operate. This meant that if you watched him closely you would get a good, relaxed picture.

Both the public and the press wanted more and more of such photographs. They proved that the Queen and her relatives were likeable people, not pompous figureheads. And as a result, they brought the Royal Family closer to the British public.

Rival newspapers were not slow to realize that they were missing good pictures and stories. In a very short time the *Mirror*, the *Mail*, and the *Daily Express* all had royal teams. And soon the competition began to hot up.

One man who had been photographing the Royals years before I began was Jimmy Gray, then working for the *Daily Mail*. Jimmy is a Londoner like myself, from Islington. He is only five foot tall, but those sixty inches are packed with fun. He has a wicked twinkle in his eye and a very saucy grin. And he never ever takes anything at face value. He never gives you any credit for doing anything good; he always rubbishes any effort you make, and turns everything, no matter how serious, into a joke. It's impossible to be in his company for longer than five minutes without laughing.

When the new technology arrived and Fleet Street changed, Jimmy didn't enjoy it. He left the *Daily Mail*, went freelance for a while then took early retirement. He is greatly missed now, especially by me.

Jimmy is also very laid-back about the Royal Family. He thinks their great status is just a result of an accident of birth and that they don't deserve any of their privileges. And as for the press covering the Royal Family he says: 'It ain't a real job. It's a fucking doddle.'

So he has no qualms about photographing them whenever and wherever he can. I was with Jimmy once, chewing the fat, sitting in his car outside Sandringham waiting for the family to appear. Suddenly we looked up and saw the Duke of Edinburgh about ten yards away, striding furiously towards us. We had the window of the car down and desperately tried to wind it up. But the Duke stopped us by sticking his head in. He said: 'Having a good snoop, gentlemen?'

Well, what can you say to that? For once Jimmy was dumb founded. But the incident reminded him of the last time he had been reprimanded by a Duke. I have dined out on the story ever since.

In the mid-1960s, Jimmy was working for Keystone, a news agency that has produced many great photographers. One day he was asked to cover the return of the Duke of Windsor to England for an eye operation. While he was recovering it was the Duke's habit to go for a walk in Regent's Park each day, so Jimmy set out to follow him. As the Duke and his bodyguard strolled along, Jimmy kept popping up out of the bushes and photographing him. The Duke would then walk on and Jimmy would bounce up again. Finally, the former King lost patience with Jimmy and said: 'Go away, go on, stop pestering me and piss off.'

Halfway through this tirade Jimmy started panicking and shot into a gents' toilet nearby, thinking he would escape. He was standing at a urinal relieving himself when who should walk in but the Duke of Windsor, determined to finish reprimanding Jimmy. 'Who do you work for?' he asked. 'If you don't stop pestering me, I'll ring up your boss. Can't you see I'm recovering from an operation?'

Jimmy was just having a quiet pee, and a former King of England was bollocking him in a public convenience in the middle of London. 'I thought I was dreaming,' he told me. 'I just froze. Everything froze in mid-stream, I felt such a nitwit. I just carried on looking at the wall, praying he would go away.'

The bollocking probably lasted about a minute, but to Jimmy it seemed to go on for ever. I reckon the Duke of Windsor won that argument, because Jimmy Gray never bothered him again.

When he told me this story I was helpless with laughter. At least he got the pictures; some of Jimmy's funniest stories are about the ones that got away.

He once went to Jersey to photograph a man wanted for questioning in England in connection with a big case of fraud. His lawyers claimed he was too ill to travel, and so he was holed up in his mansion on the island. Jimmy turned up outside the house with a *Daily Mail* reporter called Dickie Heard and they worked out a plan to get a picture of the suspect. Every morning his nurse brought him out into the garden to sit by the swimming pool. Dickie suggested that Jimmy should climb over the high garden wall and hide in the bushes near the pool.

Jimmy was too short to scramble over the stone wall, which was eight or nine feet high. So they brought up their hire car to the wall and with great difficulty Jimmy made it over the top with all his gear clanking around his neck. He crept through the bushes to the edge of the lawn where he had a good view of the swimming pool and settled down to wait.

About an hour later, when the guy was due to appear, the french windows at the back of the house opened and out walked the biggest Doberman pinscher Jimmy had ever seen in his life. As he said to me later: 'I froze. Every hair stood up on the back of my neck. The bloody dog sniffed the air then looked straight at the spot where I was hiding in the bushes. It stuck its nose up again then looked directly at me. The Doberman took two steps forward and blind panic overtook me. I tore back to the wall and I went straight up it as if I had suckers on my hands. I just flew up that high wall with the dog's hot breath on the back of my neck.'

When Jimmy collapsed in a heap on the other side, his reporter asked anxiously: 'Have you got the pictures?' Jimmy gave him a withering look and said: 'Fuck you, Dickie. Have I got the pictures? I'm lucky to have my fucking life!'

I owe my introduction to the world of the upper classes to James Whitaker, who joined the *Sun* after working for some time on the *Daily Express*'s William Hickey gossip column. I was quite impressed with him at the time because he had recently scooped all of Fleet Street with the story of actor Edward Woodward's marriage break-up. One day, soon after he joined the paper, he said to me: 'I'm going to the polo at Windsor this afternoon to watch the Prince of Wales play. Why don't you come along?'

I was astonished when I got there at being able to photograph the Prince from a distance of just a few feet without any hassle. I snapped him feeding sugar to one of his polo ponies and got a good show in the paper next day. It seemed an easy way to get my pictures published, so I kept going back.

In those days before the IRA assassination of Lord Mountbatten in 1979, access to the Royals was much more relaxed.

Today, we are forced to photograph the Prince playing polo from a distance of around 300 metres.

Having gone to a minor public school, James Whitaker had the confidence I then lacked. I'll never forget him walking up to Prince Charles the day the *Daily Express* ran a story claiming he was about to marry Princess Marie Astrid of Luxembourg. James was anxious to check the story, so boldly went straight to the only person who really would know. Luckily for him, the Prince was keen to rubbish the story and said: 'I've only ever met her twice before.' And he then proceeded to deny every word of the *Daily Express* exclusive. But he did not want to be quoted directly. 'Could you just say a close friend told you?' Charles asked.

Observing all this made me realize that the Royals were not gods, but approachable human beings just like anyone else. From that moment on I've never been fazed by any of them.

Newspaper readers probably often see a story in which a close friend of the Royal Family is quoted and think the reporter has made it up. They would never believe that the source of such information is sometimes the Royals themselves.

It's hard to describe James Whitaker, because he is such a larger-than-life character. But a reporter in Australia came close when he once wrote that James resembled 'a red-faced colonel with deaf daughters'. James (never Jim) does have a booming voice and you would never have any trouble finding him in a crowded room.

In the late seventies, James and I pioneered covering the Royals as a full-time occupation in the aggressive style that is now the normal practice. Those were trail-blazing years, when nobody else did it. I suppose we were the founding fathers of the Royal Rat Pack. Many have joined, and many have left since, but James and I soldier on.

In those early days all the colourful expressions we used gradually became the Rat Pack's own private language. Photographers were known as 'Monkeys'. I think this name was derived from a sarcastic comment made by the Duke of Edinburgh while looking at the apes who live on the Rock of

Gibraltar. 'Look at all the monkeys,' someone said to him. He quickly pointed in the direction of the press covering his visit and replied: 'Which ones are the monkeys, and which are the reporters?'

In 1988, I celebrated my birthday with the entire Rat Pack outside the Portland Hospital where the Duchess of York had just given birth to Princess Beatrice. They surprised me with a birthday present. It was a huge bunch of bananas with a card bearing a message which read: 'To my favourite monkey, with best wishes from the Queen.'

Monkeys don't 'take photographs' of the Royals; we 'whack 'em'. If we go in shooting full-lengths of them from every angle we describe that as 'hosing them down'. And at night when we use flash guns, we 'blitz' them. The pictures that result are 'smudges', a jokey expression meaning they are mostly out of focus.

In return the reporters who work with us, who may think of themselves as organ-grinders controlling the monkeys, are dismissed by us as mere caption-writers.

When James and I began working together, the Rat Pack wasn't even a Mouse Pack. But we were keen to keep breaking new stories and we were having a lot of fun. Never before had anyone covered the Royal Ascot race meeting in June and all the other ritzy royal occasions of the London season the way we did. James used to get togged up in his Ascot morning dress and topper and strut around the Royal Enclosure searching out Prince Charles's latest girlfriend. Then he would signal to me on the photographers' balcony, where cameramen were confined, that the couple were heading towards me. We got a lot of exclusives that way by working together as a really close team.

I did my first royal tour with James. We went to Yugoslavia with Prince Charles in 1978. The trip began in Dubrovnik on the beautiful Dalmatian coast. I learned a few very important lessons on my first foreign excursion with a member of the Royal Family. The first was never oversleep in the morning. And the second rule was always do every job on the royal schedule, no matter how boring it looks on paper.

The tour did not start off very well because I was not getting many pictures in the paper. The Prince was aware of this, and was trying to inject a lot of enthusiasm and animation into everything he did. But it wasn't until the final day that the picture of the tour happened. And I so nearly missed the whole incident.

I had overslept after drinking too much the night before and so missed the press coach. I woke up in an absolute panic and, without shaving, jumped into my clothes, grabbed my cameras and quickly looking at my programme to see where I could catch up, I hired a taxi.

I managed to link up with my colleagues on the bus before it set off on the long journey to Nova Sad on the Hungarian border. But when we arrived we found the Prince visiting a very boring art gallery. I thought: 'What's the point of hanging about?' The tour hadn't produced very many pictures and this place didn't look very promising. I considered cutting my losses and returning to Belgrade early, but Anwar Hussein, a freelance photographer, said, 'Come on, you never know. It might produce something.' So I went with him into the art gallery.

Prince Charles had almost completed his tour of the place when he stopped to look at a nude painting. I took a picture of this, and to my surprise, he turned to me and said: 'Why don't you put her on Page Three?'

Page Three was then, and still is, the pride and joy of the *Sun*. Each day it features a huge picture of a glamorous semi-nude model. The Page Three beauties have become the nation's favourite pin-ups and the phrase Page Three has passed into the English language.

The deputy editor of the *Sun*, then Arthur Brittenden, happened to be in charge that day and put my picture of the Prince with the nude on Page One. Above the usual Page Three beauty was the headline 'BY ROYAL APPOINTMENT'. This made the whole trip worthwhile and it ended on a high note for me.

Unfortunately, James Whitaker was not so lucky. He had gone ahead to Austria, where Prince Charles was due to go shooting the following day with Prince Hans Adam of Liechtenstein. James had missed the only decent story of the entire tour.

James soon moved on to the *Daily Star* and later the *Daily Mirror*. Since then, we have remained good friends, but as he is now working for the *Sun*'s main competitor, a healthy rivalry exists between us.

James has teamed up with the *Daily Mirror*'s top photographer Ken Gavin, known to everyone, including the Royal Household at Buckingham Palace, as 'Gavvers'.

Gavvers comes from north London and went to school with Jimmy Gray in Islington. When he is not photographing the Royals he is photographing his favourite football team, Arsenal. He is as slim as James Whitaker is fat, which inspired their former boss Richard Stott, who is now editing the *Today* newspaper, to give them both nicknames. He said James reminded him of the plump pantomime character Widow Twankey, while Gavvers had to be 'Idle Jack'.

But of course this is quite unfair, because 'idle' is the last word I would choose to describe my old mate. He is never still for a second, always on the telephone organizing the next royal job, the next royal tour or telling me the latest gossip. He takes only one holiday each year, a fortnight in August. And I don't believe he would even take that if his lady Gloria didn't insist that he has a break. He lives and breathes his work and Mike Molloy, another executive he once worked for, used to say: 'Ken Gavin *is* the *Daily Mirror*.'

Amazingly, by his own admission the best picture he ever took was not of a member of the Queen's family. In the early seventies he went to the frozen wastes of northern Canada to cover the annual seal cull. The result was an unforgettable shot of a seal-hunter with a club raised high above his head about to smash it down on a seal pup, which was helplessly gazing up at him. That picture did more to stop the slaughter in the Arctic than the millions of words written by animal-lovers.

Gavvers and I have known each other almost twenty years and only ever quarrelled once. In 1983, during Charles and Diana's first tour of Canada, we visited Newfoundland. While we were in the capital, St John's, the weather was warm and sunny, and we had all dressed in short-sleeved summer shirts.

Later that day, the royal party were scheduled to drive to Cape Spear, the most easterly point in North America, to look at whales offshore.

The idea of the Prince and Princess of Wales looking at the magnificent mammals with the similar name appealed to Gavs, so he set off in advance, while I stayed behind to finish covering the ceremonial welcome St John's turned on for them. I caught up later by hitching a ride in the official photographer's car at the tail-end of the royal motorcade.

Although the distance from St John's to Cape Spear was less than ten miles, the weather on the coast was dramatically different. Fog had swept in and the temperature had plummeted. From the seventy-plus degrees in the capital it was now barely forty Fahrenheit. And when I arrived I found a shivering bunch of pressmen standing in the fog, trying vainly to get a picture. The clammy, damp conditions were so bad you could barely see the end of your lens.

I took one look at the scene and decided I wouldn't bother to stay. We were four hours behind London time, so I thought it better to head back to my hotel, and start filing the pictures I had taken earlier. I stuck my head out of the nice, warm car and yelled at Gavvers that I was going back to the city.

About ninety minutes later, I was just starting to wire the earlier pictures to London when Ken stormed into my hotel room screaming hysterically at me. 'You fucking bastard,' he yelled. 'Why did you piss off with the car?'

I was taken aback. 'What do you mean?' I asked, perplexed. 'What's the problem?'

He was so out of control that Dennis Paquin, a French-Canadian photographer for United Press International, dashed into the bathroom and locked himself in.

Shaking with uncontrollable rage, Gavvers bellowed: 'The problem was I was freezing my bollocks off, and there was no other transport. I yelled at you to wait for us, but you buggered off. So we had to wait in the bloody cold until the Royals left and the press bus collected us.'

When I thought about all my mates shivering and shaking in their summer clothes on the freezing coastline, I burst out laughing. Suddenly Gavvers's face, which a minute ago had been twisted with anger, broke into a grin. He saw the funny side of it too and started to laugh with me.

Just then the bathroom door opened and Dennis Paquin poked his head out. 'I can't make out you Limeys,' he said with a shake of his head. 'One minute you are roaring at each other, and the next you are falling about laughing together.'

After James Whitaker left for the *Daily Star*, I teamed up with another *Sun* reporter, Harry Arnold, and thus began the greatest twelve years of my career. Harry is undoubtedly the finest reporter I have ever worked with. He not only writes well, he has great judgement and is very brave. Although short in stature he is big in confidence; his motto has always been: 'Boldness be my friend.'

The first job of any consequence I ever did with Harry Arnold was a Princess Margaret story. The office had got a tip that she was staying with her much younger boyfriend, Roddy Llewellyn, at a stately home near Newport Pagnell, in Buckinghamshire. It was June 1978, and it was an unusually hot day, the temperature soaring to ninety degrees. It was a Sunday morning when Harry and I were dispatched up the M1. We went to the stately home, only to discover that it was shut for the day. This made us think the tip might be true, but we couldn't find any access to the grounds, which were surrounded by an eight-foot wall. By luck we stumbled across the filtration plant for the swimming pool, and heard voices on the other side of the wall. Very quietly and carefully we climbed up a tree and on to the roof of the filtration plant.

We could hardly believe what we saw. There was Princess Margaret, in a one-piece strapless swimsuit, lying right underneath us. We almost fell off the roof as we quickly drew back in surprise. Silently we sat there, hardly daring to move or make a sound for almost two hours, waiting in the blazing heat for Roddy to appear.

About four o'clock in the afternoon, when it was really stinking hot, the tar on the roof of the filtration plant began to melt and stick to our smart city suits. Just then Roddy appeared carrying some tea and white wine on a silver tray. Margaret got up, walked over to the pool, eased herself in, swam one length breast-stroke, then got out again. She walked over to Roddy and helped herself to a cup of tea.

I took several pictures of the two together and Harry said: 'I've got the story to go with them. It's tea and sympathy.' This was at a time when newspapers were running stories to the effect that the couple's romance was cooling. Thrilled with our exclusive, we quietly climbed down off the roof, and made our way back to London. Our suits were ruined, but we were deliriously happy because we had what we thought was a great scoop.

I phoned in to the picture desk, and they were dancing for joy. They even agreed to replace our ruined suits. The headline 'TOGETHER AGAIN' had already been written for Page One when we arrived back in Fleet Street. But Tom Petrie took one look at my pictures and said: 'I don't think that's Roddy Llewellyn.'

I couldn't believe what I had heard. 'Why don't you?' I asked him.

'Roddy has a hairy chest and this bloke hasn't,' he said, indicating the man in my shots.

'Don't be silly, of course it's Roddy,' I said.

But he insisted that we get the file pictures of Roddy out of the picture library and check them.

When we saw the real Roddy Llewellyn I realized at once that I had the wrong guy and that the picture was unusable. The hairstyle was the same, the build and colouring were the same, but it wasn't Roddy.

It was a brave decision for any Picture Editor to make – killing a big exclusive story that all the other executives wanted to print. But next day we discovered that Tom Petrie was right. The man in our picture was a well-known barrister who owned the stately home. If we had run the story and picture suggesting he was Princess Margaret's lover we could have cost the *Sun* thousands of pounds in damages.

The final indignity came as we left the office, crestfallen, that evening. The deputy editor called out to us: 'By the way, lads, you can forget the new suits.'

But Harry and I were determined to restore our reputations. Not long afterwards, we set off for the Caribbean when Harry got a tip that Roddy Llewellyn was to holiday with Princess Margaret at her home on Mustique. Harry had a plan: we would go in advance, book into the only hotel on the island and pose as tourists. Under this very thin cover, we would, we hoped, get pictures and stories of Roddy and Margaret relaxing on the sun-kissed sands.

So off we went, arriving in Mustique via Barbados two days later. We booked in to the Cotton House Hotel and went down to dinner that evening to find to our horror that Harry, his wife Linda and I were the only guests in the hotel.

We thought it was going to be very difficult doing an under-cover operation when there was no cover to go under. An added complication was that Margaret was already on the island, but Roddy had yet to join her, so we had three days to wait before he arrived.

By coincidence, the Queen and the Duke of Edinburgh were on an island-hopping tour of the Caribbean in the royal yacht *Britannia*. We already knew that the Queen was due to visit her sister two days before Roddy arrived; what we didn't realize was the programme had been changed. Originally, the Queen's short visit was to be private, with no press allowed to cover it. Imagine the shock we got when we turned up, posing as tourists, at the quay to find most of Fleet Street there to greet her and the Duke.

Of course they recognized us, and from then on, I suppose, our cover was blown. But because we were guests at the hotel, we were invited to the dance held there that evening for the royal visitors.

The Duke spent most of the evening pressed up against the bar, while the Queen and Margaret danced with many of the guests. Harry and I were just wandering around, mingling, when Ronald Allison, who was the Queen's press secretary at that time, came up to Harry and said: 'Hello, Harry, how is the *Sun* going these days?'

Harry was gobsmacked. '*Sun*? what *Sun*? I don't know what you're talking about,' he gibbered.

This made Ron Allison laugh and start looking around for me. I shot out of the room, hoping I hadn't been spotted, but I had. The following morning we were invited to leave. Harry tried to argue with the managing director of the hotel, but I said: 'No, let's go now.'

I realized that if we got to Barbados quickly we could probably get Roddy there on his way in. So we got a plane and flew from Mustique about ten o'clock that morning, flying over Princess Margaret's villa en route to photograph it from the air.

We landed in Barbados, then booked into a hotel near the airport and started to make our plans. Harry was convinced that Roddy would arrive that night, so we went to the airport. Sure enough, Roddy landed and was met by a huge woman and whisked off in a car. We thought: 'God! Where is he going?' But it was only an overnight stop, and the following morning we began doorstepping the airport at six o'clock so we wouldn't miss him.

Harry is never very good in the morning, as it takes him a long time to wake up. But his eyes shot wide open when Roddy stepped out of a car just after 6.30 a.m. I walked over to him and said: 'OK, Roddy, we're from the *Sun* in London. Do you want it the hard way or the easy way?'

He said: 'What do you mean?'

I explained: 'Well, the easy way is you sit down and pose for a few photographs. And the hard way is I chase you all around the airport and it could be very embarrassing.'

I suppose he thought he didn't really have any choice, so he agreed to pose. Harry asked him a few tentative questions, and we walked off, thinking we had done quite well. By this time Roddy was queueing up for his flight to Mustique, and I said to Harry: 'Why don't you get stuck into him while he's in the queue and can't leave?'

Harry did as I suggested and Roddy suddenly started to open up.

Harry got the most amazing quotes out of him. Roddy said: 'I'm tired of hiding in cupboards.' Then he went on to talk about the difficulties of conducting a royal romance. He talked about his love for Margaret, and how he had met the Queen.

Then we took him upstairs for coffee because there was a photographer from the *Daily Mail* lurking around the airport. We also knew that at ten o'clock that morning the Queen was due to fly from Barbados to London on Concorde, and we were worried that, with so many pressmen covering her departure from the airport, we could lose our exclusive.

We wanted Roddy out of the way, so we took him for some tea and managed to get him on his flight without anyone else getting to him. As he flew out for Mustique, Harry and I were hugging each other with delight about our wonderful exclusive.

About an hour later, we bumped into Ron Bell, a veteran photographer then working for the Press Association in London. He is a very nice man and one of my true friends. He happened to be flying back with the Queen on Concorde, and I asked him if he would take my film with him. Ron knew I had been up to something, but he was too professional, and too much of a good friend, to ask about it. So Concorde took off with the Queen and Ron carrying back our film.

It made a terrific show in the *Sun* next day. We had Page One with the story: 'MY LOVE FOR MARGARET' by Roddy, and pictures of the villa where they were staying together, as well as Margaret meeting the Queen, and Roddy posing especially for us at Barbados Airport.

After we had been kicked off Mustique, we had been very low, but we had fought back. One of Harry's greatest qualities is that he never stays down long, no matter how low he gets. He can always lift himself, and anybody he is working with, out of the trough.

After we got this great exclusive purely by hard work and determination, Hilary Bonner, another *Sun* reporter, was speaking to the *Sun*'s News Editor, at that time Ken Donlan. 'How are Arthur and Harry getting on?' she asked.

Ken looked up and told her: 'Well, they were kicked off the island without a story, but I have just spoken to them and I know they will crack this one.'

And that is exactly what we did. We came back from the dead with a story and pictures that saved the situation. We never ever got pictures of Margaret and Roddy together, but we did get the first ever interview Roddy gave about his relationship with the Queen's sister.

That was the start of our great partnership, the *Sun*'s legendary royal team of Harry and Arthur, who scooped everybody in the eighties. We achieved a lot, we have been to a lot of places, and are great friends, even though we no longer work together.

Harry, who now works for the *Daily Mirror*, is a very funny man and always terrific company. He loves his family, cares about other people, and takes great pride in his appearance. He is always so smartly dressed that I have nicknamed him 'The little soldier'.

It amazed me that Harry could stagger out of bed early enough to catch Roddy Llewellyn, because he is hopeless when it comes to getting up in the morning. When we were abroad on royal tours, one of my great worries was making certain he was down in time to catch the press bus each day.

The first time we went to Kathmandu, in November 1980, we were due to set off from our hotel very early one day about six o'clock. When it was time to go I was quite concerned because Harry hadn't appeared.

I went upstairs and started banging on his bedroom door. As I got no reply I started shouting: 'Harry, are you up? Harry, Harry, are you up?' After about five minutes of almost beating the door down, it opened, and there stood a sixteen-stone German tourist, nearly seven feet tall. He looked down at me and between gritted teeth spat these words out: 'My name iz not Harry, but I am up.' I had woken him from a deep sleep. Apologizing, I went back downstairs to find Harry sitting on the press bus. He had changed his room the previous evening without telling me.

Another one of the earliest Rats to join the Royal Pack was Ashley Walton of the *Daily Express*. He dresses in a very English style, rather like one of the characters in the BBC TV series 'Yes, Minister'. As a result I nicknamed him Sir Humphrey. Like most of us, he has had many close encounters of the worst kind with the Royals, and many of these have occurred at Sandringham, in Norfolk.

To me, the Queen's estate eight miles from King's Lynn is the loveliest of all her homes. It is set among beautiful pine woods, dotted with lovely little villages, and pheasant dash out of the undergrowth as you drive around the back roads. But this peaceful scene is often disturbed by the sound of Royals letting unwary pressmen know that they are not welcome.

In fact, the only time the Queen has ever been seen to lose her cool was when she shouted at photographers there in 1981: 'Go away, go on, leave us alone.'

Ashley has frequently been on the receiving end of such pleasantries, but it was his turn to surprise the Queen during a state visit to India in November 1983. Ashley and James Whitaker, who have never been very close, had fallen out over some minor matter during an inspection by the Queen of St Thomas's Church of England School in New Delhi. They were arguing loudly in the press pen as the royal entourage approached. The row got so heated they began kicking each other and swearing at the tops of their voices. The Queen's press secretary, Michael Shea, was trying to announce that she would confer her personal award, the Order of Merit, on Mother Teresa of Calcutta during the tour. But his words were being drowned out by the fight. 'Please, gentlemen, please, the Queen is coming,' Shea pleaded. Ashley and James looked up to find her glaring at them, just a few feet away.

A Palace official who witnessed this unseemly squabble described it as 'two old tarts having a fight in a brothel in Berlin at the end of the war'.

But Ashley claims the worst telling-off he ever received came from the Duke of Edinburgh a few years later. He was covering the Royal Family's New Year holiday at Sandringham when he happened to come across the Duke out for a stroll near the main house. Feeling enterprising, Ashley decided to approach the formidable Philip because the royal yacht *Britannia* had rescued hundreds of South Yemeni citizens from a civil war in the Persian Gulf the previous day. As the Queen's husband was formerly a serving officer with the Royal Navy, he thought he might commend *Britannia*'s daring sailors.

'Good morning, sir,' he said. 'I do apologize for interrupting your holiday, but I thought you might like to say a few words about the wonderful job *Britannia*'s crew have just done.'

The Duke beamed at him. 'Ah, yes, I would like to say a few words,' he said politely.

Ashley could not believe his luck. Scrabbling in his coat pocket, he produced a notebook and stood with his pen poised, ready to take down the exclusive story he thought he was about to get from Prince Philip.

'Yes, I would just like to say...FUCK OFF!' roared the Duke, his phoney smile suddenly vanishing. 'Fuck off at once, and don't hang about here again!'

Totally deflated, Ashley stood in the road waiting to be picked up by his photographer as Prince Philip disappeared into the distance. He waited and waited but his lift failed to arrive. After fifteen minutes, Ashley was horror-stricken when he suddenly noticed the Duke of Edinburgh in a Land Rover heading back down the road straight for him. He stopped as he passed, wound down the car window and bellowed: 'I thought I told you to fuck off!' Ashley pulled himself together and did exactly that. He legged it as fast as he could until he came across his photographer waiting at the next crossroads.

The Queen's husband definitely has no love for the press. His elder son, by contrast, has never been quite so aggressive, even when the press are testing his patience to the limit.

In 1989, I was following a shooting party led by the Prince of Wales in the village of Anmer on the Sandringham estate. Driving his Range Rover up to my car, Prince Charles beckoned me to come over to him. 'Hello, Mr Edwards,' he said.

'Hello, Mr Windsor,' I replied cheekily.

Immediately, his friendly mood changed. I could see he had not taken my tactless quip at all well. 'I'm only having a joke with you,' I said.

At once his normal courtesy reappeared. 'Why are you following me around?' he asked.

'Because you are the next King of England, sir. And everything you do is of interest,' I told him. 'I'm not chasing your wife around Harrods, or pestering your children at school.'

He appeared to appreciate my explanation and smiled. At that precise moment Jim Bennett, the best of the British paparazzi, was summoned by the Prince's policeman to share the reprimand. 'Why is Mr Edwards the only national news-paperman here?' the Prince asked him.

Jim replied: 'Because the others are too scared to come. We do all their dirty work for them. But Arthur prefers to do his own dirty deeds.'

Prince Charles seemed to accept this. He put one arm around my shoulders and said: 'We should have more chats like this. It helps to clear the air.'

I'm sorry to say the Prince and I have not always been on such good terms. After he moved into his country home, Highgrove, near Tetbury, Gloucestershire in 1980, I was sent down to see if I could get some pictures.

Walking across a public footpath that used to run at the bottom of the estate, which has since been moved, I was confronted by the Prince on horseback riding in the opposite direction. 'This is private property,' he told me angrily.

'No, it's not,' I said. 'It's a public right of way.'

Charles disagreed.

'Look,' I said, 'I'm not here to argue with you. Go and look at the sign over there if you don't believe me.'

The Prince would not give up. 'Well, footpaths are for walking on, not for taking pictures from.'

In reply I gave him the most pathetic of answers. 'I'm only doing my job,' I said lamely.

'Some job,' snapped Charles as he galloped off.

'At least I've got a job,' I shouted after him, at the same time banging off a picture.

I found out later that he headed straight for the house and stormed into the Highgrove kitchen, where two policemen and the caretaker Paddy Whiteland were sitting drinking coffee. Charles smashed his whip on the table and coffee cups went flying. 'You're all sitting here when you are supposed to be protecting me, and I've got Arthur Edwards on my front lawn,' he yelled. 'Go and arrest him immediately.'

The police officers protested: 'But we can't. He's on a public footpath,' they explained.

'Don't argue with me, just do it,' he said and slammed the door on his way out.

The disgruntled detectives got up and hurried out to placate the furious Prince, but by the time they reached the field I was long gone.

Incidents like this have often prompted critics to attack the media for invading the Royal Family's privacy, and have resulted in calls for tighter controls on the press. After one barrage of criticism in the House of Commons, the entire Royal Rat Pack was called scum. Prince Charles, no doubt, would love to see us all thrown into the Tower of London. But he was amused when Harry Arnold, while discussing another round of criticism, characteristically treated this attack in his witty way. 'We may be scum, but we're the Crème de la Scum,' he said.

The Prince, puzzled by some of the tales that turn up in the tabloid press, once asked Harry: 'Where do you get your stories from?'

Harry promptly started grabbing pieces of thin air as if trying to catch imaginary butterflies. 'There's one,' he said, grinning, and pretended to snatch another one flying past. 'Look, there's another one!'

The Prince smiled and shook his head. 'I thought as much,' he sighed.

CHAPTER FOUR

Sarah's Story

On a bitterly cold day in February 1978, I sat in a little Chelsea mews house chatting to the woman who had been the clear favourite in Prince Charles's affections for the past eight months. Lady Sarah Spencer had invited me into her home with reporter James Whitaker to give us an interview about her long battle against the slimmers' disease anorexia nervosa. She hoped in this way to help other girls suffering from the same problem.

As Earl Spencer's eldest daughter showed us her family albums, I was shocked by the photographs revealing the graphic evidence of her illness. The lovely twenty-three-year-old redhead was just skin and bone.

She admitted to us that at one point she had lived on nothing but Coca-Cola, and had begun to lose the enamel on her teeth because her body was so starved of nourishment. She also confessed that she had regularly swallowed laxatives in a desperate bid to lose more weight. The eating disorder had caused her normally shapely five-feet-seven-inch frame to weigh a skeletal five and three-quarter stones.

She believed her drastic dieting was the result of an unhappy love affair and upheavals in her family. 'The combination of the two things was catastrophic,' Sarah explained.

For almost three years, she refused to admit she was anorexic and concealed her condition from family and friends. When she first met Prince Charles at Windsor Castle during Ascot Week in 1977, he asked her if she had anorexia. Sarah insisted that she did not, although she realized, as she did so, that the perceptive Prince didn't believe her.

45

When she had to eat normally at dinner parties, she told us she would force the meal down and then bring it up again. As Sarah poured out her moving story, not one of us would have believed that six years later her younger sister Diana would suffer from a very similar illness. And by a sad coincidence, the cause would be the same: a disastrous romance combined with an unhappy family background.

Princess Diana, just like her sister, hid her disorder from the world when she too realized that the love of her life had ended. As medical history repeated itself so soon, it is difficult to believe that the Prince of Wales was responsible for his wife's bulimia, as has often been alleged. This eating disorder, which involves bingeing then throwing up, is so similar to her sister's anorexia that a common cause seems likely. Psychologists say it is frequently the result of a disturbed childhood. Sarah tended to confirm this when she told us that 'domestic upheavals concerning my family' were involved.

Her parents had separated when she was twelve. Her sister Diana was then six years old. According to many child psychiatrists, these are crucial stages in young girls' lives. The turmoil in the Spencer girls' childhood was compounded when their father introduced a new woman into the family, his second wife Raine. When she first appeared at their home, Althorp, Sarah described her as 'an all too frequent visitor'. Later, the Spencer children dubbed her Acid Raine. Significantly, when James and I mentioned her stepmother Sarah refused to discuss her.

Soon after she began dating Prince Charles, she began to eat again, and booked herself into a Regent's Park nursing home, where she steadily regained the weight she had lost. The girl I saw in her little house off the Fulham Road was glowing with good health.

We had got to know her quite well over the past year. James and I had seen her turn up at the polo with Prince Charles, and noticed her exercising his horses before matches. On every occasion we had bumped into her she was always friendly and good fun. She seemed to enjoy being photographed with the world's most eligible bachelor.

When we visited her home she showed us how she had carefully preserved in her photo albums every newspaper report of their appearances in public together. It was clear that the Prince of Wales had a special place in her affections.

At that time, everyone thought that Charles and Sarah were ideally suited. Her father, Johnnie Spencer, had served the Queen as an equerry and she had known the Royal Family all her life. She had grown up at Park House on the Queen's Sandringham estate, and attended tea parties with Prince Andrew. She loved the outdoor life and to this day still hunts with the Belvoir each week in the winter. With this background and a sweet personality, Lady Sarah seemed to have all the qualities needed for a future Queen.

But to our astonishment, as she talked about her life and her friendship with Prince Charles, Sarah said she would never marry him. 'He is a fabulous person, but I am not in love with him,' she declared. 'I wouldn't marry anyone I didn't love, whether it was the dustman or the King of England. If he asked me I would turn him down.'

James and I couldn't believe our ears. We had just returned from Switzerland, where we had covered Charles and Sarah's romantic skiing holiday. In the Alps they had seemed to be on top of the world, enjoying the bright sunshine and perfect powder on the pistes, as well as each other's company. Both James and I had been convinced they were crazy about each other. But those ten days together were to wreck any chance Lady Sarah had of becoming Charles's bride.

I have covered dozens of ski trips with the Royals since then, but that first one with the Prince and his sweetheart still stands out in my memory as the best ever.

I had received a tip that Prince Charles was heading off on a break in the Alps with his cousins, the Duke and Duchess of Gloucester, and his girlfriend Sarah Spencer.

The Duke knew that Charles was keen on skiing so he introduced him to his old friend, the former Olympic skier Charlie Palmer-Tomkinson and his wife Patty. They regularly rented a small chalet in the Swiss resort Klosters. They all met up at a dinner party held at Kensington Palace, and got on so well they planned a holiday together.

It was suggested that Prince Charles might like to bring a chum and he chose Lady Sarah Spencer. She had learned to ski while attending a Swiss finishing school, so the Prince believed she was expert enough to keep up with the rest of the party, when they tackled the most terrifying black runs.

Unfortunately, I did not know all this when I set off for Switzerland. All I could do was head for Zurich Airport and wait, hoping to follow the royal party when they arrived.

I teamed up with my pal Jimmy Gray of the *Daily Mail*, figuring that together we had a better chance of beating the competition. So when Charles, Lady Sarah and the Gloucesters left the airport Jimmy and I quickly tagged on to the end of the royal convoy in the *Daily Mail*'s hired Mercedes, looking very official.

By dint of this ruse, we became the only photographers to find out that the Prince was spending his first holiday at the fashionable resort.

But as we raced along the mountain roads behind the Prince's car, Jimmy kept wanting to stop, because he was desperate for a pee. I kept saying: 'No, no, we can't stop because we'll lose them.' And Jimmy kept protesting: 'I must, I must!' For more than an hour, he managed to hold on, until we got to Klosters just as Charles and Sarah were getting out of their British embassy car. If only I had had a camera at the ready, because the expression on the Prince's face was priceless. He could not believe that we were there at all. His destination had been such a closely guarded secret. And even more astonishing was the fact that Jimmy nearly knocked him over as he rushed into the nearest hotel to find a loo.

A short time later, after checking into a hotel next to Prince Charles's chalet, we got our gear and began doorstepping it. Jimmy covered the back, while I hovered outside the front. Within a very few minutes the Prince and Lady Sarah came out of the main door in their ski clothes, ready for the slopes. So within half an hour of arriving I had taken the picture we had come for. And all my rivals were still in Zurich, wondering where Jimmy and I were.

In those days, restrictive union practices still affected much of Fleet Street. The *Sun* did not have an agreement with the darkroom staff to transmit wire pictures from abroad. But the *Daily Mail* did, so Jimmy and I drove all the way back to Zurich and wired my picture to his office. We shared the picture and it appeared next morning in both newspapers.

My name didn't appear under the picture in the *Sun*, because it would have caused an industrial dispute with the darkroom staff. But it didn't matter, because it was a marvellous feeling to know that I had beaten everyone.

The next day, we followed the Prince and Sarah, and I asked him if we could take another picture. He agreed, so we suggested to Lady Sarah that it would look nice if she stood close to him. She seemed really happy to be photographed with him and we had a spread of several fun-packed pictures for the next edition. Off we went again to wire the pictures from Zurich to London. And so slowly word got out that the Prince was in Klosters.

But it wasn't until the third day that our rivals on the other papers caught up with us. Every day, Prince Charles posed for pictures and, instead of being annoyed by our presence, he was friendly and encouraged us to take advantage of the wonderful facilities at Klosters. 'Why don't you take some ski lessons while you're here?' he urged.

By this time photographers had come from all over Europe to get material on the Prince and his current girlfriend. But when they got what they wanted they all drifted off again. On the last day of the royal holiday only Albert Foster of the *Daily Mirror* and I were still there, and Prince Charles asked us if we would take a picture of the whole ski party with him. As well as Lady Sarah and his hosts the Palmer-Tomkinsons, there was his cousin the Duke of Gloucester and his wife Birgitte.

They lined up together in bright sunshine on the top of the Gotchnagrat mountain, while we snapped away. But Prince Charles suddenly lost his balance and toppled on to the other members of the party, who collapsed like dominoes.

It was a great picture, as the Prince realized immediately. Quick as a flash gun, he said: 'Remember, I asked you to take these pictures for me, not for your newspapers.' It was very tempting to send one of these fun pictures back to London, but as he had done everything we had asked every day for ten days, it would have been churlish to betray him. So our picture desks never saw the best shot of the whole trip. Both Albert and I kept our word and nobody in London ever knew.

Today, photographers are always on the lookout for pictures with a difference – especially ones in which the Royals make fools of themselves, falling over on the slopes or taking a tumble from a horse. In fact, in 1988 at Klosters, the only picture published after a photo call was arranged of the Prince and Princess of Wales with the Duke and Duchess of York, was of Diana landing on her bottom. No amount of pleading by Prince Charles in these tougher times would have stopped that picture being published. It was not until twelve years later, when Patty Palmer-Tomkinson invited me into the chalet where the Prince and Lady Sarah had stayed, that I discovered how modest it was. The wooden cabin had only two double bedrooms and two small singles in the attic. The Palmer-Tomkinsons and the Gloucesters naturally occupied the larger rooms, while Prince Charles and Lady Sarah ended up in the cramped bedrooms under the roof. There was so little space that the Prince's body-guard, Inspector John MacLean, had to sleep on a camp bed in the hall downstairs.

The chalet had only one bathroom for seven people, and the hot-water tank held only enough for one bath. When they returned from skiing each evening, the Palmer-Tomkinsons as hosts insisted that Prince Charles be the first to soak his cold, aching bones in the tub. I have no idea who the unlucky one was at the end of the queue for the bathroom. John MacLean did slightly better, because he went next door to a small hotel for a hot shower.

In 1978 the Prince and the press still had quite a friendly relationship. In fact, we used to go to the chalet each evening and check with his police officer if he had been injured. And

John MacLean would say: 'No, he's fine.' Then we would discuss our chances of getting a good picture the next day. It wasn't unusual, as we stood on the doorstep, to see Prince Charles pass down the hall with only a towel wrapped around him on his way back from his bath. Far from being embarrassed, he said only: 'Don't mind me. Carry on with your news conference.'

Patty did all the cooking for the party, but I later learned that the Prince would take turns with the rest of his friends helping with the domestic chores. 'I'll be the chalet maid tonight,' he would say with a grin. And while his hostess gratefully collapsed after dinner, he and Sarah would do the dishes. Afterwards, the whole group used to play party games before going up to bed.

I have been asked many times whether Charles and Sarah were lovers. Only the two people involved really know the answer to that question, but the adoring way Sarah looked at the Prince during that holiday together suggested to me they were more than just good friends.

The only flaw in their blossoming relationship was that Sarah was not the expert skier the Prince had been led to believe. She simply could not keep up with the daredevil Charles and his party on the slopes. The Prince's disillusionment with his girl-friend's ability soon affected the rest of their relationship.

In the confines of the small chalet a member of the party could not help overhearing when Charles and Sarah had a row. 'I thought you said you could ski,' the Prince moaned at her. The next day Charlie Palmer-Tomkinson zoomed off with the Prince, while Lady Sarah was left sedately skiing with her hostess.

The Prince of Wales had never before had the chance to live under the same roof in such close proximity with a girlfriend. Sadly, their romance did not survive this testing experience. He discovered that Sarah was a chain-smoker, a habit he detested. She is also by her own admission a 'bridge fanatic' like her sister Diana, while he does not play card games at all. Perhaps it is not surprising that when they returned to London Lady Sarah told us: 'Our relationship is totally platonic.'

51

It seemed to me that the holiday in the Alps marked the beginning of the end for Sarah as the Prince's favourite. That is probably the reason she talked so freely to James and me in London two weeks later. The fact that she did so told us that their affair was fizzling out.

Sarah is now happily married to Neil McCorquodale, a Lincolnshire farmer, and is the mother of three beautiful children. She often acts as an extra lady-in-waiting to her sister the Princess of Wales.

I did see Charles and Sarah together once again, a few months later, at a horse show in Warwickshire, where the Prince was competing in a cross-country event. The interview Sarah had given us telling the world she did not love the Prince soon appeared, and she was never again considered as a future Princess.

About the same time Lady Sarah confided to a friend: 'I'm not the one for him, but I know who is. My younger sister Diana is only sixteen, but she's tall, blonde and has great legs. She would be perfect for him.'

CHAPTER FIVE

The Royal Hunt of the Sun

The very first time I saw Lady Diana Spencer I didn't take a blind bit of notice of her, which seems incredible, looking back now. I was on my way to Sandringham on a Sunday morning in February 1980 to photograph the Royals attending church, when I spotted two girls strolling near the House. 'Blimey,' I thought, 'that's Prince Charles's girlfriend Amanda Knatchbull.'

The thought immediately occurred to me: 'Christ, if she's staying here with him on holiday the romance must be hotting up.' I pulled up with a screech of brakes and instantly regretted it, because my sudden stop alerted the girls and they turned around and scarpered back into the house.

When I enquired later who the second girl had been I was told: 'That's only Earl Spencer's youngest daughter Diana. She came up for the weekend to keep Amanda company.' I was so busy clocking the girl who was, at the time, the hot tip to marry Prince Charles, that I totally ignored the baby-faced blonde in a brown baggy overcoat.

If I had known then that there was no real romance between Prince Charles and Amanda I would probably have paid more attention to the girl out walking with her. But by the time I turned my old blue Marina around and tore back along the road the girls had disappeared back inside the Jubilee Gates.

I could have kicked myself for not getting a picture of Amanda. It taught me a bitter lesson. From that day on, I started keeping a camera loaded, and ready to use, on the front seat of the car.

53

I felt even more annoyed when Amanda failed to turn up at the church service, and I toured the estate for a few hours, hoping to spot her again. Eventually, I ended up at King's Lynn railway station, and linked up with a dear friend, Alison Howe from the *Eastern Daily Press*, who often checked the comings and goings of the Royals when they were on her patch.

Alison asked the station master, whom she knew well, if any Royals had left for London. He said, 'You're too late. Lady Diana Spencer and Amanda Knatchbull went on the three-thirty.' As I was with Alison, the man assumed I was her photographer, and he added cockily: 'I've been told there's a bloke up here from Fleet Street called Arthur Edwards and I've been warned to look out for him. He's got a great big lens. If you see him will you let me know?'

Biting my lip to stop laughing, I said: 'Of course, I'll tell you.'

Then casually I enquired what time the train reached Liverpool Street. He told me it would get there around six o'clock. I sauntered off and then dashed to a telephone box to call Harry Arnold, the royal reporter for the *Sun*. I told him to get to Liverpool Street as fast as possible as Amanda was about to arrive.

With photographer David Hill he got to the station just as the train from Norfolk pulled in. But, as hundreds of passengers poured off the train, they had trouble spotting the two girls. Fast-thinking Harry figured that they would have a lot of luggage, and would need a porter or a trolley, so he waited until the two girls finally trundled out of the station with a barrow-load of baggage.

'There she is!' Harry said to David, who began to blaze away at dark-haired Amanda. Then, head down, and giggling non-stop, the girls charged through to the taxi rank, sending their cases spinning all over the platform.

Harry and David gallantly picked up their luggage, and the two young women thanked them profusely. The following morning Amanda's picture appeared in the *Sun* with a story of her romantic weekend with Prince Charles. Lady Diana's first tangle with the press didn't get a mention.

The reason I was so keen to capture Amanda was that a year earlier I had photographed Charles and Amanda on holiday in the Bahamian island Eleuthera, frolicking on the beach. It seemed Lord Mountbatten's granddaughter was being paraded in front of the Prince to see if a romance might blossom. But despite the best efforts of Lord Louis, Prince Charles always preferred blondes.

I didn't see Diana again until five months later, when I was covering a polo match at Ambersham, near Midhurst in Sussex. Prince Charles was playing for the Blue Devils team with his father, the Duke of Edinburgh, cheering him on.

I hate polo. It may be a thrilling game to play, but for someone reared on football and cricket, it's bloody boring watching men on expensive horses charging up and down a huge field with long sticks chasing a little white ball. I was so bored that I began chatting to a member of the Duke's staff, who casually mentioned in conversation that the royal party was staying at the nearby home of Robert de Pass, a lifelong friend of the Duke. And when I asked how many were in the party he said: 'Apart from the two Princes there is only a girl called Lady Diana Spencer. I think the Prince of Wales is quite keen on her even though she is quite young.'

'That's a good story,' I thought. 'I'll see if I can find her.' I walked up to the small members' enclosure and spotted her at once. She was so wonderfully good-looking that she shone out of the group. But the real giveaway was the gold initial 'D' on a chain around her neck. Although I was some distance away, looking through a long lens, she saw me and, I am convinced, posed for a picture. With her chin resting on one hand, she boldly looked straight into my camera. I fired off two quick frames of her, and witnessed, for the first time, the famous blush which would soon endear her to millions throughout the world.

She was casually dressed in a summer floral print skirt and white voile blouse with a frilled collar. Over this she wore a knitted waistcoat. My instincts told me there could be a big story in this girl, and so I phoned the reference library at the *Sun* to find out some details on her.

I discovered that she had only just celebrated her nineteenth birthday. It made me wonder what the Prince was doing with a teenager. Nevertheless, I sent the pictures back to my office in London, and asked them to file the shots, but not to syndicate them. I had a hunch these were pictures we should keep exclusively for our own paper.

Even then, Prince Charles did his best to protect her. When the game ended, he drove off in his Aston Martin sports car without so much as a glance in her direction.

From Sussex Prince Charles joined the royal yacht *Britannia* at Cowes, and I followed him there. Although I searched to see if Diana was among the other guests going aboard, I failed to find her. In fact, I later learned she had been smuggled on to the yacht.

Even the ship's photographer, who takes souvenir pictures of every guest arriving on *Britannia*, was ordered to stand down when the royal barge carrying Diana approached. Prince Charles was determined to keep this girl a secret.

She was ostensibly on board as a friend of the Prince's cousin Lady Sarah Armstrong-Jones, the daughter of the Queen's sister Princess Margaret.

Charles's valet, the late Stephen Barry, some years later remembered that Lady Diana made a great first impression on everyone below decks. 'The crew of *Britannia* fell in love with her to a man,' he said. 'The royal servants liked her and the stewards ran around saying: "Gosh, isn't Lady Diana lovely?"' What neither Diana, Charles nor the crew knew then was that exactly one year later she would sail once again aboard *Britannia* – but this time as the Princess of Wales on her honeymoon.

The following month I went to Scotland to cover the Braemar Games, where all the Royals usually turned out for this traditional Highland sports day, held on the first Saturday in September. That morning, on my way along the Deeside Road that runs past Balmoral Castle, I spotted the Prince's green Range Rover parked on the banks of the River Dee.

Reporter James Whitaker and photographer Kenny Lennox, who were then working for the *Daily Star*, were with me. 'Good

God! Look over there,' I yelled. We jumped out of the car and ran 300 yards through a field to get within shooting distance. We could see someone with the Prince.

A boyish figure hidden in an old green Barbour jacket, wellington boots and a peaked cap, was watching him fish. Just when we were getting close, an angry farmer, obviously the owner of the field, suddenly appeared, shouting: 'Get off my land. Get off my land. You're trespassing.'

This racket immediately alerted Prince Charles, who stopped fishing and made a dash for his car with his mystery companion. All I got was a boring photograph of an unrecognizable person standing by his Range Rover. The Prince quickly drove off.

Because Charles was so predictable, we suspected he might head for another spot down river, where he often fished. Sure enough, when we reached it, he was standing in mid-stream and his unknown companion was watching from the riverbank. But on hearing our car arrive she ran and hid behind a tree.

Through his binoculars, James noticed that the person we had seen earlier was watching us with the aid of a compact mirror in her hand. This meant that she could see us, but we could not get a clear look at her.

To flush out this wily bird James devised a plan. He moved off to the right with Kenny Lennox, and I moved to the left, hoping that one of us would eventually get a clear shot of her hiding behind the tree. She quickly guessed what we were up to and, with enormous cool, suddenly left her hiding place and began to climb straight up the steep hillside away from the river, without once turning her head to look back. In a minute or so she had taken cover in the car.

Prince Charles, who through all this had carried on fishing, realized we had rumbled his companion and gave up in disgust. He packed up his rods and drove off in a huff.

Suddenly, out of the bushes near us, two furious figures emerged. Top freelance photographers Tim Graham and Anwar Hussein had been patiently hiding in the undergrowth, hoping the Prince would turn up at his favourite fishing pool, as he often did. But our noisy arrival had scuppered their plans, and they were not very pleased about it.

A blazing row then broke out between the freelancers and the Fleet Street staffmen, and a lot of things were said in the heat of the moment. If we had not turned up they would no doubt have got sensational scoop pictures of Charles with his future bride. In fact, nobody pictured them together until the day of their engagement, nearly six months later.

That afternoon at the Highland Games, a very close friend who worked at the Palace told me that the Prince of Wales's mysterious lady was Lady Diana Spencer. Suddenly everything clicked. It was the third time, to my knowledge, that Charles and Diana had been together in the past month.

As I had no reporter with me I phoned Harry Arnold that evening at his home in Kent. I told him the only two exclusive facts I had: her name and some information gleaned from my Royal Household source. This man convinced me that something was going on between Prince Charles and the girl twelve years his junior, when he said: 'She follows him around like a lamb.'

The following day, a Sunday, Harry went to a charity cricket match near his home with a close friend and colleague, *Sun* reporter Vic Chapple. They discussed the events of the previous day over a few glasses of champagne, and Vic said: 'She sounds like a perfect English rose.'

Harry jumped up. 'That's it!' he said, and rushed off to a phonebox to file the whole story.

It became a front-page story which revealed for the first time the growing relationship between the future King and Earl Spencer's youngest daughter. Harry had brilliantly interpreted the information I gave him, realizing that this girl had all the qualities to be Queen.

Fortunately, the editor that day was Peter Stephens, a very experienced newspaperman, who had such great faith in his royal team that he decided to splash the story all over Page One. As he said to me afterwards: 'I knew when I read Harry's copy there was nothing else I could do with the story.' By contrast, our rivals on the *Daily Star* tucked their story away on an inside page. Lacking my exclusive tip, James Whitaker simply wrote that the Prince had gone fishing with a pretty girl.

Finally, the *Sun* was able to use the picture I had taken of Diana at the polo match five weeks earlier under the headline: 'HE'S IN LOVE AGAIN. LADY DI IS THE NEW GIRL FOR CHARLES.'

It was the first time that the nickname Lady Di, which was soon to be known worldwide, was ever used in a newspaper.

While Harry Arnold was composing his historic splash, I was flying back to London on the same plane as Lady Diana. Prince Charles had arranged for two of his closest friends, Nicholas Soames and Andrew Parker Bowles, to escort her. Of Andrew's wife Camilla there was no sign.

She had been with the royal party at the Braemar gathering, so we assumed she had stayed at Balmoral with the Prince and the Royal Family for a few days longer.

I remember that as we went through the security check at the airport Diana had her handbag searched. James Whitaker sneaked a peek inside it and told me: 'Well, she doesn't have very much jewellery.' This lack of sparklers was soon taken care of. It was also probably one of the last times she was subjected to a security search. All I noticed as I followed her up the aircraft steps was her stunning legs clad in sheer red nylon tights.

While she was waiting in the baggage hall at Heathrow I went up to her and asked if she would pose for a picture, while her gentlemen friends were off searching for their bags. She blushed but agreed. Unfortunately, in the excitement I set my camera on the wrong exposure and totally screwed up the picture. I have never told anyone until now about the great shot of Diana in her red stockings which was destined never to be seen.

After the *Sun* story everyone began digging for more information on Lady Diana Spencer. But it was not until 17 September, more than two weeks later, that Harry and I tracked her down to a kindergarten in Pimlico where she worked as a nursery assistant. The rest of the Rat Pack, who had also sussed out her place of work, joined us.

I knocked on the door and asked the woman in charge if Lady Diana Spencer worked there. When she said yes, I asked if she would come out and speak to the press for a few minutes. After passing on this request, Diana's boss replied that she would come out and pose for a picture but would not give any interviews.

A second later, Lady Diana came out of the front door with two children from the nursery and we began snapping away.

She was posing in the garden with a child on each hip and the Nikons were rattling like machine-guns when the sun suddenly came out from behind a cloud. In a trice her flimsy summer skirt became totally see-through, and it was obvious to all that she had no petticoat on.

None of the lads said anything, because the pictures were so great. They just kept blazing away while Diana patiently posed up.

A lot of inaccurate stories have been written about the way these revealing photographs were obtained, which give the impression that she was set up. The truth is that it was just a pure fluke that we got a much better picture than we had ever hoped.

We took several other shots of her sitting down with the children on the grass. But, as far as our picture editors were concerned, the only one that mattered was Diana in the see-through skirt showing off her lovely long legs. It made Page One the next day under the headline 'CHARLIE'S GIRL'.

When the Press Association contacted her for a comment Diana was horrified. 'Oh God, I don't want to be remembered for having no petticoat,' she blurted out. But she got some comforting words from Prince Charles later, when he said: 'I didn't know you had such nice legs.'

After that the hunt was really on. We were outside her Coleherne Court flat in the Brompton Road at eight o'clock every morning. Then we followed her to the nursery and at lunchtime chased after her wherever she went. By this time she was beginning to recognize the regulars who doorstepped her, and had begun to sort out the good boys from the bad guys.

One morning, her car parked outside the nursery was boxed in by dustbins and beer barrels by a couple of French paparazzi to delay her departure. As she tried to move the heavy bins, she burst into tears of frustration and anger.

I arrived at that precise moment and rushed over to help. 'Don't let them see you cry,' I warned. 'They'd love that.' I hauled the barrels away and freed her car. She thanked me and drove off.

While outside Coleherne Court one night I saw her go for a walk with her flatmate Virginia Pitman. I was waiting with a colleague, Paul Fievez of the *Daily Mail*, who is a genuinely kind man. Diana and Virginia stopped for a chat. 'Why me?' Diana asked. 'Why all the interest?'

I mumbled something about her having no past, and she blushed.

Paul noticed her embarrassment and changed the subject. 'Listen, Lady Diana, when you get the job, remember it's Sir Paul for me and Sir Arthur for him.'

She laughed out loud but gave nothing away.

Each day we learned a little more about our quarry. She drove a blue Volkswagen and had Supertramp cassettes to play on her car stereo. She liked watching the motel soap opera 'Crossroads' on television with her flatmates. And sometimes she dashed out to the local shops to buy pink grapefruit for her breakfast.

At this time the Prince was a keen amateur jockey. On 24 October 1980 he was due to ride his horse Allibar in the Clun Handicap steeplechase for amateur jockeys at Ludlow Races. Naturally, Fleet Street's finest turned up in force, hoping Diana would be there with him.

Press harassment of the Princess-to-be had begun in earnest by now, and Diana was fast becoming every photographer's favourite target. I suddenly noticed her walking towards the paddock with Camilla Parker Bowles, and snatched a couple of quick shots. Then I went over and warned her not to go to the paddock, where the Prince was parading Allibar, because it was swarming with photographers. I wanted to keep my picture of her exclusive. She heeded my advice and went into the stand to watch the race.

I stood beside her, snapping away as she cheered on the Prince, who came a creditable second. But she couldn't stop herself running to the winner's enclosure to congratulate him. Fortunately, she had the sense to stay well in the background as he unsaddled the horse. She was jumping up and down with excitement because she had placed an each-way bet on him at 10/1.

By now, Diana was deeply in love with her Prince, so it wasn't surprising that she took such a keen interest in his favourite new sport.

On 14 November Prince Charles celebrated his thirty-second birthday at Wood Farm on the Sandringham estate. The other guests that weekend were the Queen, the Duke of Edinburgh, the chairman of the Guards Polo Club, Colonel Gerard Lee and his wife, and Lady Diana.

Jayne Fincher, the only woman photographer in the Rat Pack, told me she was convinced she had seen Diana arrive in a red Mini Metro. I passed on this information to *Sun* reporter Shan Lancaster who was working with me that weekend, and she filed it.

But when I checked the story with the Superintendent of Police, Harry Parkinson, he said: 'I have just left Wood Farm and I swear on a stack of bibles she isn't there.' As a result, I reluctantly asked Shan to kill the story. Next day I saw Diana in a field watching Charles shooting pheasants and realized we had been misled.

The fact that Diana had given up her German Volkswagen for a British-made Metro was another good sign that the romance was hotting up. Members of the Royal Family normally drive cars produced in Britain.

By this time Wood Farm was surrounded by at least a hundred newspaper, radio and television reporters and cameramen. Commander Michael Trestrail, the Queen's most senior policeman, devised a plan to help Diana elude the press and escape. Most of the press were camped at the farm's front gates and the plan was that the Prince would drive down to talk to them while Diana would nip out the back gate. Fearing this, I doorstepped the farm track at the back.

I teamed up with James Whitaker to lie in wait for the Prince's sweetheart. About four o'clock on the Sunday afternoon the red Metro suddenly appeared at the back entrance to the farm, escorted by a police Range Rover.

James, who was at the wheel of his red Cortina, drove alongside Lady Diana while I hung out of the back window with my camera. Once she reached the main road the police car abandoned her, and we had her all to ourselves. At speeds touching eighty miles an hour on the single-lane road, I snapped away as we tore along side by side.

Until she spotted us, Diana was under the impression she had got clean away. And I beautifully captured her shocked expression when we roared up beside her.

When we joked about it a few weeks later Lady Diana said, 'Sir Michael Edwardes [then the chairman of British Leyland] would have been furious with me for driving at those speeds before the car had been properly run in.'

Afterwards, I went straight into King's Lynn to wire my pictures to the office. Of course, I had to share it with James's newspaper the *Daily Star*. But once again, my picture was huge on Page One next day, while my rivals tucked it away on Page Three.

Soon afterwards, Prince Charles had to leave Diana behind when he flew off to India on an official visit. It was definitely make-your-mind-up time for Charles as he set off for the subcontinent.

The Duke of Edinburgh had been grumbling for some time that if his son didn't hurry up and choose a wife there would be no nice girls left. He was also concerned that while Charles wrestled with the greatest problem he had ever faced, he was being unfair to the girl who waited for his decision. He was fast approaching the stage when he would compromise Diana if he decided not to commit himself.

This great flaw in his character, his indecisiveness, had never been so much in evidence. The Prince's office staff have always privately moaned about the fact that he can never make up his mind about anything. And when it came to the greatest decision of his life, Charles characteristically wavered.

The long list of lovelies that Charles had loved and lost was fast becoming a joke. The Queen's subjects were beginning to tire of this endless search for the right girl. And behind closed Palace doors there were muttered comparisons with the late Duke of Windsor who, when he was Prince of Wales, failed to find a suitable single girl, fell in love with a married woman and rocked the monarchy.

Like everyone else around him, the Queen, too, was anxious that he should make his mind up one way or another, and not only because she wanted Charles to produce an heir and guarantee the line of succession. The whole family had been living under siege from the press while Charles dallied over his decision. 'The idea of this romance going on for another year is intolerable for everyone concerned,' his mother declared.

With pressures mounting from all sides, Charles had very little time to determine how he really felt. The whole world approved of Diana and wanted her to be his future Queen. But did Charles?

At the start of the Indian tour in Delhi he hosted a cocktail party for the press at the British High Commission. As we were chatting over a couple of drinks, the subject of Lady Diana came up. Paul Callan, who then worked for the *Daily Mirror*, said: 'I think that Lady Diana is coping very well with the pressure, don't you?'

The Prince considered this for a moment then said: 'That's very kind of you to say so. I must say I think she has been magnificent.'

Then he looked up at the searching expressions on our faces and added: 'You mustn't rush me, you know. It's very difficult. If only I could live with a girl before marrying her, but I can't. It's all right for chaps like you, you can afford to make a mistake, but I've got to get it right first time. And if I get it wrong you will be the first to criticize me in three years' time.'

Looking back, that short comment on the media's determination to rush him down the aisle proved sadly prophetic. He did get it wrong, and how we criticized him for it. Charles was obviously looking for a woman who was right for the country as his consort, and he hoped, right for him as well. But as events soon proved, she was perfect for the job and for the country, but a disastrous match for him.

I am certain now that, if they had been able to live together for two years or so, Charles and Diana would never have married. The gap in their intellects, interests and ages was just too wide to bridge.

Diana did not spend Christmas or New Year with her Prince. The Royal Family believed that her presence among them at such a time would convince everyone that an engagement was imminent. But, unaware of this, the press still besieged Sandringham and the Queen and her relatives got a taste of what life had been like for Diana outside Coleherne Court over the past few months.

Early in the New Year, Prince Charles stalked over to a group of us standing outside the village hall in Anmer, where the Royals had stopped for lunch during a shoot. 'I should like to take this opportunity to wish you all a very happy New Year and, to your editors, a very nasty one,' he said.

I replied: 'Well, I don't wish you anything nasty, sir. Happy New Year.'

He turned around, smiled and said: 'Thank you, Mr Edwards.'

I don't think Charles was too upset by our presence. He was more concerned about the Queen, who was infuriated by the invasion of the media during her holiday at Sandringham, her favourite home.

Without giving any clues to his future plans, Prince Charles flew off to Switzerland for his annual winter holiday a few days later. Photographers had gathered at Klosters from all over the world, hoping that Lady Diana would accompany him.

But she did not turn up at the Palmer-Tomkinsons' chalet, then or any other year – perhaps because her sister Lady Sarah had once holidayed there with the Prince.

When they did make their first trip together to Klosters, they stayed at a much larger chalet in Wolfgang, six kilometres outside the town.

Interest in the royal romance was so intense that a television crew had flown all the way from Australia. One morning, reporter Ray Martin, fronting the '60 Minutes' TV show, said good morning to the Prince, who immediately noticed his Australian accent. 'Where have you come from?' he asked.

'Australia,' Ray replied.

'Bloody hell' was Charles's instant reaction. Then, realizing he was being filmed, he quickly added: 'I'm coming to Australia in March, and I'm looking forward to it very much.'

When Martin's report was shown on Australian television the phrase 'Bloody hell' made front-page stories throughout the continent. The fact that he was keen to visit Australia didn't get much of a mention.

The same crew asked me to do an interview, and I agreed on one condition. I said I would do it outside the Prince's chalet as he was walking past in the background. For years, I had been a figure in the background of news film which featured the Prince. Just for once I wanted our roles reversed.

We arranged to shoot the interview at nine the following morning, just as the Prince was leaving his chalet to go skiing. Ray Martin decided that, as the Prince emerged, he would ask me the million-dollar question: 'Is Lady Di the one?'

It all went according to plan and as I answered emphatically: 'Yes, she is,' cameraman Brendan Ward swung the camera rapidly to catch the astonished look on the Prince's face.

After the interview was over, I went off to photograph him skiing. His only comment on my prediction that he would marry Diana was an amused: 'I see you're giving interviews to Australian TV now.'

I couldn't resist telling him: 'Well, they are as interested as we are in whether you are going to marry Lady Diana, sir.' The Prince merely grinned and set off down the piste.

Harry Arnold and I were so desperate to get some definite confirmation that an engagement was imminent that we decided to telephone Lady Diana in London.

When Harry got through to her flat, he told the flatmate who answered the phone: 'I have a call from Klosters for Lady Diana Spencer.' Of course, she rushed to take the call, thinking it was her Prince. And when Harry announced who he was, she burst into a fit of giggles.

'Well, who did you think it was?' he asked in mock surprise. Diana went into another giggling fit.

He then told her he was thinking of asking Prince Charles if he was going to marry her.

'I really don't know what to say,' she said. 'You know people keep asking me questions, but I'm the last person in the world who knows what's going on.'

This conversation could mean only one thing: the Prince had not yet popped the question. While Harry pondered this, I took over the call and we chatted for more than an hour. I told her how much the Prince was enjoying his break and seemed to be missing her.

Although Diana was friendly, she was just as cagey as the Prince, and never once gave anything away. We were not to know then that, just days later on his return to London, Charles would propose to Diana.

As he admitted on the day of their engagement, he invited her to dinner two days after he flew home, and asked her if she would be his wife. But he insisted that she think of what she was letting herself in for before replying.

Twenty-four hours later, she secretly flew to Australia to talk it over with her mother, Frances Shand Kydd who, with her then husband Peter, owned a sheep ranch near Canberra. We had a tip that Diana was Down Under, but our Australian colleagues came up with no leads, and enquiries at the Shand Kydd homestead brought firm denials.

For ten days, Diana relaxed with her mother at a beach house owned by friends on the coast. They endlessly discussed what the future would hold for her. But her return to London made us even more convinced that the wedding was on.

Our sharp-eyed Heathrow staff discovered that Diana had been given unprecedented treatment for a commoner by British Customs and Immigration officials. When her Qantas jet landed, she was taken off first and a private car whisked her away to London.

Prince Charles was making certain that she would be spared the ordeal of the arrival hall crowded with curious onlookers, but – more importantly – packed with pressmen.

Within a day of her return, Diana was with the Prince at Highgrove to give him the answer he wanted to hear.

Meanwhile, Harry and I were busy elsewhere. On 19 February Prince Andrew's twenty-first birthday diverted us from the hunt to the Royal Naval base at Culdrose, Cornwall. But the Navy's establishment was put off limits to the press and, in spite of our best efforts, we didn't lay eyes on Andrew.

Cutting our losses, we made a very early start next morning to try and get the only story that really mattered. We suspected that Prince Charles might be exercising his racehorse Allibar on the gallops at Lambourn in Berkshire; he was due to ride in the Cavalry Hunters Chase at Chepstow the following Saturday. So we were secretly hoping that Diana would be on the downs that morning with him.

It was around seven in the morning when we passed the Prince, with Diana beside him in a blue Ford Granada shooting brake, racing down the M4 heading towards Nick Gaselee's stables. Unfortunately, my cameras were locked in the boot of Harry's car. Once again I had forgotten my own rule always to carry a loaded camera with me.

Imagine my frustration at that moment. No one had ever caught the two of them together. Now here they were, yards away, sitting ducks; I had no means of snapping them.

We dropped back behind them, but the Prince promptly shot off into Membury motorway services and eluded us by sneaking off via the service road, which is prohibited to ordinary traffic.

But I said to Harry: 'It's shit or bust. Let's follow them.' It was like a car chase in the movies as both vehicles roared off in a cloud of dust along the narrow track.

When we reached Gaselee's yard the normal evasive action took place. Charles's car drove in while we had to pull up outside, where a policeman prevented us from entering.

Five minutes later, Prince Charles rode out on Allibar and set off through the early-morning mist. Of Diana there was no sign. She had been smuggled out under a rug in the back of Nick Gaselee's Land Rover and was waiting up on the downs.

'You won't frighten my horse, Mr Edwards, will you?' said the Prince as I banged off a couple of frames as a matter of record. Imagine my surprise when I checked in with the office a couple of hours later and was told that Allibar was dead. The Prince's favourite mount had had a heart attack and collapsed beneath him. The boring snap of the Prince on his horse which I had taken that morning thus became a front-page picture.

When Allibar crashed to the ground, Diana was watching from the Land Rover and rushed over, weeping, to comfort the Prince. Sick at heart, they returned to Gaselee's cottage for breakfast. Unaware of the tragedy, I and several other press-men who had turned up later, were whiling away the time outside laughing and joking to keep our spirits up in the freezing weather. Our behaviour must have seemed insensitive to the Prince when he emerged from the farmhouse soon after-wards and drove back to Highgrove.

Lady Diana was bundled into the back of the Land Rover, once again hiding under the rug. Only a matter of days before she moved into Buckingham Palace as the Prince of Wales's fiancee, she was lying under a blanket on the dirty floor of a farm vehicle.

The police blocked the road so we couldn't follow and after half a mile she jumped out of the Land Rover and joined Charles in his car.

At this time of year, it was my habit to take a week off at my house in Ireland. I was relaxing there when a phonecall came from Harry Arnold in London. Buckingham Palace had just announced the engagement. 'It will be on the one o'clock news,' he told me. I sat down and listened to the next news bulletin with my wife Ann, and she said: 'You want to go back, don't you?'

I told her I did, so she drove me to the airport. I caught the next plane to London while she stayed on with the children.

As I flew back, my mind went over the last few months. Although I was gutted at having missed the big finale to our search for the next Princess of Wales, I felt very pleased for Prince Charles. At last he had made up his mind.

I comforted myself with the knowledge that even if I had been in London I wouldn't have been allowed to take the official engagement pictures. The *Daily Express* got the rota pass and the Press Association, as the national news agency, did the interview with the happy couple.

Harry met me in London and we had a few bottles of champagne to celebrate. The following day, I went straight to Coleherne Court just in time to catch Lady Diana leaving her flat for the last time. It was one of the nicest pictures I had ever taken of her. She was radiantly happy and how it showed!

The rest of the Rat Pack ribbed me unmercifully for missing the big day. 'Don't worry, Arthur,' they teased. 'Now you're back, we'll get them to do it all over again just for you.'

Harry and I sent the Prince a telegram later that day. It read: 'Congratulations on your engagement to Lady Diana Spencer. No couple deserves greater happiness.' It was one among tens of thousands they received, but within twenty-four hours we had an unexpected reply. 'Many thanks from us both for your very kind message. Trust you won't be made redundant.' It was from Charles.

It seemed then that the task of finding Britain's future Queen was over.

CHAPTER SIX

Happy and Glorious

A beaming Prince Charles did up the last brass button on his naval uniform and put on his cap. Then he turned to his police protection officer. 'How do I look, Paul?' he asked.

The Scotland Yard bodyguard checked him over carefully and laughed. 'I think you look wonderful, sir, but don't you think you should put your trousers on?'

On the morning of his wedding to Lady Diana Spencer the Prince of Wales was as excited and eager as any ordinary groom. His valet Stephen Barry remembered that when he went to wake his boss early on 29 July 1981 he found that, for the first time he could remember in twelve years' royal service, the Prince was already awake.

As Charles revealed later, he had been gazing out of his Buckingham Palace bedroom window for hours at the crowd on the Victoria Memorial and lining the Mall below. By the time Wednesday morning dawned half a million people had crammed into the roadway, carrying a vast wave of affection to the gates of the Palace.

'All night people were sitting out on the steps there singing "Rule Britannia" and every kind of thing,' Charles recalled. 'It really was remarkable, and I found myself standing in the window with tears pouring down my face.'

The wedding of the Prince of Wales and the lovely Lady Diana evoked the greatest outpouring of national joy and pride the British public had seen since the Coronation of Queen Elizabeth II in 1953.

Critics now try to tell us that Charles did not really love his bride. But in the week before the wedding I was constantly with the couple and they certainly convinced me that they were head over heels in love.

When press cameramen and spectators blazed away at her non-stop during a polo match at Tidworth, in Sussex, Diana burst into tears and ran off, unable to cope with the relentless scrutiny. This incident is now portrayed in retrospect as a clear sign that she was having second thoughts about the marriage.

But two days later, when I photographed Charles and Diana leaving a wedding rehearsal at St Paul's Cathedral, they were lovingly holding hands. Any doubts we had about her tearful exit from the polo were forgotten, and everything seemed to be on course for the big day.

I was up very early on the wedding day to make my way through the crowds to my position outside St Paul's. I had chosen to be there, rather than outside Buckingham Palace, believing that the bride and groom in the cathedral doorway would be the most important picture for the following day's paper.

It was the centre of all the comings and goings, and I quite enjoyed watching all the guests, many of whom I had got to know quite well, arriving dressed up in their best. From humble grooms and Swiss policemen, who protected the Prince on holiday, to showbiz celebrities like comedian Spike Milligan and opera star Kiri Te Kanawa, the Prince's entire life up to that time seemed to be unfolding before me.

To have a prime position there on that very special day was a thrill in itself, as so many thousands of people had camped out for days to catch a glimpse of the wedding of the century.

As it turned out, the best picture taken that day did not happen in front of me. After the wedding the royal procession returned to Buckingham Palace, where the bridal couple, along with the Queen and all her family, appeared on the balcony of Buckingham Palace.

The cheering crowd below began chanting to the groom: 'Give her a kiss, Charlie.' The Prince, an ever-dutiful son, turned to the Queen and asked: 'Is it all right to kiss?' His mother nodded and said with a smile: 'Of course.' And a great roar of approval burst from the joyous onlookers as the Prince kissed his Princess in public for the very first time.

They cried out: 'Do it again!' so the delighted bridegroom did just that. Charles pulled Diana closer and planted another smacker on her lips as the crowd went crazy with delight. It was the big climax of the great day and, rightfully, the picture of the royal kiss was the whole of the *Sun*'s front page next day. The headline, inspired by a popular song, was 'AND THEN HE KISSED HER'.

To acknowledge a great job, done by a superb professional, the editor gave my dear friend and colleague the ultimate picture credit. The byline read: 'A great *Sun* picture by Arthur Steel'.

The next time I saw the bridal couple, they were arriving in Gibraltar to join the royal yacht *Britannia* for a honeymoon cruise. Harry Arnold and I had been sent to cover it, but after two weeks of criss-crossing the Mediterranean we hadn't set eyes on them once after they sailed from the Rock. As one fruitless day followed another, our hopes of getting great stories and pictures receded further into the distance.

A good contact had managed to pass on a list of the places they were heading for. Despite this, the royal yacht proved to be more elusive than the Flying Dutchman.

First, we took a private yacht to Puerto Banus, Marbella in southern Spain but, as we later discovered, the honeymooners had cruised in the opposite direction along the north African coast. From Marbella we took a plane to Madrid, and from there flew to Rome.

An Italian agency report we received there informed us that *Britannia* had been sighted off the northern coast of Sardinia. The office in London instructed us to get down there at once, although Harry and I protested because it was not on our contact's list.

All flights were full, so we had to charter a Lear jet for £1,500. This may not seem a lot of money now, but considering the return fare from Olbia in Sardinia back to Rome was only £27, it seemed horrendously extravagant.

The twelve-seater Lear jet provided Harry, myself and free-lance photographer Tim Graham with every luxury, including fur-lined seats and a stewardess each to pamper us. The champagne they served was included in the cost of the charter, and it was the most cushy way to go hunting the Royals we had ever experienced.

If I had known then how tough the trip was soon to become, I would not have felt so guilty about travelling in such opulent style.

We flew right round the entire northern coast of Sardinia, but never spotted *Britannia*. As it turned out, our information on the yacht's course was accurate, and the agency report was rubbish. It was not Sardinia but Sicily that the Royals were cruising around.

But following orders, we landed in Olbia in the middle of the holiday season, and there was not a single hire car or cab available. I said to Harry: 'The only way we can get into town is by bus.' Harry took one look at the filthy airport coach and with mock indignation said: 'If you think I'm stepping off my private jet on to that lousy bus, you're very much mistaken.' The idea was so hilarious that I went off and eventually managed to track down a taxi.

We checked at the Aga Khan's villa, where Charles and Diana were alleged to be dining, and established that they were not there. Getting rapidly fed up, we continued our odyssey the next day, and dragged ourselves back to Rome, then flew on to Athens. There we saw a report in a Greek newspaper that the royal yacht was off the coast of Ithaca in the Ionian Sea.

Ithaca was on the list we had been given, so we didn't waste any more time. Harry and I, with Tim Graham in tow, immediately dashed off to Patras by rental car. Once there, we chartered the only craft available to cross the sea to Ithaca, which has no airport. It was an old-fashioned pleasure boat with 100 seats under a canvas awning on deck.

74

Five hours later, we were thrilled to see the royal yacht on the horizon. The buff-coloured funnel rising above the dark-blue hull seemed like a mirage to us after our long search. To think that here it was, right in front of us, was more than we could believe. Tim and I almost shoved each other overboard in our panic to photograph it. But as we got within a mile *Britannia* suddenly upped anchor and sailed away.

We were distraught, as our sturdy tub just couldn't keep up. Our hearts sank to the bottom of the Ionian Sea as the yacht disappeared around a headland. We presumed that we had been spotted and that the Royals were scarpering.

In fact, at that very moment, we had been almost on top of them. We found out later to our dismay that the Prince and Princess had left the yacht by barge and gone ashore to swim and sunbathe in a little cove called Skinios Bay, half a mile away. But the disappearance of the ship confused us. So near and yet so far.

The cards were stacked against us and the Royals held all the aces. They even had a gunboat of the Greek Navy keeping watch for press photographers.

We crawled into Ithaca to phone the office and admit our failure, then bought a bottle of Scotch and headed back on our boat to Patras. About halfway through the bottle, and halfway through the journey, one of the boat's engines failed and a bad storm blew up. The howling wind and high sea were very sobering, and by some miracle, we limped into port seven hours after leaving Ithaca.

Dawn was breaking as we arrived, but there was no time to catch up on our sleep. After a quick shower in a hotel, we set off in our hire car for Methoni, about 100 miles away on the southern tip of Greece, the next port of call on the royal list.

We knew about Prince Charles's keen interest in ancient ruins and figured they would come ashore to see the famous Fort at Methoni.

It was the most blistering heat I had ever encountered in my life. The temperature was 100-plus in the shade, if you could find any.

We arrived mid-morning, and stayed put beneath the blazing afternoon sun, scanning the horizon for our quarry until dusk. There was no sign of the yacht offshore, so we had obviously missed it or it had bypassed the place during the night.

Baking hot and browned off, we headed back towards Athens, but our car broke down in the middle of the night at a place called Tripoli. We therefore dumped it and found a cab, which got us back to Athens just after four in the morning. After two hours' sleep, we got up and chartered a plane to Crete, the next stop on the royal itinerary.

There are three grades of hotel in Crete – A, B and C. But at the height of the holiday season we ended up in E. The only rooms we could find were in a flea-bitten hostel with no air-conditioning. We hired yet another taxi and scoured the entire western end of Crete. We were trying to keep cheerful, but our lack of success was making us totally pissed off.

The only consolation we had was that our rivals on the *Express* and the *Mirror* were unlikely to scoop us, because we knew they were lazing by the hotel pool in Athens.

Somehow, however, the honeymooners eluded us once again and after satisfying ourselves they had long gone we decided to move on. We realized the royal yacht was due, on 11 August, in Port Said, where Charles and Diana were entertaining President and Mrs Anwar Sadat to dinner on board. So we went back to Athens and flew on to Egypt.

On the road from Cairo to Port Said I had a minor accident. An old Toyota loaded with Egyptians indicated a right turn, but when I tried to pass on the inside the driver changed his mind and swung left straight into us. As I screeched to a halt an angry crowd quickly gathered around, although the damage was minimal. Harry opened his door to get out. 'I'll just go and get their details,' he said.

'Don't be daft,' I screamed. 'They don't look as if they've got any fucking insurance. Get back in the car.'

Meanwhile, Tim Graham was hanging out of a back window, yelling: 'Keep going, keep going. It's only a few scratches.' But the crowd, growing more hostile by the minute, was blocking the road.

76

Fortunately for us, two Egyptian soldiers arrived on the scene. When we explained we were en route to photograph Prince Charles with their president they cleared the way for us to continue.

A few hours after we reached Port Said, the royal yacht steamed in. All my dreams of snapping the Princess in a bikini vanished as I spotted her on an upper deck, wearing a rather unflattering straw hat and Bombay bloomer shorts.

Luckily, *Britannia*'s skipper Rear Admiral Paul Greening issued a photograph of the newly-weds taken at the banquet in evening dress with their guests President Sadat and his English-born wife Jihan. The official picture, along with the shots I had taken that afternoon of the royal couple squinting into the sunlight, were enough to make a centre-page spread in the *Sun* under the headline 'THE SUNNYMOONERS'.

While we were filing this material to London the honeymoon continued through the Suez Canal to the Red Sea. At this point we went back to Cairo, on 11 August. All we had achieved after two weeks of hard slog was a collect picture from the ship's photographer and a couple of long-distance smudges of Charles and Diana. Never was so much money spent and effort made by two people for so little.

But Harry coaxed me out of total despair with non-stop wise-cracks. He insisted we stay up until midnight to celebrate my birthday. After we had downed a couple of cold beers, I was ready for bed and got up to leave. But Harry was in the mood for a long session and said: 'It's not your birthday in London for another two hours.' That was all it needed to send both of us on the old River Ouse.

Without Harry's incredible drive and cheerful nature, the trip would have been a nightmare. Early next morning, he flew home to start a summer holiday he had booked with his family, but I soldiered on with Tim Graham and Graham Wood, a photographer then working for the *Daily Mail*.

We drove 400 kilometres south through the eastern desert to Hurghada, where we knew the royal yacht would end its cruise.

The only hotel was full, but its manager made up some beds on the floor of the ballroom and we dossed down there.

When *Britannia* docked, I was waiting on the quayside in stifling heat as the suntanned royal couple disembarked to fly home to Britain. The Princess looked stunning in a peach silk outfit, while the Prince seemed a bit uncomfortable in a woollen suit, which he was obliged to wear to bid farewell to his hosts, President and Madame Sadat.

Unlike us, they both appeared happy and rested after two weeks on their floating palace. Their VC10 was taking them home to join the Queen at Balmoral, before dropping off the rest of the Prince's party in London. I managed to give my film to a member of the royal crew to deliver to my office. As it was a Saturday, there was no rush to file.

In the meantime, I had been speaking to one of my contacts who was aboard during the cruise. He gave me an exclusive story about the shipboard shenanigans of the past two weeks.

While her husband took afternoon siestas, Diana had visited every wardroom on *Britannia*, to the delight of the officers and men. One day she played the piano for the ratings and they all had a sing-song together. Another day she appeared in the crew's quarters unexpectedly and ran into a sailor, fresh from a shower, wearing nothing but a bath towel. 'You can't come in here, ma'am,' said the startled matelot, 'I'm not dressed.'

Diana grinned. 'Oh for goodness' sake, I'm a married woman now,' she teased.

On the last night aboard ship the Royal Household and ship's crew organized a farewell concert for the Prince and Princess. The highlight of the evening was Diana and Charles's personal staff singing the Rod Stewart hit 'Sailing' dressed in bathing suits, snorkel masks and flippers.

As I had no reporter with me, I relayed all these facts to the news editor. Instead of realizing that the only inside story of the entire cruise deserved to be the front-page splash, the *Sun* editor relegated it to Page Seven. What was worse, I didn't even get a byline under my picture.

This was the finale to the toughest assignment I had ever been on. The long drive though the desert while suffering from stomach problems, plus sleeping on the hotel floor and working in sweltering heat was bad enough, but what really pissed me off was getting no recognition for all my effort. But that's the newspaper game. Sub-editors never forget to credit reporters, but often omit the photographer's byline.

I wasn't terribly upset, because a few days earlier Harry and I had been given huge picture credits for our efforts in Port Said. In this business, one minute you are treated like King George, and the next like George King.

But the fun wasn't over yet. On the long drive back to Cairo our arch-rivals Whitaker and Lennox from the *Daily Star* had trouble with their ancient Fiat hire car. They set off behind me, but when I noticed that they had not appeared in the rearview mirror for some miles, I turned back to find them.

About ten miles back along the deserted road I discovered Kenny Lennox with sweat pouring off his brow struggling to change a flat tyre. James, dressed up in the white robes of a desert tribesman, was bellowing advice while refreshing himself from a large bottle of water.

One look at the bald spare convinced me it wouldn't last long on the rough road. And sure enough, two miles further on the tyre blew out. 'Push that fucking car into the desert, Kenny,' ordered James as he clambered into my air-conditioned Mercedes.

'OK old chap,' I said, 'I'll give you and Kenny a lift back to Cairo on one condition. You've got to promise me you'll never tell my editor Kelvin MacKenzie that I saved your lives.'

But there were more frequent interruptions on the journey. Tim Graham had a really bad case of diarrhoea and every few miles he begged me to stop. As flat desert stretched out on either side of us it was only when we passed burnt-out buses and lorries left over from Middle East wars that he found some privacy.

One of my lasting memories of the trip is of Tim running for a blackened wreck with a roll of pink loo paper clutched in his hand. Sometimes covering the Royals can be a really shitty job.

CHAPTER SEVEN

Bahama Mama

The celebrations broke out all over again when Buckingham Palace announced that the new Princess of Wales was expecting her first baby. A few months later, I discovered that Charles and Diana were taking a secret holiday in the Bahamas before the birth. Harry Arnold and I were naturally keen to follow them.

The editor of the *Sun*, Kelvin MacKenzie, agreed we should go, and we started to plan the trip. Two days later Kelvin changed his mind. He didn't believe we would get anything and so all our tickets and bookings were cancelled.

Our rivals James Whitaker and Kenny Lennox, then both working for the *Daily Star*, were also planning to cover the royal holiday. When they heard we had cancelled, James asked to see me. We met in the Snooker Club in Fleet Street, and James asked me for some tips on how to do the job. He knew that two years earlier I had been to the Bahamian island Eleuthera, where the royal couple were heading, when the Prince had stayed there with the Mountbatten family.

Feeling pretty peeved, as I wasn't going, I saw no harm in helping James, and so I drew a diagram to show him how it could be done. James had also previously been to Eleuthera to do the same story and had failed. He was very grateful for this information and offered to pay me, but I told him I didn't want any money, that I was only too pleased to help.

Imagine my shock and horror two days later when Kelvin MacKenzie said: 'I've decided you and Harry should go after all.'

We set off and booked in at the Winding Bay Hotel complex and made our plans. We checked the route through the jungle

81

to a spot overlooking the beach the Royals would use on Windermere Island. When we got back to our hotel we were told that because we had cancelled our booking originally there was no room for us. So we ended up moving to the Cotton Bay Country Club, a very smart golf club in the north of the island.

This proved to be a good move, because when we finally succeeded in getting the pictures, the Bahamian police rounded up all the pressmen on the island, but the one place they didn't look was our exclusive hotel.

Charles and Diana arrived on Eleuthera that evening. Next morning, we set off about four o'clock carrying a gallon of water, a monopod, a 1,200-millimetre lens, film, food and plastic bags. They were needed because on my previous trip I had got caught in a rainstorm which ruined my film, so I had had to go back and reshoot all the pictures. This time I was prepared with polythene bags and waterproofs.

We followed the sun as it was rising and smashed our way through thick undergrowth full of thorns. After about two hours, we finally came to a headland opposite their beach.

It was a public beach, and we could clearly see several other people enjoying the sun and surf. After about two hours, Prince Charles came down with his detective Colin Trimming and began to waterski. This went on for a while and we took pictures, but there was no sign of Diana.

About ten o'clock she finally appeared with Penelope Romsey, who is married to the former Norton Knatchbull, now Lord Romsey. Diana was wearing a nice beach wrap and they sat down and began sunbathing. Eventually she took the wrap off, and there was the pregnant Princess in a red bikini.

If it hadn't been a bikini but a one-piece bathing suit there wouldn't have been so much fuss afterwards. Knowing Diana as I do now, I suspect she wore the bikini because she imagined there would be photographers around.

We blazed away at Charles and Diana for about two hours as they went swimming then lay on the sand rubbing sun oil on each other. I had the Princess wading out gingerly into the cold water, then dunking herself beneath the waves. I got wonderful shots of the two of them lazing on sun loungers, chatting to their friends and reading books. At one point I even photographed them taking photographs of each other. It was a great set of pictures.

About midday we decided to split because it was five in the afternoon in London. Whitaker had just left and I suddenly realized what he was up to: he hoped to get his photographer's film to London first and screw us. Harry wanted to follow James with our film, but as I had done this hazardous journey three times before I wouldn't let him. I told him it was too dangerous. I warned him: 'You could break a leg in the jungle and never be found.' Even though the Royals were still in clear view I decided to pull out, so we set off together.

By then the sun was high overhead and it was really hot and steamy. At one stage Harry begged me to stop. He said: 'If we don't stop, we'll die.' Our hearts were racing and sweat was pumping out of us. We had run out of water and were both in danger of dehydrating, but eventually we found the trail out and got back to our car totally knackered.

Stinking, sweaty and starving, we made our way to the Beachcomber Hotel where we knew that a United Press International agency photographer called Dennis Paquin had a wire machine to transmit photographs. He was based in New York and was a very keen young bloke. When I told him what we had he couldn't get the film processed fast enough. While he was doing this, Harry and I poured Heinekens down our throats non-stop.

I got on the phone to London and told them what we had and told them the *Star* had the same stuff. Kelvin MacKenzie came on to me and said, 'I want you to put everything over and when you have finished I want you to put an axe through the wire machine. Stop those bastards from the *Star*.'

His voice was coming out of a speaker on the wire machine, and the yell from Dennis Paquin when he heard this command could have been heard in Miami. 'You go fuck yourself,' he said. 'You're not touching my machine.' And he picked it up in his arms to make off with it.

I calmed him down and assured him my editor was only joking, although knowing Kelvin, I was certain he wasn't. Eventually we reached a compromise. I asked him to keep the *Star* off the machine and in return I would give him a picture for his service in America. He was delighted, because this meant he could scoop the other agencies without doing any work.

We got over eight or nine pictures and Kelvin was delighted. The quality was not fantastic, but considering the pictures were taken at a distance of more than a quarter of a mile, and were wired 4,000 miles across the Atlantic, they were very acceptable. We went back to the Country Club. Harry and I were feeling a mixture of euphoria and sadness; we were thrilled that we had got the pictures but disappointed that we had to share our exclusive.

The following day we decided we would try to do a follow-up, because while I had been snapping the Royals we had noticed a couple bonking about fifty yards along the beach. I had taken some pictures, not of the couple actually at it, but indulging in a bit of hanky-panky. They were so engrossed in each other that they were unaware that just along the beach the world's most famous couple were sunbathing.

Next day I thought I would wire them to London, but when I went back and told Dennis Paquin I had more pictures he freaked out. 'Christ! Have you been back again?' he said.

I told the office about the sex on the sand, but they weren't interested. They told me that all hell was breaking out back in London. 'Rebase, rebase,' they screamed down the phone.

So we dashed off to the airport, got a plane to Miami and headed for London. On the way to the office from Heathrow I switched on the radio and heard a disc jockey slagging us off for getting revealing pictures of a pregnant Princess.

The whole world seemed to be against us. I arrived in Bouverie Street, where the *Sun* newspaper was then situated, and an editorial driver spat at my feet and called me scum. He said he was ashamed to work for the same paper as me.

I was feeling very low when I walked into the newsroom, but Kelvin MacKenzie raced up to meet me. He lifted me off my feet and said, 'You come back to this office a fucking hero.'

In his book *Royal Pursuit*, Douglas Keay quoted James Whitaker claiming that he beat the *Sun* by one edition. But I know that's not true. It was definitely our scoop. In fact we sold four times more than the *Daily Star*, which at that time was selling fewer than a million.

The attacks on myself and my newspaper continued. There was a question in the House of Commons, raised by Sir John Langford-Holt, the Conservative MP for Shrewsbury. He attacked both newspapers for falling short of the professional standards of journalism. The editor of the *Daily Mirror*, Mike Molloy, criticized us too on Radio Four. I think he was sick because he didn't have the pictures himself. Earlier he had told his royal snapper Ken Gavin not to go because he didn't think it was possible to get them.

And when we scooped them all Gavin, one of my oldest friends and chief rival, was in Japan on another job with reporter John Edwards. They saw our triumph on television and Gavvers freaked out. 'Fucking hell. They got 'em,' he howled.

Everywhere we went for the next few weeks there were people praising us and condemning us. The funniest thing of all was the fact that Kelvin MacKenzie ran the controversial pictures two days running. He decided that, as the people in the north of England hadn't seen them because they missed the first edition of the *Sun*, he would print them all over again.

By far the best headline in the coverage of the sensational royal holiday was dreamed up by Harry Arnold. He described the pregnant princess in the Caribbean as 'BAHAMA MAMA'. He got the idea when studying a list of cocktails in our Eleuthera hotel. He figured a rum-based drink with a parasol on top best summed up the sunbathing royal beauty. That wasn't the first time that a drink or two gave Harry the inspiration he needed.

Once another reporter looked at an unrecognizable drink in his hand and asked: 'What's that, Harry?' Holding out the glass, Harry said simply: 'That is a page lead.' Then, to laughter all round, he banged two drinks down on the counter, adding: 'And that is a splash!'

Michael Shea, the Buckingham Palace press officer, issued a statement next day condemning publication of the pictures. But I later learned that Charles and Diana knew we were on the island and were not as upset as people claimed. In fact, in one of my shots the Princess raised a hand to her forehead, as if searching the horizon for marauding press photographers.

James Whitaker, now working for the *Daily Mirror*, has made tremendous capital out of those pictures on television talk shows, and is quoted in magazines as if he was the only one who was there. But he didn't do anything except maybe carry a lens or a bottle of water and write a few picture captions. It was his colleague Kenny Lennox who took the *Daily Star*'s pictures, and he did a superb job.

I had great support from Harry Arnold, but he would be the first to admit that it was all down to the photographs. And nothing else. Without them, what did you have?

The bikini pictures were taken in February 1982, just after the Queen had summoned all the Fleet Street editors to Buckingham Palace for a quiet, friendly chat. She asked them to give the Princess of Wales some breathing space, but the editor of the *Sun* refused to attend the meeting, as he didn't want to compromise himself with the Palace.

One of the funniest sequels to this story was that, next day, the Bahamian police rounded up all the photographers and reporters they could find and banished them from the island. There were shots of German and French photographers photographing each other at the airport as their film was stripped from their cameras by angry Bahamian Special Branch officers.

I think this was to protect themselves from their angry editors in Germany and Paris, who had seen their wonderful star snappers scooped by the English.

The *Sun* is reputed to have made £100,000 out of syndicating the pictures around the world. Many people, including the Royals, thought I had pocketed all this money. Of course, I hadn't. I didn't even get a bonus. The copyright belonged to the editor of the *Sun*, who was rightfully the only person entitled to make money out of them. They appeared in almost every

The picture I cherish most: Dancing with the Duchess of York at the Hohwald
Restaurant, Klosters, January, 1992.

Top: The last tour: Charles and Diana turn away from each other in Korea, unable to find anything to talk about.

Below: The Princess engrossed in conversation with an AIDS sufferer at Middlesex Hospital, July 1991.

A shipshape Diana aboard King Juan Carlos's yacht The Fortuna at sea off Majorca in August, 1990.

Top: "Where do you want me, Arthur?" the Princess said when I asked her to pose in front of the Taj Mahal.

Below: Diana recalls the Last Days of the Raj in an elegant Thirties-style outfit in Delhi, February, 1992.

H. R. H. The Duchess of York sitting by her desk at Romenda Lodge, Berkshire - the first photo session inside her new home, April, 1993.

Top: The Prince of Wales stares forlornly from the window of a chateau near Avignon while recovering from a broken arm, September, 1991.

Below: The Queen gets a welcoming cuddle from Alice Frazier at a housing project near Washington D.C., 1991.

Top: Diana observing the Muslim dress code at a mosque in Lahore, Pakistan, during her first major solo tour, Autumn 1991.

Below: A charade of togetherness at the Garter Ceremony, only a week after Andrew Morton's best-selling bombshell blew the Royal Family apart, June, 1992.

Top: Diana adds dazzle to a banquet in Delhi on a tour of India in 1992, wearing a silver-embroidered gown and the Spencer tiara.

Below: Introducing Prince William to the people of Wales in Cardiff on St.David's Day, 1991.

Diana's darling: With Prince Harry on holiday in Majorca, August, 1987.

William's first day at Wetherby School in February, 1987. Prince Charles was snowbound at Sandringham.

Andrew and Sarah together in Calgary on a tour of Canada in July, 1987.

Princess of wows! : Diana chose a pearl and sapphire choker for a big night out in Melbourne, 1985.

Top: The kiss that missed as Diana turned away when Charles tried to plant a smacker on her lips at Jaipur, 1992.

Below: And how it used to be … in Adelaide, 1985.

Top: A Christmas present from Fergie in December 1992 - a pair of socks embroidered with the message "No Comment!"

Below: Having a laugh with Prince Charles and his policeman Inspector John McLean at Klosters, 1979.

U-turn Clarke to axe crooks' charter

By SIMON WALTERS

NEW laws branded a "villains' charter" are to be scrapped only five months after they came into force.

The get-tough move by Home Secretary Kenneth Clarke follows a storm of protest over the Criminal Justice Act.

Police claimed it tied their hands and magistrates said it let young thugs "laugh at the law."

The U-turn dumping it so soon is a massive embarrassment for the Government which is already on the rack over crime. In his new version, Mr Clarke wants to THROW young runaways into police cells overnight when they are caught red handed.

Mess

SCRAP the ban on courts punishing life-long crooks harder at first offenders.

LET jobless yobs getting away with tiny fines because they claim to be hard up.

A mother of a 14-year-old boy responsible for 200 shop burglaries welcomed Clarke's proposals.

She said: "If my son had been thrown in a cell overnight the time he ran into trouble he would not be in the mess he's in now, instead he simply cautioned.

Continued on Page Four

HIGH UNLUCKY

A plough sent to lost Giovanni Evasio, 82, in a field ran him over and killed him in Grasco, Italy.

SUN MAN IN THE BROWN STUFF

Nepal Premier says our Arthur's 'Brownie' quip was racist. Arthur says his crack was aimed at Di's copper Insp. Brown

Complaint ... Premier Koirala

Comment ... our man Arthur

SUN photographer Arthur Edwards sparked a diplomatic row last night when he was wrongly accused of making a "racist" remark to Nepal's Premier.

Snapper Arthur, 51, caused the rumpus by using the word "Brownie" as he chatted with Princess Diana when she arrived for a banquet in Kathmandu.

He told Di "You look great" and she beamed back at him.

When her bodyguard Peter Brown smirked at him, Arthur used the

From ROBERT JOBSON in Kathmandu

detective's nickname and added: "You don't look bad yourself, Brownie."

But he made the remark just as the dark-skinned Nepalese premier Girija Prasad Koirala was walking past.

The PM had heard the Sun man talking to Diana. And as he was following behind, he thought the word Brownie was aimed at him.

He looked shocked, turned away from cameramen and followed the Princess into the lavish banquet hall.

When he sat down at the top table the Prime Minister called over his private secretary and said he was upset by Arthur's comment.

The private secretary told the Nepalese Minister of Information to ask his British embassy equivalent to find out the reason for the Pressman's "gross insult."

SORRY

By then Arthur, who had no idea his light-hearted words had been misunderstood, had gone back to his hotel to process his film of Diana wearing her new ballgown.

But a British Embassy official told reporters the Nepalese had complained about the remark.

The reporters explained the Brownie was simply a nickname for Detective Inspector Brown.

The British Embassy then related to the Nepalese how the mix-up had happened.

Arthur is Di's favourite photographer and has followed her to VIP functions all over the world for more than 12 years.

He said afterwards: "I am sorry if the Prime Minister misunderstood what I was saying. I would never

Continued on Page Five

Thursday, December 24, 1992

25p

Audited daily sale for November 3,515,236

TV FREE INSIDE TODAY

4-DAY XMAS GUIDE

TV GUIDE

EASTEND KISSMAS IS SOME 'FLING' SPECIAL

QUEEN BANS OUR ARFUR

Council orkers ee their ick' pal ghting n Bosnia

By JOHN KAY
Chief Reporter

COUNCIL caretaker who took sick leave three months ago was spotted by workmates on TV — fighting as a mercenary in Bosnia.

His pals were stunned when they watched a dramatic front-line report on Sky and spotted 34-year-old Ron Warne.

Instead of council overalls he was wearing battle-dress — and in place of his broom he had a gun. He looked fighting-fit too.

Now Ron's furious bosses at London's Islington Council have launched an investigation and asked for a video of their report.

A council spokesman said: "If this is proved true he'll be Continued on Page Two

Favourite . . Sun man Arthur Edwards with Diana in Egypt in May

Favourite . . Arthur gets an Xmas present from Fergie this week

Revenge for Royal speech story

By JOHN KAY, Chief Reporter

THE QUEEN has banned Sun man Arthur Edwards from photographing her on Christmas Day — in revenge for our scoop on her annual address to the nation.

Cockney Arfur, who has been snapping Royals for 14 years, was picked to be the only national newspaper photographer outside church at Sandringham, Norfolk.

He was due to take pictures on behalf of all the national Press.

But after The Sun published the text of the Queen's broadcast yesterday, Arthur lost his prized pass. It will go to a snapper from another paper.

Last night Arthur, 52 — who is Fergie and Princess Di's favourite Royal photographer — was gutted.

He said: "I've never done anything to upset the Royal Family. I have very good relations with them all.

"I was chuffed when my name came out of the hat as it's the first time this system's been used for the service.

"I've covered the last ten Christmas Day services without any complaints."

Proud Arthur planned to take wife Anne and daughter Annmarie, 21. He said: "I'm bitterly disappointed. I think the Palace are being petty.

"They are taking it out on me just because The Sun got away with a good, old-fashioned scoop."

Now Arthur will go to Althorp, Northants, to photograph Di who is spending Christmas Day with her brother Earl Spencer.

The Princess plans to go to a church there at exactly the same time as the other Royals step out in Sandringham.

The Newspaper Publishers Association, which controls the issue of permits, known as rota passes, confirmed that Buckingham Palace asked for the ban on The Sun. Arthur's name went Continued on Page Five magazine and newspaper throughout the world. Lord Matthews, then publisher of the *Daily Star*, refused to allow his paper to syndicate Kenny Lennox's photographs.

I know Princess Diana thought I had made a mint out of her Bahamian beach holiday, because she tackled me about this when we met up in Australia the following year.

'Just think of all the money you have made out of me,' she chided me gently.

I had to put her straight, so I said bluntly: 'I get the same money if I photograph you in the Bahamas as I do for covering a court case in Bradford. The pay is the same.'

She laughed at my curt reply and moaned in mock dismay: 'Ooh, pass me the Kleenex.'

When the 'Bahama Mama' edition hit the streets, Diana's then private secretary Francis Cornish was on a train travelling north with another one of Prince Charles's detectives, John MacLean. As they pulled into Sheffield Station they spotted a paperboy shouting: 'See the lovely pictures of Princess Diana in a bikini.' Cornish rushed off to buy a paper, as MacLean, who was careful with his cash, shouted after him: 'No, don't do that. You're just giving more money to the *Sun*. And that's what they want you to do.' But he didn't stop Francis who, like everyone else in Britain, could not wait to see the 'Bahama Mama' in her bikini.

Some newsagents were returning to newspaper wholesalers three and four times that day for more copies of the *Sun*. And it has been reported that over the following two days they sold an extra million newspapers. And that represents a whole lot of money.

I never felt the photographs were intrusive, because the Prince and Princess were on a public beach. Unfortunately, this fact was never raised in our defence. There were plenty of other holiday-makers in the vicinity, but no one ever knew about them.

In the light of the sensational pictures of the Duchess of York topless in St Tropez, these pictures seem rather tame by comparison. At the time I was made to feel like a criminal, but

I still can't see anything tasteless about pictures showing a beautiful woman in the full bloom of pregnancy.

Where are those naughty negatives now? They are in a safe hiding place where nobody can get them. When the *Sun* moved out of Fleet Street in January 1985, the negatives were left locked in a huge, old-fashioned safe in the photographers' room. In the chaos surrounding the *Sun*'s rapid changeover to new technology amid riots in the streets by disgruntled printers outside the new News International plant at Wapping, everyone forgot about the three-year-old snaps.

I went back six months later when the old *Sun* offices were being demolished, and discovered that the safe containing my sensational scoop pictures was now buried in the foundations of a new, half-built Japanese bank.

Maybe one day someone will dig them up again. What a time capsule that will be. But when that day comes no one will know or care about the fuss these few rolls of film created.

CHAPTER EIGHT

The Honeymoon is Over

On a misty autumn morning at Balmoral in 1981, Prince Charles sat down at his desk and began to write one letter after another to his closest friends. Each one bore the same message: 'I'm sorry I won't be able to spend so much time with you in future. I am sure you will understand that now I am married I want to devote all my time to my wife.'

The Prince was making every effort to ensure that his wife was happy and his marriage a success. He gave up skiing with the Palmer-Tomkinsons, and cooled his close friendship with Lord and Lady Tryon. He stopped going to Iceland to fish with them every August.

But one relationship carried on as normal. The Prince's valet noted in his memoirs that his affection for old friends Camilla and Andrew Parker Bowles was as strong as ever. Stephen Barry wrote in 1982: 'The friendship, unlike the Tryons', seems to have survived his marriage.'

Despite this, it wasn't long before Diana began to feel she was not getting enough time alone with her new husband. A friend of mine who worked on the royal estate at Sandringham told me about an incident which revealed Diana's resentment.

While they were staying at Sandringham during the Royals' New Year holiday Prince Charles decided to drive off and have lunch with the Queen at a shoot, leaving his bride at home. As he got into his car, staff were shocked to hear the Princess screaming at her husband from an upstairs window. 'That's right, go and have lunch with your mother and leave me here all alone,' she yelled.

Ignoring this outburst, Charles put his car into gear and drove off to join the shooting party's picnic lunch. Minutes later, Princess Diana rushed out of the house and roared off after him in her Ford Escort. A few miles down the road, she waved him down, and forced him to pull over to the side of the road.

Startled beaters from the shoot saw her leap out of her car and dash over to the Range Rover as Charles wound his window down. Her face flushed with anger, Diana shrieked: 'Why do you do this to me? Why can't we just have a meal alone together for a change?'

News of the newly-weds' quarrel soon went right round Sandringham. The world's most famous couple had been married only six months and the new Princess was pregnant. Charles's duty to his mother and his family seemed already to be driving a wedge between them.

Twelve and a half years older than his wife, Charles was set in his ways and very close to his mother. Until his marriage, the Prince had never once gone out in the evening before calling the Queen to wish her goodnight. With the exception of his short skiing trips, he had spent all his holidays with his mother and shared her passion for country life. Their unique destiny had created a special bond between them.

But the dramatic lows in Charles and Diana's relationship were counterbalanced by moments of great tenderness. Like any other newly-married couple, they were still learning to live with each other.

Charles's loving concern for his young wife was never more evident than when, a short time later, she tripped and fell down the last three steps of the main staircase at Sandringham House. Much has been made of this incident. It has even been suggested that it could have been a suicide attempt. But eyewitnesses have since told me that any suggestion the Princess was deliberately trying to harm herself, or her unborn child, is very far from the truth. She simply tripped at the bottom of the stairs; she did not fling herself right down the staircase.

A page helped her up as Diana shouted for her husband to come quickly. The Prince rushed into the room and saw that his wife was uninjured. But, as a precaution, he summoned the local general practitioner, Dr Hugh Ford, to check that his wife and their unborn child were unharmed.

Diana rested until the doctor arrived, but after he gave her the all-clear, she went off with Charles to a picnic with the rest of the family at Holkam Beach on the Norfolk coast.

As Diana began to undertake official engagements in her new role as Princess of Wales, interest in her steadily increased. Royal Household officials had predicted the media's frenzied coverage of the future Queen would fizzle out after the royal couple returned from their honeymoon and settled down.

The Queen's press secretary at that time, Michael Shea, later admitted how wrong they were. 'We expected that, following the honeymoon, press attention would wane somewhat,' he said. 'But it has in no way abated. The Princess of Wales feels totally beleaguered. The people who love and care for her are anxious at the effect it is having.'

While Diana was endeavouring to cope with suddenly becoming the globe's most gawked-at celebrity, she had another problem. She was starting to realize how much she had given up when she had married her Prince. She could not go anywhere alone any more: for security reasons, a Scotland Yard protection officer accompanied her wherever she went.

And protocol placed a million other restrictions on her once carefree life. These ranged from being forced to wear hats on royal occasions, when she had never owned any headgear before, to driving only British cars because members of the Royal Family must always 'fly the flag'. At the same time, staff were beginning to leave the Prince's service; his new wife was blamed.

Diana's astounding popularity was also beginning to cause problems with her royal relatives. Several other leading members of the Royal Family, accustomed to hitting the headlines regularly, suddenly didn't rate a line or a picture in the newspapers. Princess Anne was more than a little miffed when she risked her life visiting troops in Northern Ireland and found the following morning that the papers were full of Diana attending a concert at the Barbican in London. Anne's brave trip didn't even rate one paragraph.

Throughout these early months of adjustment, the Queen sympathized with her daughter-in-law's struggle to come to terms with her strange new life. 'She is not like the rest of us,' the Queen explained when Diana's tears and tantrums astonished her in-laws. 'She wasn't born into our way of life.'

So concerned did the Queen become, that she called Fleet Street editors together in an unprecedented plea to give her son's new wife more privacy.

The cumulative stress of all these problems, added to severe morning sickness, had to find an outlet. There were brief flare-ups between the Prince and Princess. Staff never knew when these squabbles were likely to happen, so visitors were warned: 'If they row in front of you, please pretend it's not happening. It will be all over in a matter of minutes.'

This was also a difficult time for Prince Charles. He was unaccustomed to tantrums, as his family was not given to emotional displays. As the dutiful eldest son of a family devoted to serving the monarchy, he found it hard to understand why his young wife was so demanding. She wanted him to behave like any ordinary husband; he did not know what ordinary life was like.

In 1983, Diana freaked out while on a skiing holiday in Liechtenstein. Prince Charles had refused to arrange a photo call for all the photographers who had swarmed into the small principality on their arrival. As a result, they were followed every time they left the home of their host, Prince Hans Adam.

One afternoon, after they had finished skiing in the nearby Austrian resort Lech, they were trapped in an alleyway by three Continental cameramen. Diana began to cry, and lowered her head into the collar of her ski jacket so that the tears wouldn't show. Charles put his arm around her: 'Please, darling, don't cry,' he said gently. As they tried to walk away, one of the jostling photographers fell over. Noticing this, the Prince attempted to cheer his wife up by saying: 'One down, two to go.'

Just then about thirty other snappers, including myself, turned up and started blazing away. Completely surrounded, Charles and Diana had no escape. They were forced to stand in the street waiting for Prince Hans Adam's car to come and collect them. The Princess by this time was on the point of hysteria. She put both hands over her ears and began shrieking: 'I can't stand it, I can't stand it.'

Prince Charles was rapidly losing his cool too and said sharply to her: 'Please, darling, please, don't be stupid.' Luckily for them both, the car turned up at this point and whisked them back to the castle in Vaduz.

A similar situation happened two years later, when they were again guests of Prince Hans Adam in Liechtenstein. This time, to avoid problems with the press, they agreed to hold a photo call. They posed together at the bottom of a tow-bar, then proceeded to go up the mountain. Two-thirds of the way up, Hans Adam, who was suffering from an ear infection, was troubled by the altitude and signalled for the tow-bar to stop. Diana, travelling up behind him, was not expecting the sudden jolt and fell off. Looking furious, she picked herself up, afraid that the photographers had caught her undignified tumble in the snow. She skied straight down to the bottom, got into the Prince's car and asked to be taken straight back to the castle in Vaduz. Meanwhile, Prince Charles was wondering where she had gone. When he came down the mountain he said to us: 'Where is she? I thought we were going to go up again.' When we told him we had seen her disappear in the car he groaned: 'I suppose I'll get it in the neck now.'

Those few words told us all we needed to know about the real state of the royal marriage. If this was the way they behaved in public, their behaviour in private was even more disturbing. One of the Prince's oldest friends told me that their rows at home had become increasingly frequent. Prince Charles could not handle the way his wife ranted. 'He was not used to someone throwing things at him, slamming doors in his face and telling him to piss off,' my contact said. 'He had been brought up in a home where people bowed and scraped to him.'

Not even in the Navy had anyone had the nerve to speak to the Prince of Wales like this before. But loud screeches from Charles and Diana's upstairs windows soon had staff arriving for work at Kensington Palace saying to each other: 'There they go again.'

Instead of arguing with Diana, Charles used simply to walk away from her. She interpreted this as indifference, and they then started to go their separate ways.

In fact, the so-called fairy-tale marriage of the Prince and Princess of Wales was almost over before it had begun, triggering genuine fears that a constitutional crisis could rock the monarchy as early as 1982.

Diana, then just twenty-one and the mother of five-month-old Prince William, was suffering from clinical depression. She was threatening to leave her husband and the Royal Family just sixteen months after they had walked down the aisle of St Paul's Cathedral.

The future Queen and mother of a future King had threatened to commit suicide on several occasions in the first year of her marriage. She was hysterical, shouting and screaming with frustration and anger about the trap she found herself in. She also suspected her husband was still in love with his old flame Camilla Parker Bowles.

I now know that her own family doctor, Michael Linnett, who was Apothecary to the Prince and Princess of Wales, was the first to be called in to help the tormented Princess around October 1982.

He in turn called in top psychiatrist Dr Michael Pare, who has written papers on the treatment of depression. Other psychiatrists and medical experts were found to try to lift the cloud that threatened to smother the young Princess.

At the height of this crisis, Diana had private appointments with the psychiatrists in the sitting room of her Kensington Palace apartment four times a week, and she had dozens of appointments between late 1982 and her departure for her first overseas tour with Charles and Prince William in March 1983.

One senior aide, who has since left royal service, says: 'It was perfectly clear that the Princess had no idea what she was getting into when she got married. She was clearly intimidated by the family and she found very little support from her own husband and his relatives. The view was very much that she should stop moaning and get on with it.'

The psychiatrists and psychologists also had meetings with Diana and Charles together on at least three occasions, and Charles alone, in a bid to break down the barriers between the couple.

If it had been any other marriage, they say, it would have broken up in a very short time. There were no obvious signs of mutual love. Diana clearly adored her husband but the age-gap of twelve and a half years was simply too wide to bridge. The overall feeling was that it was their duty to stay married, regardless of whether they loved each other or not.

One courtier confided: 'The Prince of Wales did not understand at all what was going on. He was very detached from the problems and not at all psychologically minded. He did not appreciate the scale of the problem and rather assumed it would all go away.'

The sessions were aimed at helping the newly-married couple to communicate more effectively. The relationship was simply not functioning like an ordinary marriage. She had few interests, few friends and a fairly dull, lonely life with no one to confide in, although she enjoyed a higher public profile than her husband. He, in turn, was not prepared to make any changes to his self-centred life or to his personality, to accommodate his young wife.

'They were both desperately unhappy at this time,' the courtier said. 'There were various suicide threats by the Princess and on many occasions she said she was leaving him and the family. In some cases, the doctors were called in urgently when the situation reached crisis point.'

The psychiatrist assessed the possibility of her actually committing suicide as 'low-risk' and saw the threats as terrible evidence of her disillusionment and loneliness.

Her depression and fears were so consuming that the people treating her often left her to go home and switch on the TV news to make sure she had turned up to a particular event like a gala evening or a film première, and had not cried off. Her moods were that unpredictable.

In November 1982, Diana cancelled her appearance at the Remembrance Day Service at the last minute. Ten minutes after the Queen and Prince Charles had arrived at the Royal Albert Hall, the red-eyed Princess suddenly appeared in the royal box with them. Her sense of duty had overcome her fears, but afterwards she was accused of breaking protocol by turning up after the sovereign.

Diana worked herself up into a frightening state when her first overseas tour loomed. In March 1983, the Prince and Princess of Wales were scheduled to visit Australia and New Zealand together. Diana was tormented daily by the prospect of eating in front of people. She was scared of saying anything in public and she did not know what was expected of her. She was also worried about the protocol, and no one gave her any help.

One of the Prince's aides said: 'The medical people could not see the marriage lasting at all, and the only hope was that constitutional pressure would force them to make a go of it. They were from two completely separate worlds, and their expectations of one another were completely different. She was expected to behave like a member of the Royal Family right away. It was genuinely too much for her.'

Royal officials assumed that when she went to Australia, the Princess would leave her nine-month-old baby behind, as the Queen had always done. But Diana refused to consider it.

The Prince's staff went ahead with arrangements for the tour that did not include his son. When Diana discovered this, she issued an ultimatum to her husband. 'Either William goes, or you go on your own, and that's final,' she declared. For the sake of peace, the Prince bowed to his wife's wishes once again.

All these disagreements were forgotten when their plane touched down in Alice Springs, Central Australia and Prince Charles proudly showed off his wife and baby son to the

Australian nation. It was the start of arguably their most successful tour ever.

The six-week slog through heat, dust, bushfires and floods was a testing time for the royal novice, but she emerged at the end of it triumphant. The Aussies and the Kiwis loved her. Everywhere she went she was mobbed by wildly enthusiastic crowds. Even though she attracted more attention than her husband, Prince Charles seemed thrilled that the people Down Under approved of the wife he had chosen.

In Tasmania, he recalled the good-luck messages received on his last visit after their engagement and added: 'I was indeed lucky enough to marry her.' If William had not been with them, however, it might have been a different story. Diana would no doubt have been thoroughly miserable, and the tour perhaps not such a great success.

They covered so much territory, and shook so many hands in just a few weeks, that the trip became a gruelling ordeal for both of them. But it seemed to bring them much closer. On one scorchingly hot day in Maitland, north of Sydney, they were sitting in a park watching a display by schoolchildren when I snapped a magic moment between them. Instead of watching the show the Prince was gazing at his wife. I saw him place his hand over hers and give her a look which clearly said: 'I love you.'

Two months later, Diana and Charles were off again on another exhausting tour which took them to Canada. This time they decided to leave Prince William behind, because it was only a two-week trip, and they did not want to interrupt his nursery routine.

To royal watchers, the tour provided an amazing insight into the difficulties the Princess experienced coping with media attention. During a press reception aboard the royal yacht *Britannia*, she confided her feelings to reporter Diana Bentley of the *Halifax Daily News*. 'When they write something horrible I get a horrible feeling right here,' Diana said, touching her heart. 'And I don't want to go outside.'

This caused a massive row, because the main condition for admittance to any royal press reception is that every royal comment is off the record, and must not be reported.

The trip ended in Edmonton, Alberta, on 1 July, which, as well as Canada's national day, was also Diana's twenty-second birthday. And when the Prince and Princess opened the World Student Games at an outdoor stadium, some 62,000 spectators and young athletes from ninety-five countries joined in singing 'Happy Birthday' to her.

What remained of Diana's birthday was spent flying home to Britain aboard a Canadian Air Force 707. Prince Charles had arranged a special celebration and champagne corks popped at 30,000 feet as Diana cut a birthday cake he had ordered from his chef on the royal yacht. On top of the scrumptious icing was the simple message: 'I love you, darling.'

The Princess of Wales was by then the most adored woman in the world, yet her confidence was at an all-time low. She had very little self-esteem and was constantly anxious. She also confided to a member of her staff her feelings of 'jealousy and insecurity' over her husband's past girlfriends, especially Camilla Parker Bowles. She claimed that Camilla was still seeing her husband. 'This became a big issue in her mind,' said the aide.

Diana could not banish Camilla from her husband's life, but she could ban her from 'her' home. No one on her staff can ever remember Mrs Parker Bowles visiting Kensington Palace.

At a time when the young Princess needed reassurance and sympathy, there was a void. Her husband was 'unreceptive' to advice. According to those around him, he was 'not in tune with the normal feelings of someone so much younger than him. There had been a major change to her life and she simply could not adapt. Nor did she receive any help in trying to do so. She was like a lost little kid.'

Christmas Day also became a focus for her increasing anxiety. She dreaded the formality of it. She was in awe of the Queen and the protocol surrounding her mother-in-law. She was still in love with Charles, but he did not show much affection for her. 'It was a distant love,' the Palace aide concluded.

Diana also became apprehensive when holidays at Balmoral drew near. She had detested the Highland estate from the beginning, because it represented her husband's past life. She felt he was carrying on the existence he had before they married, and was consciously refusing to involve her in it.

Diana was paranoid about failure. She was constantly made aware what was expected of her, but never helped in achieving it. She found the Royal Family 'very evaluative', and full of high expectations. The perfectionist Princess felt that she constantly disappointed them.

At this time, the doctors and the team of psychiatrists and psychologists could find no evidence of the eating disorder bulimia, which later played havoc with her confidence. But she did have a hang-up about eating in public, which may have been the earliest sign of the disease which followed in later years. No inkling of these dramas behind palace doors was ever revealed in public. Diana continued to smile blissfully when she appeared with her husband, and they seemed happier than ever when Buckingham Palace announced in February 1984 that the Princess was expecting her second child.

When Prince Harry was born in September 1984, the Prince of Wales was keen to be a modern dad, involved with every aspect of his children's lives. Indeed he devoted so much time to caring for them that he was soon criticized for cutting down the number of official engagements he undertook.

In 1985, Prince Charles and Princess Diana went to Italy on a seventeen-day official tour. Their small sons were flown out to Venice at the end of the trip to join their parents for a cruise around the Italian coast. After four happy days in the warm Mediterranean sunshine, they all flew home together from Olbia in Sardinia.

Things started to go badly wrong between Charles and Diana from then on. In the autumn of that year, when I was covering their return to Australia to celebrate the 150th anniversary of the state of Victoria, I noticed that Diana looked alarmingly thin. As I photographed her dancing with Prince Charles at a ball in Melbourne, I realized for the first time how much weight she had lost. Her sleeveless dress showed her shoulderbones, protruding through her skin, and her lovely face had not an ounce of spare flesh on it.

When I mentioned this to my colleagues, most felt Diana was misguidedly trying to look like a fashion model. A few wondered if she had succumbed to her sister's anorexia nervosa and suggested this eating disorder might run in families.

But there were other clues that the Princess of Wales was growing increasingly unhappy. Her husband began spending more and more time apart from his wife.

In 1986, when they finished a tour of several Gulf states, the Princess flew home aboard a chartered British Caledonian jet while her husband cruised to Cyprus aboard the royal yacht *Britannia*. In the next year, he deserted his wife on six separate occasions. He enjoyed three solo trips to Italy, his favourite European country. He stayed on in Switzerland after his wife flew home from their 1987 skiing holiday, and returned to stay with friends in Gstaad in March of that year. In April, after a tour of southern Africa, he went trekking through the Kalahari Desert with his mentor, the author and mystic Sir Laurens van der Post.

I had become so concerned about the amount of time the Prince and Princess were spending apart that at a cocktail party in Madrid that year I asked her to explain. 'What's all this about you leading separate lives?' I bluntly demanded.

Diana was not at all dismayed. 'Ooh, that,' she laughingly replied. 'When we first got married we were everyone's idea of the world's most perfect couple. Now they say we're leading separate lives. The next thing I know I'll read in some newspaper that I've got a black, Catholic lover.'

She went on to explain that there was a very good reason why they were hardly ever together. 'My husband and I get around 2,000 invitations to visit different places every six months. We couldn't possibly get through many if we did them all together. So we have decided to accept as many as we can separately. This means we can get to twice as many places and meet twice as many people.'

It seemed at the time to be a reasonable explanation. Diana was her normal jokey self and I believed her. Later, however, I began to have my doubts. Separate jobs were understandable, but separate holidays quite another matter.

All the people who worked for the Waleses were upset by the strained atmosphere in their home. Whenever Charles and Diana were due to carry out an official engagement together, the Prince seemed to be behind schedule. His wife would turn up punctually at the front door ready to go, while staff scurried around trying to find Prince Charles. 'He's late as usual,' the Princess would fume. 'I'm fed up waiting for him.'

One evening, when they were off to a glittering première, Diana was once again cooling her heels in the hall while Charles was nowhere to be seen. Rolling her eyes to heaven, she flounced out and got into their waiting car. Some ten minutes after they had been due to depart, the Prince strolled out, looking dashing in his dinner jacket. In one hand he held a vodka martini which he carried into the car. He finished the drink, lowered the electric window and passed the glass to his butler Harold Brown as the car sped away.

Another tell-tale sign of the couple's drift from each other was the lack of fanfare about their respective birthdays. After their first five years of marriage, the celebrations had virtually dried up. One Palace worker said: 'The Royal Family set great store by birthdays and although, as one gets older, there tends to be less fuss, it is regarded as being very important. The Prince and Princess no longer regarded those days as being anything special.'

When the Prince and Princess were not together to celebrate milestones like his fortieth and her thirtieth birthdays, the Palace press office offered lame excuses to the media. We were told the Princess felt a lavish birthday party was inappropriate in a recession.

(Every royal birthday is recorded in the Royal Family's Season Calendar, which also contains dates of key events like race meetings, rugby matches and the birthdays of Commonwealth heads of state. On one occasion, when controversial Princess Michael of Kent was out of favour, the Queen banned her birthday and wedding anniversary from appearing in the calendar, causing a terrible row with Prince Michael of Kent. The Queen relented when the Princess had proved her worth in the family.)

To emphasize the growing gulf between them, the Princess began calling her staff 'The A team' and her husband's 'The B team'. They were also becoming more distant in another, even more important sense. All royal homes have unusual sleeping quarters. Each married couple has a smaller room adjoining their bedroom. This is designed to be used when a wife or husband has to leave very early, or comes home late, and does not want to disturb his or her partner.

Prince Charles began sleeping on a single bed in this room while Princess Diana occupied their vast four-poster. Whenever they stayed at Balmoral or Sandringham the same thing happened.

Why did the world's most famous married couple stop sleeping together? The answer came to me from a confidant of the Prince. 'He simply could not stand the smell of sick,' I was informed. 'The Princess was throwing up so often their bedroom was contaminated by her bulimia. He could smell it in her hair, on her clothes, on her skin. It turned him off totally.'

Like many husbands, he was revolted by this eating disorder. He could not cope with it. Despite the best medical advice, his wife seemed addicted to her illness.

Whenever they flew abroad on a tour she would be sick in the aircraft lavatory they shared. When Charles used it to change his clothes before landing, he felt nauseous himself.

Eventually, the pungent odour of vomit, whether real or imagined by Charles, came to symbolize everything he loathed about his wife. And it seemed to him a valid reason to stay well away from her.

Diana began to dread holidays, when she was marooned on the royal estates with her husband, far from her friends in London. Unwilling to join in with Charles's outdoor pursuits, she became increasingly lonely and isolated. Accustomed to a daily dip in the Buckingham Palace or Highgrove pools, she missed the regular exercise which kept her in great shape physically and mentally. Eventually, Diana began using the heated pools at hotels near the Queen's country estates.

Even though the Queen was well aware that her daughter-in-law and her grandchildren enjoyed swimming, she would not consider building a private pool at either Balmoral or Sandringham. A frequent guest at both estates explained: 'These places are for the outdoor life, for being close to nature. We all get plenty of exercise out stalking and grouse shooting. Besides, there are pools at Windsor and Buckingham Palace so the Queen doesn't see the need for any more.'

To fill her empty hours, Diana began to spend a lot of time with her bodyguard Sergeant Barry Mannakee. They were often seen together strolling through the grounds of Balmoral Castle. The handsome young sergeant pushed Prince Harry in his pram while the Princess chatted away at his side. And any passer-by might easily have mistaken them for a young married couple out for a walk with their own baby. Their friendship sparked off speculation in the Rat Pack when, in the summer of 1985, Jim Bennett, a freelance photographer, spotted them zooming along the road between Braemar and Crathie. He followed them for thirty miles along the road to Aberdeen. When the Princess finally noticed the snapper coming up fast behind them, she slammed on the brakes, did an amazing handbrake turn and drove off back the way she had come. It seemed a peculiar way to behave, and the cameraman could not wait to tell his mates.

Although a relatively junior officer, Mannakee seemed more popular with Diana than many of his more senior colleagues were. He was not very tall, but was a good-looking charmer. Everyone liked the lad from London's East End, especially the Prince of Wales. His one fault was that he tended to be a bit flash with us. When Jim Bennett later tackled Mannakee about his race along the Deeside Road, the policeman boasted with a laugh: 'My lady won't be caught by you when she's with me.'

The easy familiarity that seemed to exist between the Princess of Wales and the Cockney policeman was the talk of the Royal Protection Squad. No one was surprised when, less than a year later, the smooth-talking sergeant was transferred to other duties. His skill with firearms won him an equally responsible position in the Diplomatic Protection Squad.

At the time, Mannakee claimed that he had requested the move for domestic reasons. 'The job meant long hours away from home,' he explained. But his eye for a pretty girl was more likely the reason for his downfall.

His marriage was going through a rocky patch and he had become involved with a pretty housemaid at Kensington Palace. During this period, Charles and Diana's staff were invited to a private tour of the studios at Independent Television News in Central London. Afterwards food and booze were served. All the guests were in a party mood, and Mannakee ended up taking home another woman on his bosses' payroll. The result was a love triangle which caused ructions in the Royal Household. Soon afterwards, the handsome sergeant got his marching orders.

Tragically, in May 1987, Barry Mannakee was killed in a road accident. He was a pillion passenger on a motorbike driven by a police colleague, which was in a collision with a vehicle driven by a seventeen-year-old girl.

Prince Charles was deeply upset when he learned of the accident next day, but when he broke the news, his wife burst into tears and dashed from the room, sobbing uncontrollably. They were on the point of leaving London to attend the Cannes Film Festival. A wreath from both of them was sent to the funeral.

I photographed the Princess in Cannes and, as usual, she was on sparkling form. If she had harboured any deep personal feelings for Mannakee it certainly didn't show.

Diana was upset when the time she innocently spent with Mannakee created a lot of malicious gossip, particularly as nobody noticed what Charles was getting up to in his private life. The Prince had drifted back to his old chums. He was spending more and more time with the Palmer-Tomkinsons, the Romseys, the Wards and the Parker Bowleses.

In the autumn of 1986, when Diana returned to London to take her children back to school, Charles stayed on at Balmoral for eight more weeks. The Rat Pack failed to notice this long period apart, as we were too busy following the Queen and Prince Philip around China.

It wasn't until the following year that the *News of the World* began to keep count of the nights the Prince and Princess of Wales spent apart. When the total reached thirty-three, speculation that the marriage was heading for the rocks reverberated right around the world.

Even when the Prince flew down from Balmoral to accompany his wife on a tour of floods in Wales, he dashed straight back to his pals in the Highlands immediately afterwards. It seemed that Charles and Diana simply could not bear to spend even one night under the same roof. From then on, it was a marriage in name only.

Diana began cutting down the time she spent at Highgrove, while Charles rarely spent a night at their London home. For company, he turned increasingly to the woman who shared so many of his interests. Camilla Parker Bowles, a great horsewoman, rode out with him in the Beaufort Hunt, and loved fishing and stalking with him at Balmoral. She was a frequent guest at Highgrove, occasionally acting as the Prince's hostess in the absence of his wife, and Charles was often seen at her home in Wiltshire.

In fact, they were so often together that the writer Tina Brown, then editor of *Tatler*, noticed that Camilla had picked up many of the Prince's speech mannerisms when she interviewed her. She talked of a 'hice with some virry virry nice pictures'.

This seemed a dead giveaway. The only other person who spent so much time in the Prince's company was his senior bodyguard, Superintendent Colin Hayward-Trimming, who has also adopted the Prince's phraseology and body language.

At this time, the general public were not aware of his closeness to the wife of an Army officer, but the members of the Royal Protection Group could talk of nothing else.

The Prince thought he was being terribly discreet when he gave orders for the police back-up car containing two sergeants not to follow him after Exit 17 on the M4 motorway when he headed for Camilla's house. He drove on with only his personal protection officer, having arranged to rendezvous with the back-up men at the same spot next day.

What the Prince never knew as he sped off to meet Camilla was the hilarity he left behind. As the police officers he left behind watched him tear off, they used to sing in unison: 'We know where you-'re go-ing.'

CHAPTER NINE

Heir-raising Tales

Prince William was learning how to fly a kite on a beach in west Norfolk in a half-term school break in 1986, while his two-year-old brother sat watching. As usual, their nanny Barbara Barnes was making a big fuss of William, leaving Harry to entertain himself.

Feeling sorry for the younger boy, who always seemed to be treated as second best, their Scotland Yard bodyguard Andy Creighton said: 'Come here, Harry. I'll build you a sandcastle. It's the only bleedin' castle you're ever likely to get.'

This kind-hearted gesture by the bluff, Cockney copper summed up the enormous difference between Prince William and his younger brother. William will one day be master of Windsor Castle, Balmoral Castle, Buckingham Palace, Sandringham and the vast estates that go with them. But what will Harry have?

Under the British Royal Family's system, the eldest son gets the lot. This means all the property, and all the money, goes to Prince Charles's first-born son, William. Harry, like the Queen's second son Prince Andrew, will probably have to get a job or rely on the trust fund his parents have set up for him.

But it's not just a matter of material wealth. The ever-widening gulf between William and Harry is reflected in the attitudes of the people around them. William has occupied a special place in history from the moment he was born, while Harry is doomed forever to live in his shadow. The great divide between a boy born to be a King and his brother affects every aspect of their lives.

Eventually, William will become not just head of the family firm, but head of state, while Harry, although working for the same institution, will have only a supporting role. The milestones in William's young life have been marked by special photo sessions for the royal archives and the media. At nine months old his first crawl-about made the world's front pages.

I remember going to Kensington Palace to record the fact that William had become a toddler, running around everywhere. Then I went back to do the official pictures for his second birthday. But less important Harry's progress was not so well documented.

The first session with William was the best. A flowery rug was spread out on the manicured lawn of Government House in Auckland, on the second leg of Charles and Diana's first tour together Down Under. The proud parents sat down with their young son and watched him crawl around at alarming speed.

The Nikons rattled as forty photographers blazed away at the baby Prince's antics. He was dressed in an apricot-and-white romper suit and had brought along his favourite toy, a clockwork bee. It was just an ordinary family scene, the kind stuck in millions of photo albums around the world. But because the man and his son sitting on the rug would one day sit on the throne of Great Britain, it was a memorable and historic occasion.

The photo call was arranged by the local tour officials for 9.30 on a Saturday morning for the benefit of the New Zealand and Australian Sunday newspapers. But the thirteen-hour time difference between England and New Zealand meant that there was still time to get these very special pictures into the later editions of Saturday's *Sun* in London.

Outside, I had a cab waiting to rush me back to the *Auckland Star* newspaper, so I could quickly process and transmit my film to my office. Unfortunately, the Prince and Princess were so engrossed in showing off their son's progress that the session dragged on and on.

The reporters were as pleased as the cameramen. They had heard Prince Charles calling his son 'Wills', a nickname that gave them a nice little story to accompany the pictures. But I was getting increasingly anxious as the minutes ticked by. I already had so many great shots of William crawling, sitting, standing, blowing raspberries, and in his parents' loving arms, that I decided to make a fast getaway. So I legged it while the session was still going on. My partner, *Sun* reporter Harry Arnold, then started worrying that if the photo call continued much longer, a more spectacular picture than the ones I had shot might materialize. So, thinking quickly, he decided to call it all to a halt.

'Thank you very much, sir. Thank you, ma'am,' he told the Princes and Princess. 'We've got some superb pictures.'

Hearing this, Diana scooped up William and with Charles headed back to the house. But the other photographers went hysterical and began shouting and swearing at Harry. 'Why the hell did you do that?' screamed Tim Graham, a freelance photographer. As he wasn't working for a newspaper, he was under no pressure to file and would have been happy to stay there snapping away all day. The other freelancers angrily joined in. But Harry was unrepentant. He knew that by stopping the picture session he had prevented the *Sun* from being scooped.

'Now my monkey's gone, I've got to protect his back,' he explained. And with that he cheerily went off to file the story of the first ever royal crawl-about. The end result was a splash that made Page One plus a double-page spread of pictures in the later editions of our paper. My colleagues might have been irate, but the editor of the *Sun* was delighted.

From the day he was born Prince William was God's gift to the media. I photographed him for the first time when he was less than twenty hours old. And now the poor little sod is doomed to have us chasing him for the rest of his life.

When he was a toddler his mischievous antics kept reporters busy for several years. He was a normal two-year-old tearaway trying to flush his dad's Gucci loafers down the loo, and he once had police rushing from all over Aberdeenshire when he pressed an alarm bell at Balmoral. He caused another rumpus in the

Highlands when he wrecked the Queen Mother's afternoon tea party by pulling off a tablecloth complete with china, cakes and teapot.

I got a lot of fun pictures of Wee Willie before he became the rather reserved and self-conscious schoolboy he is today. He once came back to London from Sandringham on a cold winter evening wearing a knitted bonnet. That picture screamed into the *Sun* under the jokey headline 'WILLIE WARMER'.

Another great shot came the day he walked out of his nursery school on his way to perform in a Christmas concert with his classmates. A little girl walking beside him had unknowingly hitched her skirt above her knickers. My pun-loving Picture Editor Paul Buttle conjured up the perfect caption: 'WILLIAM'S PANTY-MIME'.

I went to Kensington Palace for an official photo call arranged to mark William's second birthday. I had been lucky enough to draw the national newspaper pass to record this event. The young Prince happily ran into the garden wearing dungarees and a little stripey tee-shirt. As I focused on him, I noticed that he scratched his head with his left hand. This picture appeared on the front page of every daily newspaper the next morning and prompted the *Sun* to run a story suggesting that the little Prince was left-handed.

This assumption proved to be correct. On 1 March 1991, Prince William was in Cardiff with his parents celebrating St David's Day. When he signed the visitors' book at the Town Hall everybody was able to confirm the truth of what the *Sun* had predicted seven years earlier: the next Prince of Wales was indeed a southpaw.

The fierce spotlight focused on all the Royal Family is now beginning to have an effect on William. This is the price that he is paying for being heir to the last surviving major monarchy and to one of the greatest fortunes in the world.

Unlike his younger brother Harry, William dreads every encounter with cameramen. A man who has known the little Prince since he was born told me: 'He hates the press. He hates being on show.' The truth of his words became obvious in

110

Austria when Princess Diana took her sons on a skiing holiday in March 1993.

One afternoon, while out shopping for sweets, they were surrounded by at least two dozen paparazzi, mostly French and Italian freelance photographers, who were 'monstering' the Princess and her children. When she tried to escape with her sons back to their hotel by crossing the street the 'Europaps' closed in for the kill. Blazing away at close range, they must have appeared very threatening to the young lads.

Traffic screeched to a halt and tourists stared in amazement as Princess Diana's policeman, Inspector Ken Wharfe, scuffled with the photographers. One Italian snapper, who would not move out of the way, was thrown bodily to the ground.

Both young princes were visibly shocked. But it was William who was affected most. His mother put a protective arm around him as she ushered the boys back into the safety of the Arlberg Hotel. It took Prince William three hours to recover from the trauma of the incident.

'I wasn't worried for myself, only for the boys,' Diana told me the next day. 'People forget that they are only eight and ten years old.'

When they first went to Lech, in 1991, Harry acted as if he had been born on skis, whereas William struggled through his first few lessons. One morning, when things went hopelessly wrong for him, the eight-year-old Prince started to cry, and went back to his hotel with his nanny. Next morning he was unfairly dubbed 'Willie the Wimp' in the *Sun*. In fact, William wasn't very well, as he was suffering from a sore throat. It must be very hard to learn anything when every mistake is filmed and photographed for the world's consumption.

Like all children, he has to be disciplined sometimes. And I got a cracking picture when William's nanny Olga Powell chastised him for misbehaving at a polo game one Sunday afternoon in May 1987. At the end of the match he decided to dash out on to the pitch to join his father in the winners' line-up. Olga, the deputy nanny who was on duty that weekend, grabbed the little runaway to haul him back, but he kept trying to wriggle out of her clutches. Finally, Olga gave him a stern ticking-off and William's little face crumpled as he burst into tears.

I had my 600-millimetre lens focused on him throughout this episode, and banged off half a dozen frames. One of these was the splash picture next day on Page One of the *Sun*.

The *Sun* editor Kelvin MacKenzie, who very rarely praises any member of his staff, told me: 'Every kid cries when he is told off, but it's rare to picture a royal child in tears. Well done; your picture carried the paper today. It will go down in the royal archives.'

It must be tough trying to raise two well-adjusted children when they are surrounded by so many adults, all telling them what to do. Diana once severely reprimanded a member of her staff who took it on himself to give William a whack for mis-behaving after twice being warned for playing with a sharp knife. The little grass immediately ran off and told his mum that he had been walloped.

Minutes later, Diana appeared and asked what her son had done. When told he had been ordered out of the kitchen because he could have come to harm, the Princess understood. 'I'm sorry he was getting in your way,' she said. 'But in future, when William is naughty don't smack him. Instead, please come and tell me, and I will deal with it myself.'

While William is reserved and rather timid like his father, Harry has a sunny, fun-loving personality. He is a born comedian and mimic. Kensington Palace staff laugh at the way he stands behind important visitors, pulling faces and imitating them. With his red hair, he looks like a real Spencer. His mother says: 'Everyone tells me he could easily be my sister Sarah's son. He has a real Spencer look about him.'

With his little pink cheeks, and neat, glossy haircut Harry looks like an angel, but can be a little devil at times. At one Horse of the Year show he was introduced to a colonel's wife, who asked him if he was enjoying himself. 'What have you been doing?' she enquired.

'What's it got to do with you?' the royal rascal replied.

He is so cheeky that one person who looks after him tells him off constantly. 'You're a rude, horrible little boy,' he says. 'What are you? You're 'orrible!'

'Yep,' says Harry, grinning from ear to ear, 'I'm horrible.'

Every scolding is like water off a duck's back. 'Yep,' he answers every time, and runs off laughing.

Once William was mischievous too. I remember the best pictures taken at Fergie's wedding were of William poking his tongue out at the little bridesmaid beside him during the service in Westminster Abbey. He was just four years old, and a normal kid who then had no idea what the future held.

When I reviewed the papers on BBC TV's 'Breakfast Time' show next morning I had to admit that *Daily Mirror* staff photographer Brendan Monks's pictures showed that William had stolen the show. Today that high-spirited kid has totally disappeared and William is a completely different youngster.

He seems shy and withdrawn whenever he appears in public now. Although he may get up to all sorts of pranks with his chums in private, he is always self-conscious in front of the press. His head goes down the minute he spots a camera. If he is ever to carry out the role he is destined to fulfil, somehow he must learn to live under the glare of the spotlight.

In the early years of their lives, I had lots of opportunities to photograph the young Princes. Now they are boarding at Ludgrove School, near Wokingham in Berkshire, we are staying out of their hair. Every child has the right to an education, and it would be unfair to disturb their studies. But as soon as they are old enough to start dating girls, the press will resume their hot pursuit.

The girl Prince William marries will have to be very special indeed. The whole world thought Princess Diana was the perfect partner for a future King, but look what happened to that fairy-tale marriage! When, or if, the young Prince gets around to choosing a wife, the entire Royal Household will want to be assured he is making the right choice.

William is already very keen on girls. In fact, he had his first serious romance at the age of seven. I don't think his parents ever realized he was so besotted that he proposed marriage.

The little Prince was on holiday at Balmoral when he first laid eyes on Anna McCart while out riding with Prince Harry and their groom. She was a gorgeous little curly-haired blonde, around the same age. He took one look at the Balmoral gardener's daughter and was instantly smitten. Anna shyly said hello and asked where he was going, but William couldn't utter a word. He was dumbstruck. And, as she walked away, he could not take his eyes off her. An amused estate worker told me later: 'He turned around and leaned so far out of the saddle to stare at her that he almost fell off his pony.'

Like his father, Prince William could not resist a blue-eyed blonde.

After that first meeting he was with her every day until their summer holiday was over. As soon as his morning ride finished he would dash back from the stables to play with his new friend. And within a week he boldly gave her a kiss and said: 'Will you marry me?'

Anna, like most seven-year-old females, was not too keen on little boys, and just laughed. But William wanted to assure her he was not joking. 'When I come back next year I am going to marry you,' he insisted. 'My papa told me if you kiss a girl you have to marry her.' With that, he gave her another smacker on the cheek just to make sure.

Anna took the proposal very seriously. As far as she was concerned they were engaged. 'William and I are getting married next year,' she rushed around telling the other estate workers' children. Everyone at Balmoral laughed when the story of the young Prince's romance went the rounds, but it was clear proof that Prince Charles was teaching his son from an early age that when you make a pass at a pretty girl, your intentions must be honourable.

Royal staff who have known William all his short life know how close Prince Charles is to his sons. They have always ignored reports that the Prince neglects his children. They have heard him affectionately calling William 'Womble', the special nickname he has used far more often than 'Wills'. And they have seen the boys helping their father weed his Highgrove garden, encouraging them to produce their own organically-grown vegetables.

Their unique destiny as first and second in line to the throne has created a very special bond between Prince Charles and his elder son. The Prince is realistic enough to recognize that he is unlikely to become King until his late seventies, and therefore will probably reign for a very short time, if at all. Therefore nothing has a higher priority in his life than preparing William to continue the Windsor dynasty into the twenty-first century.

All parents find raising their children a difficult task. But for the Prince of Wales it is even more daunting. The young Prince must be able to combine the traditions of a medieval monarchy with the demands of our technological age.

Over the past fifty years, the social and ethnic composition of Great Britain has been utterly transformed, and Prince Charles realizes that his son will reign in a different world. Who knows if Royal Ascot, the Trooping of the Colour and all the other ceremonial trappings of the present sovereign will survive Queen Elizabeth II's reign?

After the woes of the Windsors at the end of the twentieth century, the Prince of Wales must ensure that William has a throne to inherit. Britain is no longer the centre of a great world-wide empire. Even its historic ties with the Commonwealth are gradually breaking, as the nation takes on a more integrated role in the European Economic Community. If a Federal Europe eventually arrives, the British monarch may become just like a provincial governor in a United States of Europe.

The Prince is conscious that he must chart the course William will one day follow. He realizes this is a tricky job because sons don't always listen to their fathers. 'I didn't listen to advice from my own father until I was in my late teens,' he once revealed.

But he went on to say that he hopes William will learn a lot just by hanging around with his dad, 'rather like a farmer's son, by following his father around the farm, picking things up, he will do the same'. The best advice of all he could give his son, the Prince added, 'is to make sure that he has got advisers around him, to choose the right people to help him do the job'.

Charles loves his son, of that there can be no doubt. Sailors on the royal yacht *Britannia* during a visit to Canada in November 1991 vividly remember how the Prince behaved when it was time for the boys to leave him and fly home to England. William and Harry had joined their parents on the official tour, but had to return to school two days before the trip ended. As they prepared to board the royal barge that would carry them ashore on Lake Ontario, the little Princes were clearly upset. But so was their father, as a crewman later told me. 'I looked at Prince Charles as his sons disappeared down the companionway and set off in the barge. I saw tears rolling down his cheeks. It was obvious how he felt about saying goodbye to his children.'

As the Princes and their nanny reached the jetty at Oshawa, where a car was waiting to whisk them to the airport, a few enterprising photographers were waiting. Their pictures showed a distressed William, red-eyed and tearful, unable to keep a stiff upper lip. His younger brother, who was not then at boarding school, looked much more cheerful.

But the picture from that royal tour which was flashed around the world was of the children greeting their mother on the deck of *Britannia* after her arrival with Prince Charles in Toronto. After driving from the airport to the yacht berthed on the lake shore, the Princess brushed past the Admiral and crew waiting to welcome them, and dashed towards her boys with arms outstretched. A photograph of this happy scene later won an award for my colleague Jayne Fincher.

Minutes later, the Prince, who had politely stopped to meet the top brass, also warmly hugged his sons. But no editor wanted the picture. It just simply did not compete with the theatrical sequence of the Princess tossing her hat aside as she rushed forward to throw her arms around the boys and kiss them. This is another example of how continually Diana upstaged her husband. When this further proof of the Princess's love for her children was splashed all over the front pages of British and Canadian newspapers, Prince Charles was hurt. 'I love my sons, too,' he said. 'Why was my wife the only one pictured with the boys?'

It was no coincidence that, a few months later in March 1992, when Prince Charles joined his boys in Austria, the press was permitted to witness their reunion. The little Princes had arrived earlier with their mother in Lech for a skiing holiday. But the Princess was nowhere to be seen when Prince Charles's car drew up outside their hotel. Instead, two excited little boys dashed out of the front door into the snowy street and leaped into their father's arms. The bliss on William's face as he flung his arms around his father's waist and hugged him tightly showed the great love between them.

The day that Prince William was born was undoubtedly the happiest of Prince Charles's life. I remember the beaming new dad walking out of St Mary's Hospital, Paddington two hours after he had witnessed his son's arrival. None of us who were there that night, covering the birth of another heir to the British throne, had ever seen the Prince of Wales so ecstatic.

The crowd in the street was singing 'Nice one, Charlie, nice one, son. Now give us another one.' When he heard this Charles said: 'Bloody hell! I think my wife would have something to say about that.' But he admitted he was 'over the moon'.

My partner Harry Arnold had the presence of mind to dash across the street from the press position, and he congratulated the new father before he stepped into his car. I was right behind him snapping away, as Harry shook his hand, and asked how mother and baby were doing.

The Prince said his son had fair hair, sort of blondish and blue eyes, and his wife was very tired. 'Some sleep is urgently needed,' he explained. It had been a long wait. The date, 21 June 1982, was coincidentally Midsummer's Day and when evening came we went off to grab something to eat in a curry house around the corner from the hospital. Just as a dozen dishes were being served, Harry, ever the true professional, decided to make a check call to the Palace, before we ate. He was asking the press office if there was any news. The Queen's press secretary Michael Shea told him that there would be an official announcement from the Palace within a very few minutes.

Overhearing this, every snapper and reporter made a dash for the door to get back to St Mary's. When Harry turned around after finishing his call, all he could see was a table loaded with plates of steaming curry, with no one to eat it. He wanted to run out after us, but the irate restaurant owner would not let him leave before the £50 bill was paid.

The next day Diana surprised everyone by leaving hospital less than twenty-four hours after giving birth, at a time when most first-time mothers stayed in at least a week. At six o'clock in the evening the new parents walked slowly down the front steps of the Lindo Wing with Charles holding his son snugly wrapped in a lacy shawl. The crowds, who had been lining the street all day, got only a glimpse of a white bundle as the royal couple posed for the rows of photographers lined up on the opposite pavement.

I knew the most important picture of the day would be of the baby's face, so I instructed another *Sun* photographer, Barry Beattie, to climb as high as he could up a wall behind us, and using nothing but a 500-mm lens, concentrate only on the baby's face.

The result was the *Sun* had the only clear shot of the new heir to the throne next day. With his eyes tightly shut and one finger in his mouth, the as yet unnamed little Prince slept soundly in his father's arms, unaware that he was meeting the press for the very first time.

When Prince Harry was born two years later, every newspaper had a photographer whose only role was to get a good snap of the baby's face. Beattie did a superb job on William, and his picture was splashed all over Page One, while my more mundane shots of the royal threesome were relegated to an inside page. Barry Beattie received a bonus from the boss for his excellent efforts, while I had to console myself with the thought that my idea had given the *Sun* the best coverage of William's first photo call.

Although I didn't take the front-page picture that day, I did get several shots which were published inside the paper next morning. And in my pocket I had a hero-gram from my boss, the *Sun*'s Picture Editor, congratulating me on the excellent pictures of Prince Charles celebrating the new arrival the night before.

At least I was outside St Mary's Hospital when Diana took her baby home. One of my chief rivals, James Whitaker of the *Daily Mirror*, decided that the Princess would not leave hospital so soon. He had gone to Cirencester, where Prince Charles was scheduled to play polo, so he missed the whole show.

But the most touching story of the day, which everyone missed, including me, was something that happened a few minutes after the new Royal Family left the hospital. A friend of the Princess later told me the happy scene the cameras recorded was a painful ordeal for Diana.

'When I came out of the hospital I could barely put one foot in front of the other. My stitches were killing me,' Diana confided to her chum. 'It was such a strain to stand there and smile even for just a couple of minutes. As soon as the car disappeared around the corner out of sight of the photographers I burst into tears.'

Most new mothers have a bit of a weep a day or so after giving birth. It's a normal come-down after such a highly emotional experience. But the Princess of Wales wasn't any ordinary mum leaving hospital. The world's media were waiting to document the momentous occasion. And Diana was definitely not looking her best. She was wearing an old green maternity dress, the only outfit her still bulky figure could squeeze into. And instead of tights she wore pop socks, which wrinkled and fell down around her ankles. It was a bit much to expect a girl who had been an unknown nursery school assistant eighteen months earlier to cope with such media scrutiny at such a time.

By comparison, when she left hospital with Prince Harry on 16 September 1984, Diana had learned a lot. She cleverly wore a vivid red jacket to conceal her thick waistline, had her hair styled and looked far more glamorous the second time around.

The biggest drama in William's young life was the day he fractured his skull, but the real drama of that day has never been revealed until now.

It was just after lunch at Ludgrove School, where William and some pals were practising their golf swings. A careless school-chum raised his club to hit a ball and accidentally whacked William on the forehead. When he was taken back to the main house, the staff were about to put the young Prince in the infirmary, but William's personal protection officer, Reg Spinney, insisted on an ambulance being called. One of the masters suggested a doctor should be summoned.

Sergeant Spinney would have none of it, and didn't mince his words. 'I'm getting him out of here,' he said firmly. 'You are in charge of his education, I'm in charge of keeping him alive.' And he called an ambulance.

The Prince and Princess of Wales were alerted as William was rushed to Reading General Hospital. There doctors decided that this was no minor bang on the head. They felt they were not qualified to deal with such a serious head injury to such an important child.

Within half an hour of his parents' arrival, the still conscious William was back in the ambulance on his way to the world-famous children's hospital, Great Ormond Street in London. The Queen's physician, Dr Anthony Dawson, and several other consultants told his parents that William was suffering from a depressed fracture of the skull and needed an immediate operation to relieve the pressure on his brain.

The Prince and Princess of Wales were warned that William's injury was far more dangerous than was at first believed, and Reg's swift action had probably saved his life. Charles and Diana expressed their gratitude to him for looking after their son so well, and the Police Comissioner gave him a commendation for his rapid response in an emergency.

While his son was in surgery, Prince Charles went off to attend a performance of Puccini's *Tosca* at Covent Garden. He got a lot of flak in the press next morning for not being a caring father. While Princess Diana stayed by her son's bedside, Prince Charles claimed he could not let down a group of visitors from the European Commission in Brussels, because he had already cancelled a meeting with them once before.

Unknown to his critics, the Prince had a pager in his pocket so that he could be summoned immediately if his son suffered a relapse. And at the opera he was only ten minutes away from Great Ormond Street. His staff later revealed this information to prove that Prince Charles was not a cold man who had neglected his son, as his critics had claimed. But I could not forget that he had also refused to come home from a painting holiday in Italy when Prince Harry was rushed to hospital three years earlier for a hernia operation.

As a result of William's accident he is now discouraged from playing certain risky sports. Princess Diana has revealed he no longer joins his classmates in the Ludgrove golf class. But I have learned that the young Prince has also stopped riding lessons and is not at all keen to become a polo player like his father.

Prince William is unhappy in the saddle, just as his mother always has been. This is the reason he appeared in the BBC TV documentary 'Elizabeth R' taking Princess Beatrice pony-trekking on a leading rein, rather than riding alongside like his little brother Harry, and cousin Zara Phillips.

Now that the Prince and Princess of Wales have separated and the boys are at boarding school, the time each parent gets with them is limited. As a result, Charles has made a tremendous sacrifice. His favourite way to unwind has always been a game of polo. He once claimed: 'If I didn't get the exercise or have something to take my mind off things I would go potty.'

Although the sport is more of an obsession than a game to him, he is aware that his sons are bored by afternoons watching him play polo. Year after year, his entire summer programme was once planned around the polo fixtures. Now, he has decided to cut his polo programme in half so that he can spend more quality time with William and Harry during their summer holidays and weekend breaks.

In fact, both lads were often so bored on summer afternoons at Smith's Lawn Windsor that they used to play in horseboxes and parked cars. I spotted them once pretending to drive the ambulance that always stands by during matches in case of a mishap. As the match ended, Diana hauled them out and started to tidy them up.

Instilling respect for their dad in them, she told them: 'I'm not letting you see your father looking like that.' And she quickly tucked in William's shirt and pulled up Harry's socks. The young Princes seem more interested in motor sports than horse-riding. This may be the result of the influence of their mother's friend James Gilbey, who works for the Lotus sports-car company.

On almost every school break, you can find them down at Buckmore Park, Kent, whizzing around with their school pals on a go-cart track. Both boys are now regular visitors to the Grand Prix circuit in Britain.

Until they discovered the thrill of the speedway, both William and Harry used to take their bicycles everywhere. On holiday at Sandringham and Balmoral they used them to dash around the Queen's huge estates. Prince William once scared his nanny witless when he popped the then baby Princess Beatrice into the basket on front of his bike and cycled off with her. Alison Wardley, who was caring for the Duke and Duchess of York's little daughter, was apprehensive. And William's nanny Ruth Wallace called out: 'I'm not sure this is a good idea, William.' But the fearless Prince was not going to be prevented from giving his little cousin a ride. 'It's all right, I'm allowed,' he called, as he disappeared from sight down a path through some trees.

When he didn't return after ten minutes or so, the two women began to worry. But about fifteen minutes later the cycle and its beaming rider returned with a gurgling baby Beatrice still safely in her precarious seat.

The same summer I learned that these carefree kids were being indoctrinated with the Royals' loathing of the press. A groom told me he overheard the Wales brothers discussing where they would go to play one morning after their riding lesson. Harry wanted to set off for the riverbank to look for their father, who was out fishing. But older and wiser William stopped him. 'You mustn't go down there, Harry,' he said. 'The press are there and they mustn't see you.'

Even at this young age, royal children are taught to be wary, if not contemptuous, of the royal Rat Pack. Perhaps William's instinctive hatred of photographers is the right attitude. Top London psychiatrist Dr Dennis Friedman believes the boys are being damaged by exposure to the media.

'Children should not be expected to perform,' he says. 'But royal children are expected to behave not just for their parents, but for the press and the public. It's not fair and it may be damaging.'

I am concerned about the effect photographing the children could have. So I thought quickly when I spotted William watching me from the window of his Austrian hotel as I sat across the street on the terrace of my own hotel in April 1993. Instead of grabbing a camera and snapping away at him, I lifted an imaginary camera up to my face and signalled to the young Prince to photograph me.

William immediately understood and grinned. He picked his camera up and hastily shot a picture of me as I posed for him with thumbs up laughing. His detective came out later and thanked me. 'It's good for him to see a friendly face,' he explained. 'He thinks he has turned the tables on you. And if it makes him feel better about cameramen it can't be a bad thing. Thanks very much.'

I never imagined, when I first started photographing the Royals more than twenty years ago, that the day would come when I would get just as much satisfaction from allowing them to photograph me.

CHAPTER TEN

Behind the Smile

The staff at Kensington Palace are still talking about the day Princess Diana climbed up the horse-chestnut tree at the main gates of her London home. Prince William wanted to play conkers at school, and his mother knew just where she could find some, so on a sultry September afternoon Diana strolled out of her front door, bare-legged in a blue denim mini-skirt and white tee-shirt. She found a ladder in the garages and propped it up against the tree. Then, hitching up her skirt, she began to climb up into the branches. Unfortunately, the ladder was not high enough to enable her to reach the best horse chestnuts. No matter how far she leant from the top of her perch the best conkers were still beyond her grasp.

Noticing a Range Rover parked nearby, she asked the driver to move it under the tree. Then, with his help, she lifted the ladder on to the roof of the car to gain some extra height.

The sight of the long-legged Princess scaling the ladder in her daringly short skirt drew chefs, chauffeurs, butlers and even the cops from the police lodge next door. They gathered around the car, gazing upwards, pretending to offer advice, but secretly enjoying the royal peep show.

The more Diana strained to grab conkers, the more the thin fabric of her tee-shirt stretched against her figure, revealing that she had not bothered to wear a bra. The temperature of every man watching below suddenly soared, for reasons totally unconnected with the warm weather.

125

Apparently unaware of her audience's enjoyment, Diana proceeded to throw the conkers to the ground. She yelled at the staff to collect them for her before they rolled away.

So many onlookers gathered within a few minutes that it gradually dawned on Diana what was attracting them. Knowing she was turning the men on, she giggled but finished her task. Then she slowly descended the ladder, thrilling the assembled staff with her feline grace.

After she recovered her composure, she decided to punish the men for their impudence. She ordered them to drill holes and put string in each conker. 'I've done my bit,' she said, laughing, 'now you can do yours.'

Diana is a good-looking woman with legs that go on for ever. And she knows it. When I heard how she conkered the Kensington Palace staff my mind went back to April Fool's Day 1986, when the Prince and Princess of Wales opened Terminal Four at Heathrow. Airport chiefs felt really foolish when they suddenly realized that Diana would travel up a steep escalator, giving photographers below a very good shot up her legs.

The Princess was wearing a stewardess-style outfit with a long split in the back of her skirt which increased the danger of over-exposure. When she was warned of this, Diana turned to me and said: 'Hello, Arthur, I suppose you want to take a picture right up my legs?'

In an instant, I replied: 'I will if you'll let me, ma'am.'

Before she could give me an answer, two royal policemen swiftly moved in behind her, totally blocking our view as she ascended to the next level. I didn't get a great picture that day, but I got a front-page story in the *Sun* under the headline 'KEEP YOUR EYES OFF MY THIGHS'.

When her staff ribbed her about the story of our chat next day, she denied ever mentioning the subject to me. 'I was talking to Arthur about eggs, not legs,' she said. A royal aide who had been with her could not believe his ears. He wondered if the Princess was referring to some April Fool's Day joke he wasn't party to. 'But I distinctly heard you say "legs", ma'am,' he said. Diana only laughed and walked off, insisting she was right.

Twelve years at the top have taught the Princess of Wales a lot of tricks. She can now wiggle her way out of any sticky situtation with a big smile and a little white lie. But her employees at the Palace don't mind when she tries to mislead them with the occasional pork pie, because she is such a wonderful boss.

A former butler at Kensington Palace once told me: 'She is as beautiful on the inside as she is on the outside. When she is at home with us she is grateful for every little thing you do.' He added: 'When a vacancy occurs on her staff, Buckingham Palace servants fight tooth and nail to move over on to her team.'

After returning home with a bouquet she has been given at a film première or banquet, Diana often gives it to her chauffeur Simon Solari. 'Take this home to your wife Lyn,' she says. 'I've kept you out late tonight, so maybe this will make amends.'

Wherever she goes, Diana is showered with gifts and small mementoes. Her ladies-in-waiting carry them back to the office, where they are stored in what Diana calls 'my charity box'. The toys and clothes are passed on to hospitals and charities, but if a member of her staff needs something for a good cause Diana always says: 'Help yourself to something from the box.'

She often includes the children of staff members in outings with her sons William and Harry. Her chauffeur's son went to the Royal Tournament and her butler's young boys joined the Princess and her boys on their annual trip to Thorpe Park, a leisure centre in Surrey.

And when the former head of her personal protection squad, Chief Inspector Graham Smith, was hospitalized with cancer of the lymph glands she went along when he had chemotherapy. She treated him just like one of her family. And as he recovered she invited him to join them on the Waleses' summer-holiday cruise around Italy on a millionaire's yacht.

Every December, the Prince and Princess of Wales hold a Christmas party for all their employees. More than fifty travel up to London from Highgrove, the Prince's country estate, in specially hired coaches. In 1986, the venue was the Carlton Tower hotel in Knightsbridge. When the guests arrived they were amazed to find the room decorated with thousands of silver balloons bearing the Prince of Wales's feathered emblem. Balloons bobbed above every table and hundreds more floated around the walls.

As the party was breaking up, Diana said to her staff: 'It seems a shame to leave all these lovely balloons behind. Help yourself. After all, we've paid for them, so let's get them.' To show she meant what she said, Diana began stripping the walls of dozens of balloons.

Just for a laugh, she asked a waiter to tie them to her arms. Then she floated off to her car giggling as she tried to squeeze herself and all the balloons into the back seat. As the guests waved goodbye, they couldn't see the royal couple at all because the car was crammed with shiny silver balloons.

Any ordinary vehicle travelling through London with the driver's vision obscured like this would have been pulled up by the police. But the registration numbers on the fleet of cars used by the Prince and Princess of Wales are listed on the Police National Computer in a special category, which means they are not to be stopped under any circumstances.

Diana may still be the same thoughtful, kind-hearted girl who married Prince Charles, but she has changed in other ways. Once she was astonishingly frank when she talked to people. Now she is quite guarded. Any question that provokes a too-revealing reply gets the Sly Di treatment.

I once asked her if she had enjoyed the London film première of the Hollywood blockbuster *Wall Street*, which contained some steamy sex scenes. Immediately she came over all innocent. 'It was much too grown-up for me,' she said, fluttering her eye-lashes. 'I didn't really understand any of it.'

I imagined she was referring to the complex dealings of Wall Street traders. I know that raunchy bedroom scenes would not faze her.

A secret known only to Diana's closest friends and household is she loves risqué jokes. The racier they are, the harder she laughs.

When the Essex Girl jokes were all the rage, she enjoyed repeating them to her friends, but as she kept forgetting the punch-lines she decided to write every one down. By the time she finished she had four closely-written pages of unbelievably blue gags. I won't repeat them here, but simply say they are more suited to the men's room than the drawing room of a royal palace.

It seems nothing shocks her insatiable sense of humour. She is always asking palace employees: 'Have you got any jokes for me?' Her wit is never malicious, but almost always designed to cheer herself up.

Even when she started referring to her stepmother the Dowager Countess Spencer as 'Purple Raine', it was just a jest. The pop song of the same name, recorded by the American pop singer Prince, was topping the charts at the time. Diana claimed to see some similarities between the garishly dressed rock star and her father's widow.

The public did not gain an inkling of the naughty way the Princess behaved in private until her taped telephone call to James Gilbey was made public. The world learned then that Diana told lies to cover her tracks when slipping off to meet Gilbey and blew kisses to him down the phone. She discussed arrangements for a clandestine meeting with him and warned him that she did not want to get pregnant.

Such revelations did little to dent her popularity, and less to shake her late father, Earl Spencer's faith in her. In the late 1980s, he asserted: 'My daughter's only ever slept with one man in her life. That is the Prince of Wales. She tells me she doesn't enjoy sex.' Even those who were more cynical felt Prince Charles's neglect had forced her into the arms of another man.

The Princess has learned the hard way not to give too much away. She continues to chat to journalists at cocktail parties held at the end of every tour abroad she undertakes. Prince Charles, on the other hand, has banned all contact with the media. Diana thinks his attitude is counter-productive. 'I do enjoy our chats,' she once told me on a trip to France. 'My husband refuses to have these parties with the press, but I think they are a good idea. After all, you only need to tell people what you want them to know.'

Prince Charles has not held a meeting with the press since 1987. But the Queen seems to agree with Diana; she has continued to hold press receptions for the last forty years.

After all, most of our conversations are not state secrets, but lighthearted chit-chat. We both love a good joke. And when it comes to delivering deadly one-liners Di can shoot it out with the best.

When being shown around the Botanical Gardens in Melbourne on a visit to Australia in 1985, Diana saw prize blooms and rare orchids. Then she walked on past the press position where I was standing. Giving us an impish look, she said to her guide: 'I suppose these must be the weeds.'

I was gobsmacked when I heard that. But I have always been prepared to come up with a quick quip ever since. Our knock-about routines have since become a regular part of tours overseas and official jobs in Britain, and often make good copy for the *Sun*. Diana never minds when I publish our conversations. 'As long as they continue to be so accurate I don't mind,' she tells her staff.

Our double act really got off the ground in Italy in 1985. All the photographers were hoping she would arrive at La Scala in Milan in a fantastic new frock. You could have heard the groans in Rome when she turned up in a pale-pink organza gown first seen two years earlier and worn many times in between.

Back in London, the office was keeping a page open for this special picture and when I rang them and explained that the dress she was wearing was an old one they didn't even want me to transmit the picture.

Next evening I decided to tackle her about our disappointment over her gown. I walked up to her and said: 'Why did you have to wear that boring old dress at the opera last night?'

Diana laughed. 'Oh, I suppose you'd like it better if I came naked,' she teased.

'Well, I would definitely get that in the paper,' I cracked. I turned to Prince Charles: 'Why don't you buy your wife a new frock?' In mock dismay, the Prince joined in the joke: 'We simply can't afford it,' he declared.

130

'Well, sell one of your polo ponies, then,' I replied. We all joined in the laughter that followed.

I can't resist complimenting her when she looks wonderful, but I'm no boot-licker. If I don't like her outfit or hairstyle I say so, often with hilarious results.

In spring of 1991, her first job after getting a very short new haircut was a visit to RAF Scampton in Lincolnshire to meet wives of airmen serving in the Gulf War. I was appalled when I saw her her boyish hairdo, but at the time *Vogue* model Linda Evangelista had made short crops ultra-fashionable and the Princess seemed to be following this stylish trend.

At the end of the job she walked over and said: 'Hullo, Arthur, this is a long way for you to come.'

I didn't waste time with pleasantries. 'If you keep cutting your hair short you'll end up looking like that pop star Sinead O'Connor,' I warned.

Diana reddened to the roots and pointed at my thinning scalp: 'At least I've got some hair, Arthur,' she snapped back with a wicked grin.

I laughed and admitted defeat as she got into her car. Then she turned to her chauffeur and said with a chuckle, 'That soon shut him up.'

It was the third time in a few months that we had swapped wisecracks. The comedy act had begun the previous November in Japan when Diana was visiting the Honda factory near Tokyo. A few weeks earlier she had been stopped for speeding on the motorway to her West Country home Highgrove. So when I saw her inspecting Ayrton Senna's Honda McLaren racing car in which he had just won the World Championship, I couldn't resist saying: 'They would never catch you on the M4 motorway in that, ma'am.'

Diana roared with laughter and said, 'I'll tell the jokes, Arthur, thank you.'

I got my own back two weeks later on a wet afternoon in Norwich. I was wearing an old tweed flat cap to keep my head dry and while on a walkabout Diana looked up and giggled. 'Are you wearing that hat for a bet, Arthur?' she teased.

131

Quick as a flash, I stole her line: 'I'll tell the jokes, thank you, ma'am.'

When I compliment her on how lovely she looks, whether she's dripping in jewels or in jeans and sweatshirt, I know this makes her feel great. She in turn has also given me a boost just when I needed it most.

In 1991, I had an accident while I was covering her skiing holiday in Lech, Austria. I lost my concentration on an icy bend, hit a mogul and landed on my head. I was unconscious for twenty minutes with a bad gash over one eye, so my colleague James Whitaker called the ski patrol. They took one look at my head injury and radioed for a helicopter to whisk me off to the local clinic. There they diagnosed concussion and and two broken fingers.

The Princess soon found out about my mishap. Not ten minutes after I hit the slope, my son Paul, a photographer working for the *Today* newspaper, bumped into the Princess at the bottom of the mountain. He was white-faced with shock. 'What's happened to your father?' she asked. When Paul told her the details and how worried he felt she cheered him up with a quick quip. 'What? Helicoptered off just for two broken fingers? Oh dear, it must have been serious.'

When it was explained that I had needed a brain scan she became really concerned. 'Give him my best wishes; I hope he's better soon.'

Next day I was back on my feet, despite a crashing headache and I somehow managed to complete the assignment. The Princess was genuinely sympathetic when she met me. 'Are you all right now?' I showed her my fingers plastered up in splints and told her I was on the mend.

Ten days later, we met up again while she was on a tour of Brazil with Prince Charles. At an open-cut mine she came over, wiggled her fingers and said: 'How's your hand now, Arthur?'

The following year I was laid low by a stomach bug in Cairo. As soon as she heard of this the Princess sent her own doctor to visit me. He gave me the right advice to get me back on my feet. Later, she sent her police officer, Peter Brown, to give me some powders containing mineral supplements to help me regain my strength.

After a few days in bed I managed to stagger back to work. I had lost seven pounds in four days and this must have been obvious when I arrived at the Cairo Museum to photograph the Princess looking at the treasures from King Tutankhamen's tomb.

As she walked in she asked me: 'How are you feeling?'

I told her: 'I'm still a bit feverish but the pain in my legs has gone.'

Cheeky Diana said: 'I'll tell you this. It's done wonders for your waistline.'

All the time she was taking the mickey out of me and swapping wisecracks, her private life was utterly miserable. She hid her sadness behind a beaming smile and never let the world guess how trapped she felt behind closed palace doors. I like to think that our gags and giggles helped her to cope. When her self-esteem was on the floor I inadvertently gave her a much-needed boost. But I little knew then that the jokes we laughed at when on jobs together distracted her from the pain she suffered at home.

For five years Diana and Charles continued to keep up the semblance of a united couple. The Prince always called his wife 'darling' in front of the media and even kissed her in public, but I couldn't help noticing that the kisses he gave his missus had changed. The normal smacker he used to give her on the lips became a quick peck on the cheek.

The Princess did not need any show of affection from the man she loathed. There were other men in her life only too willing to give her the comfort and support she craved. As the notorious 'Squidgy Tape' revealed, Diana had a long-running liaison with car dealer James Gilbey.

She had known him in her bachelor-girl days and their friendship was revived when they met up again in the mid-1980s at a dinner party. She turned to him because he was a link with her old life and, as a friend of her sister's, she knew she could trust him.

But Diana never allowed their warm, close relationship to go too far. It was intense and often contained the sexual innuendo of young sweethearts, or long-distance pen pals, who fantasize about making the ultimate move to have sexual intercourse, but fear the repercussions.

One mutual pal, in whom they both confided, says: 'James Gilbey put the Princess of Wales upon a pedestal and looked up to her like a goddess. He worshipped her. The Princess was lonely and tortured. She unloaded all her misery on to his shoulders and he helped her at a crucial time, when she had no idea where her life was going. He lifted her spirits, made her laugh and reminded her that there was life outside.'

The old chum went on: 'But she was never in love with him in the way he was with her. The Princess is a terrible flirt. If she likes someone, she can turn it on, almost at the switch of a button. She uses her eyes and her smile and she can trap an innocent admirer like a spider within a web. That is the real actress in her. And that's all she was doing in her conversations with Gilbey, acting out her fantasies.

'For Diana, the relationship was like phone sex. It suited Diana's obsessive personality down to the ground. She is a self-confessed phoneaholic, and can spend hours talking to her pals. They teased and tantalized each other in the way people talk on 0898 telephone sex lines, where the cheap thrill of saying what you would "like to do" to your opposite number always gives more satisfaction than the deed itself.'

Backing up this friend's belief is the expert opinion of psychiatrist Dr Dennis Friedman, whose book *Inheritance* provides amazing insights into the Royal Family. In an interview with *Woman's Own* magazine he said: 'The "Dianagate" recording suggests to me that she prefers love at a distance. She would rather have a telephone romance than the real thing.' He believes she now gets the love and affection she yearns for from her devoted public. For this reason he feels she will never marry again.

According to her friends, the Princess often considered the act of being unfaithful but said she was 'scared to death' of the consequences.

Gilbey was a perfect telephone lover. He talked about becoming aroused by her voice and 'playing with himself', giving the lonely Princess a long-distance kick. She relished having the power to excite someone to such passion even though they were miles apart.

The key section of the 'Dianagate Tape' which pinpoints the exact nature of their peculiar relationship begins:

DI: How wonderful!

GILBEY: I know, darling, uh! More. It's just like sort of...um...

DI: (*interrupts*) Playing with yourself.

GILBEY: What?

DIANA: (*giggling*) Nothing.

GILBEY: No, I'm not actually.

DIANA: I said, it's just...just like –

GILBEY: Playing with yourself.

DI: Yes.

GILBEY: Not quite as nice. Not quite as nice. I haven't played with myself actually. Not for a full forty-eight hours.

DIANA: (*giggles*)

GILBEY: Not for a full forty-eight hours. (*funny voice*) Umm. Tell me some more. How was your lunch?

Then there is a break and this exchange:

GILBEY: All right...I got there Tuesday night, don't worry. I got there. I can tell you, the feeling's entirely mutual. Umm, Squidgy...what else? It's just like unwinding now. I am just letting my heartbeat come down again now. I had the most amazing dream about us last night. Not the physical, nothing to do with that.

DI: That makes a change.

GILBEY: Darling, it's just that we were together an awful lot of the time and we were having dinner with some people. It was the most extraordinary dream, very vivid, because I woke up in the morning and I remembered all aspects of it. All bits of it. I remembered sort of what you were wearing and what you had said. It was so strange, very strange and very lovely too.

DIANA: I don't want to get pregnant.

GILBEY: Darling, it's not going to happen.

DIANA: (*half laugh*)

GILBEY: All right.

DIANA: Yah.

GILBEY: Don't look at it like that. It's not going to happen. You won't get pregnant.

DIANA: I watched 'EastEnders' today and one of the main characters had a baby. They thought it was her husband's but it was by another man. (*burst of laughter*)

GILBEY: (*moaning*) Squidgy...kiss me. (*sounds of kisses by him and her*) Oh God! It's wonderful, isn't it? This sort of feeling. Don't you like it?

DIANA: I love it.

GILBEY: Umn.

DIANA: I love it.

As with all such clandestine relationships, they plotted and schemed together to arrange rendezvous. But when they actually met, it was often awkward and an anti-climax, with the previous sexual promises never mentioned. Gilbey's words over the phone became like the love letters she could never receive, calling her by the nickname she adored, Squidgy, and repeatedly telling her how much he loved her.

Diana, although grateful for such loving attention, was naturally cautious. But she could never have imagined that the whole intimate saga would be published all over the world three years later and remembered throughout history as 'Dianagate' and the 'Squidgy Tapes'.

She frequently thanked Gilbey for being part of her life. He would never know how much good he had done her, she told him during their late-night conversations. She made clear her frustrations with life in the Royal Family, and although Gilbey never offered a real way out of the mess, he did offer a glimmer of light in her darkest days.

Looking back on the days when their friendship was strongest, Gilbey now believes he provided a crutch for Diana when she was at the lowest point in her life, depressed and suicidal. They remain friends but are no longer close friends.

Three years after the 'Dianagate Tape' was recorded, they were driven back together when it became public knowledge. United in their shame at being exposed, they were also indignant, because they were not guilty of the sin everyone imagined.

On first reading, the 'Dianagate Tape' suggested that the Princess and Gilbey were enjoying a physical relationship. But a deeper examination of their ambiguous dialogue indicates otherwise. Their love talk is decidedly one-sided. And Diana's insistence that she does not want to become pregnant spells out her reluctance to commit herself fully to Gilbey.

Within two weeks of the tape being proved authentic, Gilbey was confronted by journalists, who asked him about his conversations with the Princess of Wales over New Year's Eve 1989. Mr Gilbey was outside his London flat in Lennox Gardens, around the corner from Kensington Palace, when they approached him. He went as white as a sheet. His jaw dropped and he refused to make any comment as he leapt into his flashy Saab car, containing the car phone – number 0860 354661 – which had been his crucial link to his secret mistress of the mind.

He only flinched at the mention of the word 'Squidgy', and from that moment, about 8.15 on a winter's morning in London, James Gilbey has never said a word about his late-night phone-calls, either to a journalist's face or on the phone.

It is a safe conclusion that soon after that confrontation, panic-stricken Gilbey was on the phone again to Diana to tell her what had happened. He would have been desperate to warn her that an eavesdropper had tuned into their midnight call.

So from that moment on in 1990 Diana knew she was sitting on a time bomb that could explode at any time. Her critics accuse her of co-operating with Andrew Morton's book so that she could get her version of the sad story out first. It would not be surprising if she had wanted to defuse the situation before she was blown out of the water with publication of the tape-recordings.

Indeed, Gilbey was a principal source of information for Morton's book, telling candidly of Diana's miserable marriage and her isolation. He passed on the fact that she had contemplated leaving the Royal Family altogether, and he helped to portray the Prince of Wales as an emotionally empty man.

Diana's relationship with dashing Life Guards Major James Hewitt was more meaningful and more intimate. Although never a sexual affair, it was the closest the Princess ever came to committing adultery. His fun-loving personality, his affection for London social life and his story-telling made him a perfect suitor for the lonely Diana, and a substitute father-figure for her sons, William and Harry. To them he was a *Boy's Own* hero who had fought in the Gulf War, and he became a patient instructor when he gave them riding lessons.

Princess Diana was never more relaxed in public than on the day she presented flame-haired Hewitt with a prize cup at a polo match. Throwing her head back and laughing easily, she revealed the sexual chemistry between the pair. An unmistakable message was again in evidence as she slumped back on an army vehicle during a private visit to his barracks. Her body language screamed an invitation to Hewitt that she could not put into words in front of others.

Hewitt, who was then thirty-one, received intimate letters from the Princess while he served in the desert. She also later recruited him as a trusted confidant when she was torn in all directions about her marriage and her future with the Royal Family.

Some of her friends claim that Hewitt was standing by ready to tell his version of their relationship to a newspaper. He was acting on her instructions and, friends say, would be instrumental in helping her leave the family if that was what she chose to do. An associate of Hewitt says: 'James was at her beck and call but her moods changed violently almost from day to day, and in the end she seemed to work everything out without his help.'

The Princess spent a small fortune on Hewitt, as she did with other men, including members of her staff. On the 'Dianagate Tape' she makes clear her delight at choosing clothes for men.

HIM: I like those ordinary Italian things that last a couple of years and then I chuck them out. It was a sort of devotion to duty. I was seeking an identity when I bought my first pair of Guccis twelve years ago.

HER: Golly!

HIM: And I've still got them. Still doing me proud like.

HER: Good!

HIM: I'm going to take you up on that, darling. I will give you some money. You can go off and spend it for me.

HER: I will. Yah.

HIM: Will you? (*laughter*)

HER: I'm a connoisseur in that department.

HIM: Are you?

HER: Yes

HIM: Well, you think you are.

HER: Well, I've decked people out in my time.

HIM: Who did you deck out? Not many, I hope.

HER: James Hewitt...entirely dressed him from head to foot, that man. Cost me a lot, that man. Cost me quite a bit.

HIM: I bet it did. At your expense?

HER: Yeh.

HIM: He didn't even pay you to do it?

HER: No!

HIM: What an ext...very extravagant, darling.

HER: Well, I am, aren't I? Anything that will make people happy.

HIM: You mustn't do it for that, darling, because you make people happy. It's what you give them...

Hewitt's personal batman has claimed he saw the Major and the Princess in fond embraces. She arrived for regular riding lessons with only her personal bodyguard, Inspector Ken Wharfe, and Hewitt was always respectful, addressing the Princess as 'ma'am'. The batman, Malcolm Leete, a former Life Guard, said Hewitt was 'obsessed' with her. He had pictures of her and the children in his room. They were signed 'Love, Diana', or 'Love, Dibbs' (his pet name for the Princess).

The impact of the 'Dianagate Tape', although devastating at the time, swiftly subsided in the tide of scandals that swept through the House of Windsor. When Prince Charles's 'Camilla-gate Tape' hit the world's front pages, Squidgy's chat with Gilbey seemed tame by comparison.

The Prince of Wales had been – metaphorically – caught with his trousers down on the phone to Camilla Parker Bowles – the woman Diana branded the 'Rottweiler'. Charles had been taped two weeks earlier declaring his love and desire to do various naughty things to Camilla. Well-known for his love of talking to plants, this episode made him appear even more eccentric when he told her he fantasized about coming back in the next life inside Camilla's trousers. But he felt with his 'luck' he would probably come back as a tampon.

The two tapes evened the score, but by this time the game was over because the marriage was dead. By this stage the Prince and Princess could not be bothered to carry on their charade any longer.

All the play-acting ended in Jaipur in 1992 when Charles and Diana were on a tour of India. After winning a game of polo in front of a crowd of 60,000 Indians, Charles was presented with a vast silver cup by his wife. He leaned forward to thank her with a kiss, and at that precise moment she swiftly turned her head away. His lips ended up somewhere near her ear, making him look a complete idiot. I knew then how much she hated him. To humiliate him like that in front of so many people was the act of a bitterly unhappy woman.

From then on, their pretence of togetherness fooled no one.

Every editor in what used to be called Fleet Street knew their marriage was a sham.

I have never believed, as many people do, that the press drove Charles and Diana apart. The simple truth is that they loathed each other. If they had been genuinely devoted, no amount of outside pressure could have come between them.

Prince Charles was simply more comfortable with a bachelor lifestyle, surrounded by servants and sycophants. He selfishly spent every Saturday and Sunday in the summer playing polo, and in the winter he went hunting at least three days a week.

He often stayed in Balmoral for up to eight weeks after his wife and children returned to London. He snatched every opportunity to take a few days off on his own at the end of most tours abroad. And every spring he spent a solo week in his favourite European country, Italy. He seemed to enjoy being anywhere but with his wife. Members of his staff began to mutter: 'He doesn't even seem to know that she exists.'

For years we had enjoyed an unusual relationship, swapping jokes and snappy one-liners so often that the *Sun* called it 'The Di and Arthur Show'. And whenever we had a verbal sparring match, delighted Diana always snapped back with a royal rib-tickler.

Throughout this time, there was not a single clue that this fun-loving lady was so desperately unhappy at home. It was an Oscar-winning performance that convinced almost everyone. But the day came when she could no longer play the part.

CHAPTER ELEVEN

Windsor Tours

Princess Diana glided in to a state banquet in Kathmandu without so much as a glance at the press eagerly waiting to photograph her. Desperate to get a picture I called out to her: 'Excuse me, ma'am. Would you stop a minute?' She immediately turned in my direction and lined up with her host, Crown Prince Dipendra, and the Nepalese Prime Minister, Girija Prasad Koirala.

To express my thanks, I said: 'You look great tonight,' and she beamed back at me. At that moment, her policeman, Inspector Peter Brown, smirked. In retaliation I said: 'You don't look so bad yourself, Brownie.' Overhearing this, Princess Diana looked back giggling at both of us.

I did not notice the startled expression on the dark-skinned Prime Minister's face as the royal party moved on into the banqueting hall. He had heard my throwaway line and thought it was aimed at him.

Unaware of this, I rushed off to wire my picture of the Princess in her new white designer gown to London. It never entered my head that I might have sparked a diplomatic row.

As I found out later, the Prime Minister had been highly offended when I used the word 'Brownie'. He thought I was referring to him, not the Princess's police officer. As soon as he sat down to dinner with her, he summoned an aide to investigate further. A British diplomat explained that I had not intended to make a racist remark, that I was merely having a joke with Inspector Brown.

143

The Prime Minister saw the funny side of it, and nothing more was said. That is, in Nepal. Back in London, Kelvin MacKenzie cracked up laughing when *Sun* reporter Robert Jobson sent the story to our office. 'I want this on Page One,' he shouted, and began to write the headline himself.

'SUN MAN IN THE BROWN STUFF' screamed out of the paper next day, alongside a picture of me and another of the Prime Minister. In the later editions, the editor managed to squeeze my picture of Princess Diana on to the front page too.

In the dozens of royal tours I have covered for the *Sun* it is the funny stories like this one that stand out in my memory. The trip that produced one of the funniest pictures was Prince Charles's skiing holiday at Klosters, Switzerland in 1979.

All we had, after a few days at the resort, were boring pictures of the Prince skiing down various slopes. As a result, we decided we would have to create something better. One of the Rat Pack had just covered the Miss World contest in London, and had learned that Miss Switzerland, Barbara Mayer, would be in Klosters towards the end of the Prince's holiday. We therefore hoped to get a picture of them both together somehow.

In the meantime, Prince Charles decided to play a trick on us. One morning his hostess, Patty Palmer-Tomkinson, announced that the Prince would not be skiing that morning. She told us that her Uncle Harry would be joining the ski party instead. Out walked the Prince of Wales, wearing a false nose, moustache and glasses, talking in a high-pitched toffee-nosed voice.

We realized immediately that this was a great picture and blazed away. Photographers were falling over themselves to get it. Charles kept the mask on for only thirty seconds, but that was all we needed.

We thanked him and immediately left for Zurich to send our pictures to London. On our way back, we had an idea that we would get some funny noses and hats and surprise Prince Charles the next day. The following morning when he left his chalet he took one look at us and burst out laughing. I seized this opportunity to ask him to pose with us. He said: 'Will this be published?' I told him there were no guarantees about that, but in his typically generous way he agreed. 'It's against my better judgement, but I'll do it,' he said. This picture also made a big splash in our papers the next day.

Then Miss Switzerland turned up, expecting us to arrange an introduction. We knew where the Prince would stop for lunch and positioned Barbara on the piste nearby. As he came into view she skied straight into him and fell over at his feet.

Always the perfect gentleman, Charles proceeded to pick her up, while we snapped away. Wanting to make sure we got good pix, she promptly fell over again, and once again, the Prince chivalrously helped her up. Meanwhile, the Prince's policeman was screaming: 'It's a set-up, sir! It's a set-up.'

Realizing he had been duped, Prince Charles angrily turned to us and said: 'Oh, you boring people, why can't you do something original?' We thought it was very original, but quite a mean trick after his kindness to us earlier in the week.

Occasionally, a lot of effort goes into getting what turns out to be a very ordinary picture. The only way this has any chance of appearing in the newspaper is if it is accompanying a hot story.

In 1988, the Duke and Duchess of York were in Australia to celebrate the nation's bicentenary. One night, Sarah met up with her sister Jane Makim for a private dinner in a suburb of Sydney. I followed them over the Harbour Bridge, racing along way over the speed limit, but lost them in the early-evening traffic. After that, all I could do was check every top restaurant in the city to find my quarry. After several disappointments, I finally found her in a smart area called Paddington, and about midnight I pictured the two women leaving the restaurant.

But when I looked at my photo in the cold light of the following day I realized it was a boring shot. Then it dawned on me that to get to and from the restaurant Fergie had been driven through Sydney's notorious red-light district, Kings Cross. She could not have failed to notice all the scantily-dressed prostitutes and transvestites parading their wares on the streets.

I got reporter Harry Arnold to dig out some colourful facts on the area and file a story about Fergie's eye-popping tour of the seedy suburbs of Sydney. In the meantime, I raided the Picture Library of the *Sydney Daily Mirror* for recent shots of Kings Cross trollops. The results of our efforts were on Page One of the *Sun* next morning.

The *Daily Mirror*'s Ken Gavin was woken that night by his London office demanding to know why he didn't have the same story. Determined to get even with me, he concocted a story in league with some Aussie photographers. They told me the hooker whose picture I had sent to the London *Sun* had quit the streets to become a nun. I was taken in by this tall tale for all of five minutes. Then I saw the wicked smile on Gavin's face and knew I had been conned.

Following members of the Royal Family on overseas trips is mostly exhausting, often exhilarating, but always good for a laugh. Sixteen-hour days are not unusual, often starting at six in the morning or earlier and finishing close to midnight. Regular meals are unheard of, and a good night's sleep is a luxury. If it's not jet-lag or the office phoning at ridiculous hours of the night, it's the mosquitoes and cockroaches that keep you awake.

Once, when we were touring southern India, we spent an unforgettable night at a run-down hovel that was called a hotel in Bubineshwar. After checking in with my colleague Harry Arnold, I discovered that the strict Indian liquor laws applied in the state. I turned to him and said: 'I've got bad news, Harry. You can't get a drink in this hotel.'

Harry said: 'What about room service?'

I told him: 'Harry, when you see the state of our rooms you'll need a drink to go there.'

A few days earlier, on a five-hour journey through Rajasthan in the middle of the night, we had been stopped by the local police for drinking bottled beer without a liquor permit. Our Indian driver intervened. 'If you give the policeman some cigarettes, he will let you go,' he said. Harry Arnold was the only smoker in the car, and I knew he had some small cigars.

'Give him your cigars, Harry, so we can get going,' I ordered.

'Fuck off!' said Harry, 'they're all I have left and we've still got three hours to go.'

The policeman then made us pour the beer we had left out on to the dusty road before he would let us continue our trip.

Soon after the 1980 tour of India had started in Delhi, Harry and I attended a party for the press at the British High Commission. As I had injured my back the previous day during a student riot at Delhi University, Harry wanted to take a taxi on the short ride from our hotel to the reception. No cabs were available, so he suggested we hire the hotel's decorated elephant instead.

It was easy to climb some wooden steps to reach the howdah where we rode on top, but getting off the animal was a totally different matter. Even when the elephant knelt down it was still a long way to the ground for me with my bad back. 'Hang on to its ear, then climb down the trunk,' Harry advised. I tried to do as he suggested but lost my grip and crashed painfully down to the dusty ground.

Harry was helping me up and trying to brush the coloured chalk from the elephant's body off my blue velvet jacket, when Prince Charles drew up in a car. He got out, took one look at me lying in the gutter and said: 'What on earth are you doing there?'

I groaned and said: 'Carry me inside, give me a gin and tonic, and I'll tell you.'

We had been desperate to take a picture of the Prince with an elephant on that tour, but it wasn't until the last week that we saw another one. We were speeding ahead of Prince Charles to an engagement when we came across another highly-decorated elephant by the roadside. We persuaded the Mahout who owned it that the Prince adored elephants and would love to meet his. We talked him into blocking the road with the huge animal so Charles had no choice but to stop and look at it.

When he arrived, his police officer sussed out what was going on and said: 'I think they want a picture of you with the elephant, sir.' The obliging Prince got out and walked over to pose for us beside it.

But the elephant, not realizing who this safari-suited VIP was, suddenly shook his trunk at Charles's head. By a miracle, the Prince managed to duck out of the way. If he hadn't, he might have been history. As a result, we got a better picture than we had hoped for, and it was published with the headline: 'THE PRINCE TAKES A TRUNK CALL'. None of us realized when we set it up that we might be endangering the life of our future King.

Some days on these tours are action-packed, others just bloody boring. One of these happened in New Zealand the following year when Prince Charles was visiting one factory after another in Rotorua. When we arrived at the third of the day, a woodchip plant, not many people could be bothered to get off the press bus.

Tim Graham and I decided we had better have a look, just in case something happened. We strolled around, following the Prince without taking a single shot. He was talking to one particular operator and I noticed the local newspaper photographer taking lots of shots. That made me say to Tim: 'God, I remember when I worked for a local paper. Whenever a Royal came on to my patch I would photograph every angle like crazy.'

Prince Charles moved off to chat to some other workers and the man he had left suddenly turned around. 'Christ! look what's on his shirt,' said Tim. I turned and saw the words 'I'M WITH STUPID' above an emblem of a pointing finger aimed just where the Prince had been standing.

I immediately grabbed the local photographer and gave him $100 for his film, not knowing whether he had the picture I needed or not. When the roll was processed there it was, crisp and clear, and I transmitted it immediately to London. Meanwhile, my colleagues, who had seen me disappear with the local snapper, were in a panic wondering where I had gone. 'What's he up to?' they asked Tim. When he explained, they forced the press bus to chase me.

From New Zealand, we flew on to Australia, then Washington, where Prince Charles was to be President Reagan's first visitor since he had been shot in an assassination attempt. So many cameramen and television crews were keen to cover this event that the White House press secretary split the job into three parts. American news agencies went first, followed by British and US TV crews, and finally the British newspapers.

As we queued outside the Oval Office waiting for our turn, I asked one of the American photographers what sort of picture he had taken. 'Oh, it's just the usual one of the Prince and the President sitting either side of the fireplace,' he told me. I thought that sounded pretty boring and was determined to get something different. So when we were finally admitted and started to take the same picture I asked President Reagan if he would mind standing up. His gunshot wounds had barely healed and he was still feeling rather fragile.

'You want me to stand up?' he laughed.

'Yes, please, sir,' I replied.

Prince Charles gave me a filthy look as they both rose to their feet. 'I'm afraid the British press are so demanding,' he said.

But I thought the end result was a much better picture, and couldn't wait to see it in the paper next day. Imagine my disappointment when the American agency picture, which had hit the *Sun* picture desk well before mine, got used instead. It only goes to prove my favourite saying: 'Better a load of crap early, than a Botticelli late.'

We get close to the Royals and the heads of state who entertain them on these foreign trips. But on one particular tour some of us got closer than we ever expected to the heavily-guarded King Hussein of Jordan.

At the end of a state visit by the Queen and the Duke of Edinburgh in 1984, the King threw a farewell party for the press in Aqaba. As it drew to an end, we all lined up to shake his hand and thank him for his hospitality. Although we had only been drinking fruit juice in the Muslim monarch's palace, London freelance Jim Bennett was feeling a bit daring. He couldn't resist seizing the opportunity to be photographed with the longest-reigning King in the world. He promptly threw an arm around Hussein's shoulders and asked me to take a snap.

The King loved it. Within minutes, there was a long queue of pressmen waiting to be pictured with this charming Arab leader.

Like any other people, Kings and Queens keep souvenir photos of the places they visit and the people they meet. On her 1986 tour of China with the Duke of Edinburgh, the Queen was no exception.

The day they visited the Great Wall of China was a historic occasion. More than a hundred British pressmen and technicians, plus the same number of Chinese journalists, took the long drive from Beijing to report it. ITN and the BBC had even erected giant satellite dishes to beam the event live to their breakfast shows back in Britain.

But when the Queen and the Duke posed for a commemorative picture on top of the Wall it was a disappointingly stiff and formal shot. After this, the royal party proceeded to stroll further along it and were soon out of sight. Harry Arnold discreetly tagged on to the tail-end of the official entourage and in his smart Savile Row suit was mistaken for a Palace aide by the Chinese guards.

Several hundred yards away, where the massed ranks of the other journalists could not see them, the Queen stopped to gaze down at the countryside. 'Take a picture, Philip,' she called to her husband, 'otherwise, no one will know I've been here.'

The Duke reminded her that five minutes earlier her image on the Great Wall of China had been beamed live to Britain. 'Yes, I know,' she said, 'but I want one for us.' Her police officer, Jim Beaton, stepped forward with a small camera and snapped away as the relaxed sovereign smiled into his lens. Quick as a flash, Harry pulled out his own miniature camera and took several frames.

Later, he slipped me the film and next day the *Sun* had outstripped the opposition, thanks to Harry's enterprise. Two days later in Xian, Harry was to break the best story of this tour. Through diligent digging he discovered the Duke had made a diplomatic blunder when he told British students: 'If you stay here much longer you'll get slitty eyes.' The fuss that followed on two continents prompted the *Sun* to come up with two

150

magnificent headlines: 'PHILIP GETS IT ALL WONG' and 'QUEEN VELLY VELLY ANGRY'.

I am often asked if we travel on the same aircraft as the Queen and her entourage the way American journalists fly with their President on Air Force One. The answer is that we did once, but the Queen never wished to repeat the experiment.

For logistical reasons we were invited aboard the Tristar taking the royal party from Nairobi to Bangladesh after a tour of Kenya by the Queen in 1983. There were no direct flights to take us across the Indian Ocean in time to reach Dacca for her arrival.

For security reasons, we were asked to be seated ready for take-off fifty minutes before the Queen departed. As it was a British Airways charter, the hand-picked stewardesses began serving champagne at the top of the aircraft steps as we walked into the main cabin. The moment a glass was empty it was refilled, as is the custom with first-class passengers.

By the time Her Majesty had buckled on her seatbelt we were all roaring drunk. Sing-songs and loud laughter floated through from the rear to the Queen's private quarters. The press section was clearly where the fun was to be had, and several of the Royal Household joined in our party.

We drank the plane dry. For the next leg from Dacca to Delhi, British Airways had to fly more crates of champagne out from London. It was one of the best flights I have ever had. But it's probably not surprising that we were never invited to fly with the Queen ever again.

On these tours, we are always at the mercy of the Buckingham Palace officials who arrange them. Even their best-laid plans come unstuck sometimes, and they inadvertently create a picture that can be embarrassing. This happened when Prince Charles visited Bergstrom Air Force Base outside Austin, Texas.

A ten-gallon hat had been specially made for the Prince, but the Stetson hat company had been given the wrong size by the British embassy. When he put it on it was so big that if it hadn't been for his jug ears, he would have gone blind. We gleefully smudged the flustered Prince wearing the twelve-gallon hat. I rushed off to send the picture to London, leaving red-faced embassy officials arguing with the Prince's private secretary about who had been responsible for the cock-up.

When people are travelling long distances and working hard, they often get very fractious and fall out with each other. I had a terrible row with my pal Jimmy Gray while covering a tour of Italy by the Prince and Princess of Wales in 1985.

New technology was about to transform the working practices of newspapers in Britain. Up until then, draconian union rules prevented photographers from processing their own films and transmitting their own pictures back to their offices. But in 1985 the *Sun* pioneered a much faster method of moving photographs quickly. I was allowed to take a negative transmitter to send my own pictures to London from abroad for the very first time. No other newspaper had this arrangement with the National Graphical Association, the most powerful of the print unions.

This revolutionized royal tours. Instead of taking my film to a news agency or newspaper office when overseas, I was able to process and transmit my film from my hotel room. The difference was that I could send pictures much faster than anyone else and scoop my rivals.

Halfway through the tour, when we were in Livorno, in northern Italy, I had done just that by taking the transmitter with me on the job. When everyone stopped for lunch I processed my films by the side of the road and sent them to London from the phonebox in a tiny café. The rest of the Rat Pack almost choked on their spaghetti when they realized what I had done. They had a five-hour journey back to Rome before they could send anything.

A few days later, lucky Jim had got a great picture of Diana stepping off an aircraft at Catania in Sicily. The wind whipped her skirt up, exposing her lovely long legs. I had a similar picture, but it did not show so much.

As we were in Sicily, I made Jimmy an offer he couldn't refuse. I had the only transmitter, so I told him I would wire his picture to the *Sun* and also to his paper, the *Daily Mail*. His only alternative was to fly to Rome and send his picture very late in the evening from there, missing all the early editions. Several hours later in Syracuse, after consulting his office, he reluctantly agreed, on condition that I got no byline in my paper.

Grabbing his film, I hired a cab to take me the forty miles back to Catania, where the telephone lines were clearer. I got the picture over in a matter of minutes, but missed the press flight to Rome, and so stayed in Sicily overnight

The following morning I linked up with the Rat Pack again. As soon as Jimmy saw me he began dancing with rage: 'You bastard,' he screamed. 'My picture is all over the front of your paper with your fucking name under it.'

I looked blankly at him and said: 'What are you talking about?'

Barely able to refrain from hitting me, he explained that the *Daily Mail* had used the same picture very small on Page Twenty-three and left off his byline. He told me he had already phoned the *Sun*'s Picture Editor, Paul Buttle, in London to complain.

I asked: 'What did he say?'

Choking with fury, Jimmy said: 'He just fucking laughed!' And he refused to speak to me for two or three days afterwards.

By this time, I was pretty angry myself. I thought I had done what I had promised. The way each newspaper treated the picture was not under my control. Bylines are secondary, anyway, and are just a reward for effort. I reckoned I had made as much effort as he had, and I deserved the credit.

Jimmy and I didn't stay bad friends for long. He is a kind-hearted man, as he proved later that year when we were in Melbourne following Diana and Charles. He had drawn the most coveted pass of the entire trip, to cover the Prince and Princess dancing together at a society ball. After a day in Echuca, northern Victoria, we were flying back to the capital when our charter plane suddenly hit an air pocket and plunged more than 1,000 feet.

There was chaos in the aircraft as drinks, papers and cameras crashed all around us. Ken Gavin, who hates flying, screamed out: 'Oh my God! We're going, we're going!' But with a nervous smile Jimmy just said: 'Oh, that was a near thing.'

After we had levelled out, he turned to me and said: 'You have the pass for the ball tonight. You care much more than I do!' Thanks to Jimmy, I got one of the greatest ever pictures of the Princess. She had left her tiara behind in London and used an emerald necklace instead as a headband. Her unusual way with jewellery was another big front-page story.

In 1992, Prince Charles and Princess Diana went on a Mediterranean cruise with their children aboard the luxury yacht *Alexander*, owned by Greek billionaire John Latsis. On this adventure the Rat Pack was unmercifully scooped by an Italian paparazzo, Massimo Sestini, who took arguably the sexiest picture of Diana in a swimsuit that I have ever seen.

The following year, when we learned that the Royals were spending their second summer holiday on the same ship, we were determined not to be beaten again. The royal teams on five tabloid newspapers got together and decided to charter our own luxury yacht at vast expense to chase them around the Greek Islands.

We were assured by the ship's brokers that our yacht, the *Electra*, was equipped with the latest navigational and communication aids. They guaranteed we would have no trouble keeping up with the Latsis yacht.

From the time we set off from Athens we became the leading actors in our very own Greek tragedy. We never saw the *Alexander* once. The *Electra*'s radar didn't work, the crew insisted on resting after eight hours at sea, and we had to keep stopping to refuel. On top of this, the ultra-modern communications equipment was non-existent, so we had to go ashore each day to keep in touch with London. Our old tub just wasn't in the same race. We were like a milkman's horse chasing a Derby-winner.

Growing increasingly desperate, as each fruitless day passed, we began to argue and bicker about where to look. The row continued one evening at a restaurant in Ithaca. *Daily Express* photographer Mike Dunlea insisted that the crew be allowed to rest after a twelve-hour day. James Whitaker disagreed at the top of his voice. 'The welfare of the crew is no concern of mine,' he bellowed. Dunlea, a softly-spoken Irishman, was incensed. 'If you feel like that, you can fuck off!' he said. From then on Mike was known to the Rat Pack as 'The Fisherman's Friend'.

We combed island after island, but were soon running out of time. Eventually, we decided to give it one more try. We hired a helicopter and flew from Ithaca around the southern tip of Greece, checking every bay and island. After a whole day searching we thought the *Alexander* must have sunk.

As I took off in the helicopter with Mike Dunlea, my son Paul turned to his reporter Charlie Rae. Anxious to speed up the search, he said: 'Do you think we should get another helicopter?' Charlie, a barrel-chested Scotsman with a short fuse, was worried about the soaring costs of the trip. 'Why don't you get the fucking Red Arrows as well?' he said, referring to Britain's top aerial-display pilots.

Eventually, we were forced to abort our disastrous odyssey and fly home with our tails between our legs. We found out later how Charles and Diana had managed to elude us so easily: we had been scouring the Ionian Sea, where they had arrived, and all the time they had been cruising the sparkling waters of the Aegean.

Often we travel huge distances for just one picture, with disastrous results. This happened when Princess Anne, as patron of Save the Children, was on a tour of Africa in 1982. It is rare for the prickly Princess ever to agree to pose for the press, but she promised to do so at Victoria Falls, in northern Zimbabwe.

As she was visiting Africa's most famous tourist atttraction on a Saturday, we made a monumental effort to get the original film back to London for Monday morning's papers. We chartered a small plane to send our film to Harare where it was put on a British Airways jet to London. We even bribed the local news-agency photographer not to send his picture for twenty-four hours.

Imagine my disgust when my picture of Anne standing against the magnificent panorama of the foaming waters was cropped to just a tiny head shot in the *Sun*. It was Anne minus Africa. The editor had lost interest in the tour and we were recalled earlier than planned.

Such disappointments are often outweighed by the rewards that come our way. In 1984 we were waiting at Dubai International Airport for Princess Anne to arrive on an official visit to the United Arab Emirates.

Several of the photographers, who had received a gold watch on the last tour of the UAE with the Queen, politely asked the Head of Protocol if we would be so lucky this time. He was a very diplomatic Arab, who simply said: 'You mustn't ask, you must wait and see.'

To our delight, at the end of the trip a junior British Embassy official, Tim Flear, turned up with a carrier bag full of Omega watches, worth at least £1,000 each.

Princess Anne then flew to Balmoral to join the Queen on her autumn holiday. She was strolling across a grouse moor when one of her mother's guests happened to mention what superb coverage of her trip to the Gulf had appeared in the press. He went on to say: 'I heard the journalists had all been given expensive watches. Maybe that had something to do with it.'

The Princess nodded. 'Do you know what?' she said. 'Those shits asked for them.'

Other tours lack promise at the start, but unexpectedly produce excellent pictures. The most recent one like this was the Queen's 1991 tour of the United States. With the Duke of Edinburgh, she flew first to Washington to meet President Bush at the White House.

But the great picture everyone remembers from that trip happened at a run-down housing project in one of the roughest areas of the Capitol. The Queen was visiting a black family in a small house. Inside the cramped rooms there was space for only two photographers and a TV crew.

As Her Majesty walked in with Mrs Bush a fifteen-stone great-grandmother, Alice Frazier, suddenly rushed forward and

156

hugged her. I had time to shoot just one frame, and the Reuters agency photographer with me completely missed this magic moment.

Two people from two totally different worlds, a poor black woman from a Washington ghetto, and the richest and most famous lady on earth, came together in friendship. Through the centuries, her ancestors had behaved like gods, aloof and untouchable, but my picture showed the human side of her.

Realizing the importance of the photograph in America, I decided to let my distraught colleague from Reuters have a copy of it. Next day, every major newspaper in the United States carried my shot on the front page. It also got a good show back in Britain in almost every paper except one. The *Sun* filed it in the wastepaper bin.

CHAPTER TWELVE

A Loyal Friend

The Prince of Wales was driving back from a hunt in Leicestershire in his brand-new Bentley turbo one Friday evening when he came to a flooded road. In a hurry to get back to Highgrove, he pushed on, not realizing that the overflow from recent heavy rains concealed a deep ditch.

He started to ease the car through the muddy water when suddenly the engine cut out. He looked out and discovered the flood was up to the Bentley's windowsills, and within minutes it began pouring into the £100,000 limousine.

Noting the Prince's plight, the police officers in the back-up Rover following him rapidly backed out of the torrent. But the Bentley would not move an inch.

By this time, Prince Charles and the personal protection officer beside him were waist-deep in icy water. As they struggled out of the half-submerged saloon getting soaking wet, they suddenly saw a recovery truck on the opposite side of the stream. Like two vultures, the driver and his mate were waiting to pounce on any unwary motorists who crossed their paths.

''Ere, George, look what we've got in our flood,' said the driver to his grinning companion. 'It's the Prince of Wales.' Feeling foolish, Charles yelled for assistance and asked them if they would tow his car to a garage.

Then, as fast as he could, he splashed back through the water and clambered dripping into the police Rover. Without a backward glance he set off to find another route home.

The following Monday he was due to carry out an official engagement, so his staff needed to find a replacement car quickly. As the Prince of Wales was their most valued customer, Bentley wanted to get him back on the road as soon as possible, but in the winter of 1984 very few turbos were available. With great difficulty, they managed to find one over the weekend and had it driven down to Highgrove in time for the Monday job.

When the Prince looked at it that morning he did not seem to appreciate the fantastic effort that had been made to procure another car. He turned to his Scotland Yard bodyguard and said: 'Oh dear, it's black. I don't like black.'

This thoughtless remark was typical of a man who expects to get exactly what he wants when he wants it. When it was explained that there was no other Bentley of any shade available, Charles sighed heavily and got into the car.

He never drove the flooded Bentley again. Even after extensive repairs and refitting, which cost Bentley £30,000, it wasn't considered good enough for the future King. The dark-blue luxury limousine ended up on loan to the pop star Paul McCartney, and the Bentley distributors sent the Prince an identical car.

It wasn't the first time the Prince had had a prang. Once, while driving away from the Queen Mother's Highland home, Birkhall, in a late-model Range Rover, he turned to wave at her.

He was so busy saying goodbye that he wasn't looking where he was going. With an almighty crash, the Range Rover hit a dry stone wall, ripping the side of the car open like a giant can opener.

Cursing his stupidity, the Prince left the wrecked Range Rover for someone else to sort out, climbed into another car and continued his journey.

His cavalier attitude to expensive cars may be understandable. At that point in his life, the Prince had more than twenty cars in his garages, but owned only one of them. The rest were leased.

On his twenty-first birthday, the Queen gave him a hand-built, dark-blue Aston Martin DB6. This is the only car he really treasures. He once told a girlfriend of the thrill he feels each time he gets behind the wheel. 'When you sit in it and look through the windscreen, it is just like looking up a woman's thighs,' he told her.

This collector's dream car has been magnificently serviced and maintained by Aston Martin at Newport Pagnell, Bedforshire. When he was in collision with a Land Rover once at the Guards Polo Club, Windsor, the right wing was slightly dented. Aston Martin sent down a skilled panel beater, who worked all night to restore the car to its pristine condition. When I saw it next day I could not believe the sports car had been involved in a shunt. And the Prince was so pleased with the rapid repair that he chastised Princess Diana when she idly sat on the wing. Diana slid off the car, laughing, as she watched her husband check to see if she had made another dent.

With such a famous owner and driver, the DB6 must be worth at least one million pounds today. But this is one car that will never be put up for sale. The clever old Queen ordered a spare engine for the DB6, so that it will last the Prince a lifetime.

He now owns a newer Aston Martin Volante, a gift from the Sultan of Brunei in 1986. He loves to drive it to the polo every summer, but somehow it doesn't mean as much to him as the DB6.

His love of gas-guzzling luxury cars seems at odds with his reputation as the green Prince who worries about our polluted world. In early summer 1991, he made make a speech in which he described motor vehicles as 'voracious beasts and monsters, ruining the environment'.

A week later he had his Bentley turbo driven out to Czechoslovakia so he could use it on an official visit. On the round trip of more than 2,000 miles, the car averaged fourteen miles to the gallon on the open road, but around only nine miles per gallon in cities.

The press accused him of failing to practise what he preached, and he really took the criticism to heart. His private secretary, Richard Aylard, consulted the engineers at Bentley to see if there was any way the car could be run less expensively. He told them that if they couldn't work something out, the Prince would have to switch to a more economical vehicle.

Spurred on by this, Bentley developed a fuel-efficient gearbox which improved the model's performance by 27 per cent. The prototype was fitted to the Prince's saloon.

Until then, Royal Household sources say that Prince Charles would think nothing of sending a car from London to Highgrove to pick up some of his organically-grown carrots. The cost of the petrol alone for the 240-mile round trip would have bought a hundredweight of the vegetables in Harrods' grocery department. This paints a picture of an impractical Prince. The royal conservationist wastes money and resources at a fantastic rate, yet has miserly habits.

His late valet, Stephen Barry, once told me about the Scrooge-like character of his boss while we were on a royal flight from Hobart, Tasmania to Adelaide. 'Prince Charles is so mean he makes me wash his dirty handkerchiefs on overseas tours,' Barry said. 'When he sends them out with the rest of the laundry they often go missing. He suspects this is because they have the Prince of Wales three-feathered emblem embroidered on them. And rather than buy new ones, he makes me wash them by hand.'

Stephen Barry went on: 'He has no idea what things cost. He will return to Highgrove from a magnificent banquet, then look at the household bills and complain about the high cost of cheese.' The steep cost of furnishing his country home appalled the Prince too, making him grumpy when the accounts came in, his valet said. 'Do things really cost this much?' he used to asked Stephen.

His staff say he is not a mean-spirited man, that in fact, he is quite the opposite: the kindest, most understanding person most of them have ever met. So why is he so mean with money? 'It's my Scottish blood,' Charles explains with a grin. 'I just can't help it.' This is not quite true, because whenever he goes out to a restaurant, he likes to leave generous tips for the staff.

He has a system by which he signals to his policeman how much money should be left. If he likes the way they have looked after him, he indicates that the officer should be generous. If he has not been impressed, he gives another signal warning the policeman not to overdo it. Once, they got their signs scrambled and Prince Charles was furious when the bodyguard left a bigger gratuity than he wished.

His penny-pinching ways are probably a result of never having had to handle money or earn a living. But most people close to him say the Prince is not a grudging giver; they feel he is miserly only with himself, as if trying to experience going without to know what life is like for ordinary people.

They believe he is riddled with guilt about the comfortable life he leads when he sees such deprivation in Britain's inner cities and in Third World countries.

He is very much aware that his privileged position is an accident of birth, and feels he has to justify it endlessly. This is the reason that most of his time is devoted to fund-raising for charities such as the Prince's Trust, the organization he founded. Aware of his cushy start in life, he wants to give young people who have not been so lucky a chance of fulfilling their dreams.

In an effort to keep a sense of proportion, he disappeared from London once to spend three days living with a crofter on the island of Berneray in the Hebrides. To earn his keep he planted potatoes, helped to build a dry stone wall, and went fishing for his supper. In 1983 and again in 1984 he took time off to work as a farmhand on Duchy of Cornwall properties, milking cows, delivering calves and building stone fences.

He often bombards his staff and friends with questions about the real world. 'What's it like to live on the dole?' he asks. 'Do neighbours help each other out when they are hard up?' He tries desperately to understand the people he will one day reign over.

He has also sought my opinion, sometimes on the strangest topics. In June 1979, soon after Mrs Thatcher had swept into power the previous May, we were walking the cross-country course at Andoversford in Gloucestershire.

As usual, I was walking backwards in front of him snapping away when he asked: 'What did you think of the General Election result?'

I was surprised, and said: 'Unfortunately, I was in France on polling day and could not vote.' I added that I was disappointed because I thought the best party had lost.

He then asked: 'Why do you think Mr Callaghan lost?'

I gave him my honest opinion. I said I thought the fact that Mr Callaghan could not promise to fulfil a full parliamentary term as prime minister damaged Labour's chances as much as the extreme left wing of the party.

His answer stunned me. He said: 'Do you know, Mr Callaghan is a fine, fine person. It's such a pity that Mrs Thatcher can't find a job for such a wonderful politician.'

I thought this was a pretty naïve statement. It just goes to show how close the Prince of Wales was to the fomer Labour leader. They had corresponded regularly when Charles was serving in the Navy and struck up a lifelong friendship.

The Prince also asks the people around him for advice sometimes, but rarely listens when they offer it.

In 1986, in the second ITN documentary on the Prince and Princess of Wales's lives in private and in public, Charles made a remark which has haunted him ever since. He talked about his love for the garden he had created at Highgrove, and said of his plants: 'I go round and I examine them very carefully and occasionally talk to them, which I think is very important – they do respond in a funny way.'

He was advised by his then press secretary, the late Victor Chapman, a straight-talking Canadian, that it would unwise to leave this sequence in the TV film. The Prince overruled him and has been paying for it ever since. The minute reviewers heard that he talked to his plants he was labelled a crank. The fact that he made the comment with tongue in cheek was completely ignored. Since then there have been countless cartoons and sketches about the Prince nattering to his nasturtiums or chatting up his chrysanthemums.

Like anyone else, he is sensitive about personal criticism. Cartoonists who exaggerate prominent facial features have always portrayed him with elephant ears, something that understandably rankles with the Prince. A good example of this came when he and Princess Diana were visiting the Keeler marmalade factory in Dundee.

A large crowd lined the street outside the plant as their motorcade approached, and slowed right down to negotiate a roundabout. It was a warm day and the windows of the royal car were open so its occupants could be more easily seen by the well-wishers. Just then a booming Scots voice bellowed out of the flag-waving throng: 'Oi, Big Ears.'

Prince Charles's face visibly stiffened and his sunny smile vanished. For the rest of the morning he was in a foul mood. All the Scotland Yard bodyguards in the world can't save a Prince from someone who wants to puncture his pride.

He likes to keep well informed. When Rupert Murdoch was negotiating to buy *The Times* and *The Sunday Times*, Prince Charles was skiing in Klosters, and as usual I was with him. Each day he would ask me how the deal was going. After checking with my office, I would report back to the Prince and give him the latest news. *The Times*, which has long been his favourite paper, was finally sold to the Australian media tycoon, along with its Sunday sister paper. When I told Prince Charles, he said: 'I wish Mr Murdoch all the success in the world with *The Times*.'

His most admirable quality is his loyalty to his friends when it really matters. In August 1990, Prince Charles was photographed comforting the wife of one of his oldest friends, Norton, Lord Romsey. He was embracing Penelope Romsey as they stood beside a swimming pool in Majorca. The reason for her distress soon became public knowledge. Her younger daughter Leonora, then aged four, had just been diagnosed as having cancer of the kidney, and had to be rushed back to England. Prince Charles put his private plane at the Romseys' disposal so they could fly little Leonara home to London. On their arrival, the Prince's Bentley was waiting to drive the family to St Bartholomew's Hospital, where Leonora was admitted for treatment.

By the following summer, Leonora was well enough to join her family when they were the Queen's guests for the Trooping the Colour ceremony in London. Afterwards, the excited little girl, wearing a hat to cover the baldness caused by chemotherapy, stood on the balcony of Buckingham Palace with Prince William and Prince Harry watching the Royal Air Force flypast to celebrate the Queen's official birthday. Two months later, the Romseys, with Leonora and her older brother and sister, accompanied the Prince and Princess of Wales on a summer-holiday cruise of the Mediterranean. At the time there were high hopes that Leonora would be cured. Tragically, her condition deteriorated soon afterwards and she was readmitted to St Bartholomew's. From then on Prince Charles was a constant visitor to her bedside. He quietly slipped in and out of the hospital without attracting any publicity whatsoever. Depite the best medical care, Leonora lost her fight for life in November 1991.

The night she died Prince Charles was preparing to leave next day with Princess Diana on an official tour of Canada. When he heard the sad news, he rushed straight down to Broadlands, the Romseys' home in Hampshire, and stayed there all night comforting the distraught couple. Norton and Penelope will never forget that when they needed a friend most, the Prince of Wales dropped everything to be with them.

He showed the same compassion when his friend and mentor Sir John Higgs, Secretary of the Duchy of Cornwall, suddenly became ill in 1986. On one occasion he drove hundreds of miles out of his way to see the man he admired so much in St Thomas's Hospital. He even knighted him on his deathbed and later helped his widow to arrange a service of thanksgiving for his life at the Queen's Chapel, St James's Palace.

There are perhaps only a dozen or so other friends to whom the Prince of Wales shows this degree of devotion. These people are known in the media as the Highgrove Set, although in the last few years of Charles's marriage they never went near Highgrove.

They were more often seen at Birkhall in Scotland, and Sandringham or Wood Farm in Norfolk. As well as the Romseys, this charmed circle included Nicholas Soames MP; the Prince's skiing pals Charles and Patty Palmer-Tomkinson; the daughter of the Earl of Dalhousie, Lady Sarah Keswick, who is married to merchant banker Chippendale, 'Chips' Keswick; as well as millionaire farmer Gerald Ward and his wife Amanda.

But the founder members of this select group were Lord and Lady Tryon (Anthony and Dale) and their chums Andrew and Camilla Parker Bowles. Australian Dale, nicknamed 'Kanga' by the Prince, had known him since they met when he was Down Under in the seventies. But Camilla, as we now know, was an even older and closer friend. For several years some newspapers hinted that it was Dale, and not Camilla, who was the centre of the Prince's affections.

Once, when the Prince was staying at Birkhall, he was snapped from a long distance with an attractive blonde. At the time it was reported that the mystery woman was Dale Tryon. This was untrue; the lady at the Prince's side was actually Amanda Ward. But for weeks thereafter the hapless Kanga was pursued around London by paparazzi.

The *Daily Star* ran a front-page story comparing an unflattering picture of Dale with a glamorous shot of Diana, suggesting that Charles would be crazy to prefer the older woman. Lady Tryon's picture was so unflattering that for a week afterwards she summoned her hairdresser to her London home so she would always look her best when photographers were on the prowl.

This once warm friendship has cooled in recent years. Now Dale and her husband no longer join the Prince's house parties. They see each other only at occasional society events, but stay in touch on the telephone.

With these friends the Prince created his own world, separate from his wife. If it seems odd that a married man should need such close women friends, a top London psychiatrist may have the answer. In his book *Inheritance*, Dr Dennis Friedman says Charles developed a need for more than one close relationship as a result of his upbringing. He was forced to love his mother from afar, as she was preoccupied with affairs of state, and gained the affection she could not give him from his nannies.

'This pattern of a loving, intimate relationship with his nannies, and a more formal one with his mother, led to a need for two simultaneous partners throughout his life,' Friedman says. As he is now middle-aged, the psychiatrist believes the Prince is too old to change, and will go on needing two separate relationships for the rest of his days.

CHAPTER THIRTEEN

A White Wall of Death

The morning of 10 March 1988 dawned beautiful and sunny in the Swiss ski resort Klosters. A photo call with the Prince and Princess of Wales and the Duchess of York had been held two days earlier, but several newspapers had kept staff on the scene in case there was an accident. This is cynically known in the newspaper business as a death watch. By the end of that lovely spring day that is exactly what it had become.

We had a deal with the Royals. If they agreed to pose for us on the first day we would stay well away from them afterwards. This meant we were just hanging about the village, keeping our heads down. A few of the press party went skiing, but I suggested to the *Daily Mail*'s royal snapper Mike Forster that we do something completely different. It was the perfect day for a walk in the mountains, I thought.

Mike had originally planned to fly back to London that day, but with amazing foresight his editor, Sir David English, had ordered him to stay put. In light of what followed, Mike decided that Sir David was a prophet and might even walk on water as well.

With the warm sunshine and clear blue skies, the mountain scenery was breathtaking, but the rise in temperature had started a thaw in the densely-packed snow. This triggered an avalanche that ripped through the royal party a short time later.

Mike and I took a cable car halfway up the Gotchnagrat, the largest mountain towering above Klosters. As we were riding up in the cable car, we were raving about the magnificent view across the valley.

Then we began to walk slowly down a toboggan run through the trees. We had no idea there had been an avalanche, because children on sledges were whizzing past us as we sauntered back down to the village two miles below.

Suddenly we heard a helicopter clattering above us. I remember turning to Mike and saying: 'Look, some poor bastard must have broken a leg.' We watched as the red mountain-rescue chopper lifted off again and headed for the hospital at Davos.

But we carried on our leisurely stroll, chatting away, when the helicopter returned. Mike said: 'Christ, Arthur, they're busy up there today. They must be falling over like ninepins.'

We were both carrrying cameras and could have quickly got to the scene had we realized that the royal party was in danger. The Prince and his friends often skied off piste in this area, but I believed that he was such a good skier, and the conditions that day so perfect, that he would never have an accident. The thought of an avalanche did not occur to us.

There was not a single clue that rescuers were searching high above us for buried bodies. Laughing schoolkids were still sledging past us, so we kept walking down the mountain.

When we reached the bottom, I saw a good friend, Elizabeth Sutter, a reporter working for the Swiss daily newspaper *Blick*. 'Quick, Arthur, get into my car,' she said. 'I think one of Prince Charles's bodyguards has been killed.'

We tore off to Davos Hospital and covered the twelve kilometres in record time, but we were too late. Two people had gone in on stretchers but no one knew who they were.

I then went to doorstep the Prince's chalet four miles away at Wolfgang. There, I learned that Major Hugh Lindsay, the Queen's former equerry and an old friend of Charles and Diana, had been killed instantly. Another member of the party, Patty Palmer-Tomkinson, was close to death.

Charles, Diana and Fergie were all inside the chalet in deep shock. It was freezing cold as darkness fell, but I stayed on photographing the comings and goings of their royal staff. I remember the Prince's assistant private secretary, Commander Richard Aylard, returning ashen-faced from the hospital. Then

Patty's husband, Charlie Palmer-Tomkinson, turned up looking shattered after visiting his wife.

In the midst of this tragedy there was an element of farce. The *Daily Mirror* reporter James Whitaker, who had been out skiing with his wife Iwona, jumped into his car still wearing his cumbersome ski boots when he heard about the avalanche.

As a result, his foot slipped on the brakes and he crashed into another car driven by a Swiss tourist. In his haste to get the big story, he refused to wait while the police took down details. They promptly hauled him off to the local nick and detained him for four hours. The *Mirror* executives in London went hysterical when they heard about this, because they had no one else on the story. Their royal photographer Ken Gavin, who hates skiing, had flown back to London the previous day after the big photo call. Because James was out of touch for so long and no agency copy was landing on the *Daily Mirror* news desk, they were desperate. Their flamboyant publisher Robert Maxwell immediately decided to send out his private plane, packed with a team of reporters, photographers and senior executives led by deputy editor John Penrose. A sheepish Ken Gavin was among them. Later that week we all joked that 'Gavvers' flew to the Alps so often that year that he had been made an honorary member of the SwissAir frequent fliers' club.

While all this drama was unfolding my partner Harry Arnold was filing his socks off in an icy phonebox a hundred yards away from the Royals' chalet. Meanwhile, I was concentrating on obtaining the first newspaper rights to pictures of the tragedy. They had been taken by freelance photographers Mauro Carraro, who was working for the *News of the World*, and Parisian Jean-Paul Dousset. These two just happened to be in the right spot on the mountain as the disaster struck.

The spring sunshine had loosened tons of snow which had been packed on to the steep slopes all winter. When Prince Charles, his guide Bruno Sprecher, Hugh Lindsay, the Palmer-Tomkinsons and a Swiss policeman ventured across the treacherous mountainside their movement apparently triggered the avalanche. The first rumblings alerted the experienced guide

Bruno, who screamed at Prince Charles: 'Go, sir, go.' Then a white wall of death thundered down the mountain, sweeping away the two stragglers in the party, Hugh and Patty, who could not get out of the way in time.

The pictures Mauro and Jean-Paul had taken were sensational. They showed Prince Charles helping to carry Hugh's body to the waiting helicopter. One of the best shots captured him weeping in the snow as Charlie Palmer-Tomkinson and Bruno consoled him.

I rang the *Sun*'s deputy picture editor Glenn Goodey at his home in Twickenham, but he had gone out that night to his daughter's school play. 'Sally, get him out of there,' I told his wife. 'And tell him to phone me immediately. It's very urgent.'

By this time the freelancers' material was in Paris and Glenn sprang into action. He despatched photographer Peter Simpson, along with reporter John Askill, to rush over and negotiate a deal for the *Sun*.

Despite their best efforts, our sister publication the *News of the World* bagged all first rights, but I was kept busy taking plenty of other pictures next day.

The following morning, flurries of snow enveloped Prince Charles as he arrived to visit Patty in the hospital. The weather had turned as overcast and gloomy as everyone felt. A shiver went through me as I photographed him, and it was not simply a result of the plunging temperature. The thought had crossed my mind that had Mike and I gone higher up the mountain we too could have been lying in that hospital or even in the morgue.

Afterwards, the Prince drove off with Diana and Fergie to Zurich Airport. There was only one thing left that they could do for their dead friend. In a final act of friendship they escorted Hugh's body home on the Queen's Flight back to London. Before the plane left, Prince Charles's press officer, Philip Mackie, read out to all of us a very moving statement that his boss had hand-written. It described how his friends were 'swept away in a whirling maelstrom as the whole mountainside seemed to hurtle past us into the valley below'.

This was not just an expression of the Prince's feelings of grief and loss, but his way of vindicating his ski guide Bruno Sprecher. Many observers felt that Bruno should have shouldered most of the blame for the catastrophe, as he was the most experienced skier in the party, and knew the mountains better than anyone else. But, as the Prince explained in his account:

> It was all over in a terrifying matter of seconds. Herr Sprecher reacted with incredible speed and total professionalism. He skied down to the bottom of the avalanche as fast as he could, having called to the Swiss policeman to radio for a helicopter.
>
> Having reached the foot of the avalanche, he located Mrs Palmer-Tomkinson using the Autophone Radio Detection System and dug down to her. Mr Palmer-Tomkinson and I skied down and just arrived as Herr Sprecher had reached Mrs Palmer-Tomkinson's head. He had given her mouth-to-mouth resuscitation and revived her. He gave me the shovel to dig her out but I tried using my hands as well.
>
> At this point I stayed with Mrs Palmer-Tomkinson while he quickly went to try and locate Major Lindsay with Mr Palmer-Tomkinson. They found him about fifteen yards above Mrs Palmer-Tomkinson, but tragically he had been killed outright during the fall, despite Herr Sprecher's valiant attempts to revive him by mouth-to-mouth resuscitation.

In fact, Bruno was the hero of the hour. As I found out later, he had made all the correct checks before the party set off. He had phoned the Alpine ski patrol and was told that all the slopes were open.

Although the photographs at Zurich Airport were dramatic, the best picture of the day came when the royal party landed at RAF Northolt near London. Jason Boland, an Australian freelance working for the *Sun*, perfectly captured the sad scene on the windswept tarmac. Hugh's widow Sarah Lindsay stood with her head held high, flanked by a sombre Fergie, a tearful Diana and a grim-faced Charles, all united in grief.

Back in Switzerland, Patty Palmer-Tomkinson was battling for her life. The most horrifying part of her agonizing ordeal had been remaining conscious throughout the rescue, despite suffering a collapsed lung and having both legs smashed. Later, when she was being examined by top Swiss orthopaedic surgeon Peter Matter, she bravely asked him: 'Will I lose my legs?' He put a comforting hand on her arm and said: 'First, we save your life, then we'll save your legs.'

He did such a superb job that Patty not only walked again, but two years later skied again. And I was there to take the exclusive pictures the day she did it. When she nervously glided just 100 yards down a small slope without falling, then turned and stopped, her three children squealed with delight and hugged her.

Her husband Charlie stood looking on, bursting with pride at her courage. Word quickly spread across the mountain that Patty was back on the slopes, and crowds of her old friends, including Bruno Sprecher and his wife, rushed to congratulate her. All of us there were touched by her bravery, especially when she said: 'I must go and see Professor Matter. He will be so pleased.'

Prince Charles flew back three times to visit Patty as she underwent repeated operations in the hospital. A year after the avalanche, he also made a brave pilgrimage back to ski again at Klosters. Patty said: 'It's exactly what I expected of the Prince. I'm sure Hugh would have wanted him to go back.' And she added: 'I know it was the right thing to do.'

But she was angry about claims that Prince Charles was to blame for the accident which almost claimed her life. And she stoutly defended his love of going off piste into deep, powder snow. 'All Prince Charles did was invite us to go skiing. He was simply the host. He was not in charge of the party that day,' she explained.

Prince Charles still returns to Klosters each winter. But when he skies off piste his guide insists that he wears an avalanche

Four months later and twenty pounds lighter, Diana leaves St. Paul's Cathederal two days before her July 29 wedding.

Top: Standing up Down Under Prince William finds his feet in Auckland, New Zealand on Charles and Diana's first overseas tour together, 1983.

Below: At a photocall for William's second birthday he left us all scratching our heads wondering if he was left-handed, June 1984.

Dazzling Melbourne with an emerald necklace worn as a headband when her tiara got left behind in London, November 1985.

Eye-catching Diana looks as elegant as a Vogue cover when she attends a wedding in Norfolk, 1984.

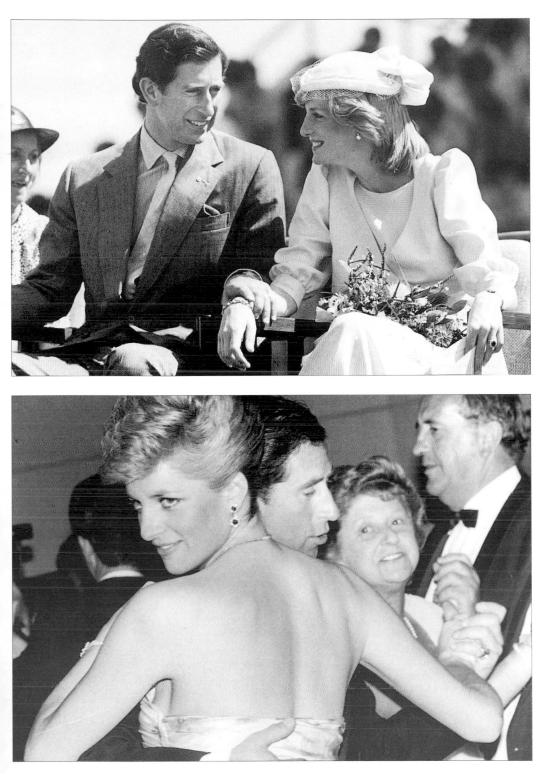

Top: The look of love: a tender moment in Maitland, New South Wales, as proud Charles tells his wife how well she is coping with her first overseas tour.

Below: A smoulder over the shoulder from Princess Diana waltzing with Prince Charles in Melbourne, 1988.

Top: A touching moment: Prince Charles's "Uncle Dickie" puts an affectionate arm around his great nephew at Tidworth, Wiltshire in July, 1978.

Below: The Queen Mother walking on the beach at Holkham, Norfolk, near Sandringham in July, 1981.

Top: Diana keeps her cool at a desert picnic in the sweltering heat of Saudi Arabia, 1986.

Below: Reviewing the cadets when she substituted for the Queen at the Sovereign's Parade in Sandhurst, 1988.

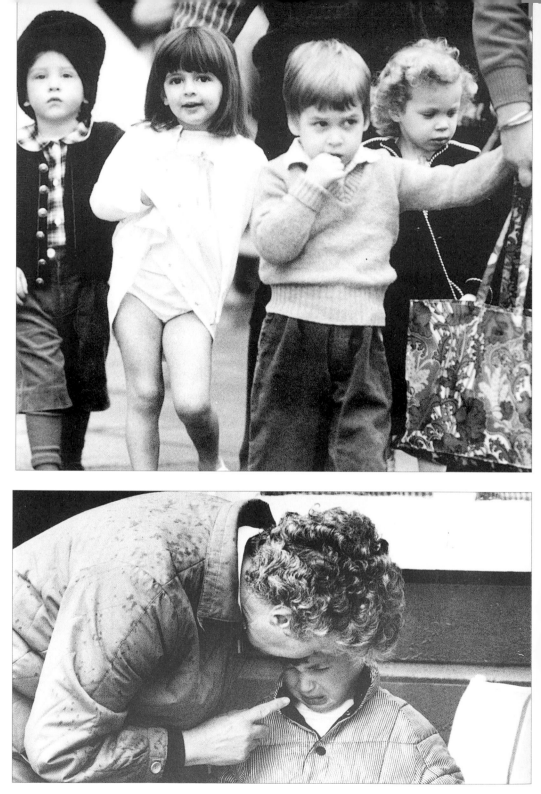

Top: William's panty-mime: Off to his school Christmas play, the little prince did not notice a classmate flashing her knickers.

Below: A tearful William gets a ticking off from his nanny Olga Powell for running on to the polo field at Windsor, 1987.

My first photo of Diana watching her Prince play polo at Midhurst, Sussex, on July 29, 1980. Exactly one year later she was the Princess of Wales.

Lady Diana Spencer in the see-through skirt which showed the world her lovely legs outside the Pimlico kindergarten where she worked, September 1980.

My conversation with Prince Charles when he ticked me off for publishing a picture of his bald spot taken a few days earlier at Cirencester Park, 1977. (Inset picture of Bald Patch)

Top: The newly-engaged couple relaxing at Smith's Lawn, Windsor after the Prince had played a game of polo, June 1981.

Below: Prince Charles and Diana's older sister Lady Sarah Spencer who told me: "He is a fabulous person, but I am not in love with him."

The Clown Prince disguised as "Uncle Harry" in a false nose, moustache and glasses. And a few hours later he toboggans down a slope behind his chalet at Klosters, 1980.

The Ice Prince cometh ... shoving ice cubes down the back of a pretty groom at Cowdray Park, Sussex, 1979.

Prince Charles with close friend Lady Sarah Keswick and Camilla Parker Bowles at Andoversford, Gloucestershire in August, 1979.

Inset picture: The two women in the Prince's life Diana and Camilla watching him racing at Ludlow in 1980.

Diana's breathtaking black evening gown emphasised her curves at her first official function with Charles at the Goldsmiths' Hall in March 1981.

survival pack. As Bruno himself showed me, this is contained in a small haversack on his back. If disaster strikes again, all he has to do is give the ripcord a sharp tug and a large balloon will inflate. This will float him to the surface of the crashing ice and snow.

When Bruno first demonstrated the life-saving gear Prince Charles said: 'I don't care what it costs, get one for everybody in the party.' He has vowed that if he can help it his dear friends will never again undergo such a horrifying ordeal in the mountains.

CHAPTER FOURTEEN

Sisters-in-law

The phone rang at Romenda Lodge, Berkshire, just as the Duchess of York was preparing to take her children to school. It was the Princess of Wales calling from her penthouse suite at the Hyatt Hotel overlooking the Korean capital Seoul.

'What's the matter, Duch?' Sarah asked, using the nickname favoured by all Diana's friends.

On the other end of the phone Diana sounded distraught. 'I can't stand it any longer. I've just got to get out.'

It was the third time the Princess had phoned her old friend that week, as she grew increasingly desperate to leave her husband.

One man who was with her entourage in Korea later explained why she turned to the Duchess in her distress. 'She was clearly at a stage where she was making a crucial decision about her future, and she wanted to know what the Duchess thought about it. 'Their friendship was still very curious. They could never be described as close, but they do have lots in common. They are both mothers of the Queen's grandchildren. The only real difference in their situations is that the Princess is the mother of the future King. The Duchess is a good listener and had urged the Princess to leave the Prince on numerous occasions before.'

From the minute Diana and Charles had arrived in Korea their misery had been impossible to hide. They did not exchange a single word on the three engagements they carried out after flying in to Seoul. Next day, the British tabloids headlined what

177

had happened over pictures of their gloomy faces. The *Daily Mail*'s front page said simply: 'TORTURED'.

It was obvious to everyone that Charles and Diana could not stand the sight of each other. One look at them convinced every journalist that this would be their last tour together.

Ironically, when they met the Korean President at his official residence, the Blue House, he welcomed them in words that made us all wince. 'You are a beautiful couple,' he said, 'and we are very glad to have you here.'

As the Princess sat listening, it was clear from the expression on her face that she wasn't at all glad to be there. Peter Westmacott, the Prince's assistant private secretary, tried to defuse the steadily worsening situation by pouring scorn on the stories in the British papers. When I asked him if this was the Waleses' last tour he said: 'Oh no, there are a couple already planned for next year.'

I told him that if he wanted to stop newspaper claims that the Prince and Princess were on the verge of a marriage break-up he should announce the tours at once. 'Perhaps we will,' he said. Later the Prince's press secretary Dickie Arbiter said he would make an announcement at eight o'clock that evening. When it came, his non-statement only fuelled the rumours. Dickie merely told us: 'No details of any tours can be announced before the host governments have been informed.'

I already knew that Charles and Diana were scheduled to tour Mexico and Poland, and could not understand why the Palace didn't say so. The reason soon became clear.

Diana had had enough. As she poured her heart out to Fergie on the phone, she insisted there was no way she would ever again go on a tour with the man she loathed. As the Princess told friends afterwards, bombarding Sarah with phonecalls was the only way she could cope.

Throughout the four-day trip to Korea she constantly needed to talk to the one person in the world who would understand and sympathize. The Duchess of York had already made the brave break with the Royal Family that Diana was planning.

For months, they had confided in each other their determination to leave their husbands. At one point they had decided to do it together. But Sarah's plans came unstuck when a woman courtier close to the Queen leaked the news to a newspaper contact. Months before she had planned to announce it, her marriage break-up was front-page news. The Royal Household immediately turned on Sarah for walking out on the Queen's second son. She was stripped of her privileges and cast out into the cold.

As a result, Diana suddenly got nervous and delayed her decision to split with Prince Charles for another nine months. Like that between any two friends, Diana and Sarah's relationship has had its ups and downs. They had been introduced to each other in 1980 after a polo match at Cowdray Park. Diana, then on one of her first outings with Charles, had gone for tea to the nearby home of Hector and Susan Barrantes. Susan's daughter Sarah was there and the two young women got chatting. They quickly discovered they had a lot in common and became firm friends.

The day after her engagement to Prince Charles was announced, in February 1981, Sarah Ferguson was her first visitor. While doorstepping Buckingham Palace, I recognized the attractive redhead who drove up to the wrought-iron gates, gave her name to the waiting police constable then parked in the forecourt and walked in through the Privy Purse door.

From then on, I often saw them together at polo matches. Whenever I snapped a picture of the Queen or Prince Charles when Sarah happened to be with them I sent her a print. And I always got a cheerful 'Hello, Arthur,' as she thanked me for the pictures.

Every one of these early photographs has been carefully preserved by the Duchess in dozens of huge leather-bound albums she keeps at home. She has filed away every newspaper report and every photograph of her royal life. 'It's all here,' she said as she showed me when I visited her Berkshire home.

Next time I saw Sarah with Diana was at Royal Ascot in 1985. I found out later that the Princess was asked to suggest suitable guests for the Queen's Ascot Week house party at Windsor. Diana named her friend Fergie.

Aware that her brother-in-law Andrew was lonely after the end of his romance with actress Koo Stark, she hoped he might take a fancy to Sarah. When he was immediately smitten, Diana encouraged the romance. She acted as a go-between and arranged dinners at Kensington Palace, where Andrew and Sarah could meet without arousing suspicion.

Finally, when they decided to go public, the Princess arranged for the three of them to attend an Elton John concert at Wembley. Andrew and Fergie sat together and held hands for all the world to see, but to their amazement no photographers spotted them.

After spending New Year at Sandringham with her Prince and his gleeful sister-in-law, Sarah returned to London. Princess Diana was due to visit Prince Andrew's ship, HMS *Brazen*, which was moored in the Pool of London. Journalists awaiting her arrival were stunned when she turned up with Sarah Ferguson. It was a clear sign that Fergie was soon to join her friend in the ranks of the Royals. Diana had even given Sarah one of her designer coat dresses, a black-and-white woollen check creation, to wear for the occasion.

The two young women laughed and giggled as they toured the ship with a delighted Prince Andrew, well aware that the Fleet Street newshounds could detect the sound of wedding bells. They laughed even harder when they saw the ship's shop sold knickers with the word 'Brazen' embroidered on the front. Diana could not resist buying two pairs, for herself and her soon-to-be sister-in-law.

The jokey underwear appealed to their Sloaney sense of humour. Diana waved hers about, showing what she had bought on board. But before she went back on deck to depart she had carefully hidden them in her handbag.

Next day the Prince and Princess of Wales arrived in Switzerland for their annual skiing holiday. Journalists were amazed to discover that Sarah Ferguson was with the royal party. There could no longer be any doubt that she would soon be Andrew's bride. And the day Sarah and Andrew's engagement was announced was a triumph for their matchmaker.

Her dream of having a pal at the Palace had come true. By 1986 Diana's private life was in turmoil. Increasingly unhappy with Charles, and alienated from his family, she looked upon Fergie as an ally inside the Windsor camp.

They were two modern girls in an archaic institution. Each became dependent on the other for advice and comfort. But their friendship came under fire after they dressed up as police-women in an attempt to gatecrash Prince Andrew's stag party. Their antics the following year at Ascot also attracted criticism, when they poked friends with their umbrellas. Inevitably, the press compared them. Diana was in no danger of losing her hold on the nation's hearts to the royal newcomer, press pundits decided. The Princess of Wales was prettier, slimmer and more elegant. No one stopped to consider that by comparison with the Duchess, Diana seemed a sweet old-fashioned girl, whose main interests were children and charity work.

I always thought feisty Fergie was far more dynamic, a royal action woman, much more in tune with her times than any of the other Windsor wives. She was the first woman in the Royal Family to gain her pilot's wings, she had back-packed around North and South America, and was the London director of an international publishing company when she met her Prince. I loved Diana, but I really admired Sarah. She could ski faster, fly higher and dare to do more than her best friend any time.

For a few years, Diana and Sarah were like Sooty and the fingers: inseparable. They watched the Wimbledon finals together, shared jokes at the Derby, and frequently went on winter holidays together.

One afternoon in February 1987 I walked into the Confiserie tea shop in Klosters, desperate for a cup of tea. Before I could order one, Princess Diana and Fergie walked over from their table on the other side of the room. As they strolled towards me I groaned out loud: 'Oh no!' Four days earlier I had broken two ribs, falling off my ladder while photographing the Princess on a tour of Portugal. At the end of the trip a doctor had strapped me up so I could follow Diana and Charles to Switzerland, where they were skiing with Andrew and Sarah.

But I was in a lot of pain. The slightest movement sent knives shooting through my lungs. Earlier that day, with the help of pain-killers, I had struggled out of bed to snap the royal skiers on the slopes of the Gotchnagrat mountain overlooking Klosters.

As soon as I finished working, I had limped into the tea shop, where I found the Princess with her sister-in-law. I made an effort to stand as the two royal ladies approached, then flopped down again. 'I'm sorry, I can't properly get up,' I apologized as they said hello. 'I broke a few ribs falling off my ladder while taking your picture in Lisbon last week. And the pain is killing me.'

Diana laughed. 'Oh, I knew it would be my fault,' she said. As we chatted I noticed she was wearing a golden medal pinned to her jacket and asked what it was for.

'Well, nobody would give me one, so I awarded it to myself,' she joked.

Just then Fergie peererd over her shoulder. 'Hullo, Arthur, aren't you talking to me?'

'As a matter of fact, I want to tell you, I've sent a lovely picture of you to the *Sun* today,' I said. 'Unfortunately, it wasn't so nice of your husband. He was walking around with a wavy line under his nose.' The Duke of York had been in one of his grumpy moods at the photo session that morning.

Sarah cracked up. 'Oh, that's great. A wavy line! I'll tell him that,' she promised.

The following year, Diana and Sarah returned to Klosters again. Sadly, it turned out to be their last skiing holiday together. One morning, while out on the slopes with Prince Charles, the Duchess fell heavily and slid into an icy stream. She was four months pregnant, and Diana, concerned about her friend, sat with her until she recovered. This minor accident may have saved Sarah from death or serious injury. An expert skier, she normally went out with Prince Charles and their guide Bruno Sprecher.

Later that day, the avalanche which killed Major Hugh Lindsay and seriously injured Patty Palmer-Tomkinson thundered down the Gotchnagrat mountain.

Next morning, the Duchess and the Princess, both dressed in black, joined Prince Charles to escort Major Lindsay's coffin on its long journey home.

Diana refused to return to Klosters afterwards, claiming that to do so would stir up heartbreaking memories for Hugh's widow. The Duchess disagreed. Like Prince Charles and the Palmer-Tomkinsons, she believed that Hugh Lindsay would have wanted them to go back to the place where they had all been so happy together. As Patty Palmer-Tomkinson explained, after her long recovery: 'In Klosters they understand about death in the mountains. My father-in-law was killed there, yet we go back. I know Hugh would have wanted us to return.'

The two friends continued to take their children swimming when on holiday together at Balmoral and Sandringham. And the little York sisters were still top of the guest list when Prince William and Prince Harry had birthday parties. Then slowly the sisters-in-law began to drift apart. The coolness between them by the end of 1989 is evident in the 'Squidgy' tape recording.

In a recorded conversation with her friend James Gilbey the Princess referred to Sarah as 'the redhead' and spoke disparagingly about her.

Around that time, the Duchess was the chief target of the tabloid royal watchers. Attacks on her weight, her wardrobe, her holidays and her apparent neglect of her baby daughter Beatrice filled endless column inches. Her husband was not sympathetic when she told him of her woes, and by the end of 1991 Sarah could stand life in the Royal Family no longer.

When she finally walked out on Andrew, she was on the verge of a nervous breakdown. Friends who visited her at Sunninghill Park sadly noted that her normal sparkle was missing. She did not make up her face or bother much about what she wore.

Fun-loving Fergie, the girl who had seemed a breath of fresh air within the stuffy world at court, had disappeared. The Queen and the Duke of Edinburgh had summoned her to Sandringham and read her the riot act.

Princess Diana sat back, watching what happened to her sister-in-law; she vowed she would not endure the same ordeal when she parted from Prince Charles.

For a brief period after her separation from Andrew, Sarah relished her new freedom, She stayed on good terms with her husband, who was anxious to win her back. They were frequently seen at local restaurants and London clubs. But when friends asked if a reconciliation was likely Fergie always said no with a sad shake of her head.

It seemed she had won a new dignity and respect when the Queen arranged for her to spend the August summer holiday at Balmoral. The estranged Duchess was even welcomed aboard the royal flight taking Prince Charles to Scotland. Then disaster struck.

Compromising photographs taken while she was in the south of France with her financial adviser John Bryan were published in Britain and on the Continent. Within days they were on sale around the world.

How could anyone be so unlucky? To be under her mother-in-law's roof when every magazine and newspaper throughout the world was running topless pictures of her frolicking by a pool with another man made her humiliation even harder to bear.

At the lowest point in her life, Sarah was in the enemy camp. Her only friend throughout the seven days she spent with the Royal Family at their Highland home was the Princess of Wales. She spent hours comforting and counselling Sarah.

At times the Duchess was so inconsolable that Prince Andrew had to call the local doctor to attend to his wife. Normally, the Duchess would drive into the nearby town of Ballater to go swimming at the Craigendarroch Hotel's pool with Diana and their children. But not once did Sarah venture outside the castle during that awful week.

When she flew back to London aboard a commercial flight, it seemed she would be banished for ever from the royal circle, although events proved otherwise.

Determined to be her own person, the Duchess refused to cave in under the pressure. With great personal courage, only a month later she attended a conference in Birmingham as patron of the Motor Neurone Disease Association. And the wave of affection that greeted her when she arrived reduced her to tears. In a speech to 500 delegates from all over Britain, Sarah explained that only days earlier she had visited a totally paralysed woman dying from the disease.

Her plight became clear to the Duchess as she explained that a wasp had flown in through a window and landed on her nose, but that she had been powerless to brush it away. 'Meeting her put all my problems into perspective,' Sarah said. 'It made me realize I had to carry on.'

Just a few weeks later, it was Diana's turn to undergo the agony of separation. Three weeks after Diana had phoned Fergie from Korea, Prime Minister John Major announced that the Prince and Princess of Wales were to part.

When the Royal Family gathered at Sandringham two weeks later to celebrate the Christmas holiday, Diana declined to join them. But the Duchess of York, to everyone's surprise, was invited to stay at Wood Farm on the Sandringham estate. No longer a member of the family, she was not welcome at the big house where her in-laws had taken up residence.

Sarah stayed at the remote farmhouse for the sake of her small daughters. To banish feelings of isolation, her mother Susan Barrantes and her sister Jane Makim were invited to stay with her.

The Duchess and her family did not go to Sandringham House for Christmas dinner, but Prince Andrew drove over to visit them on the morning of 25 December. He returned next day with Prince Charles and his sons William and Harry. Afterwards Sarah, her daughters, along with her mother and her sister, were invited to a Boxing Day lunch the Queen held in the royal shooting lodge at Flitcham Hill.

'Fergie is back in the royal fold,' the tabloids declared. But the reality was very different. Beneath the seasonal goodwill shown to the Duchess was a strong undercurrent of ill-feeling.

One man attached to the Royal Household told me later: 'It probably looked very civilized, but it was a hideous ordeal for Sarah. One or two senior members of the Royal Family almost reduced her to tears. They accused her of being in league with the Princess of Wales. They told her point blank they believed that she and Diana were conspiring to bring down the monarchy.'

The Princess of Wales was at Althorp, enjoying her first Christmas with her own family for eleven years. After the break-up of her marriage two weeks earlier, Diana did not relish the thought of another strained holiday with her husband's relatives. In her absence the Royals vented all their fury on Sarah. What should have been a relaxed reunion became a horror story. Although Andrew did his best to make amends, his wife was very distressed.

Only two years before, they had all celebrated the Christmas christening of her younger daughter, Princess Eugenie, at Sandringham. At a party after the church service champagne had flowed as they ate christening cake and posed for photographs for the family archives. Now she was a royal outcast, invited only so that her children could be with their royal relatives.

Sarah had planned to stay until the end of the week, but desperate to escape from her tormentors, she packed her bags and left three days early.

On 28 December the Duchess flew to Zurich with her daughters to start a skiing holiday at Klosters. She could no longer bear to spend another minute at the Queen's Norfolk estate.

Christmas 1992 will haunt her for the rest of her life, like a royal version of *Nightmare on Elm Street*.

CHAPTER FIFTEEN

Goodbye Camilla

Westminster Abbey was packed for the El Alamein Service held in October 1992 to mark the fiftieth anniversary of the famous battle in the north African desert. The Prince and Princess of Wales were due to arrive within moments, when suddenly down the aisle came a figure who sent a shocked murmur through the entire congregation.

Dressed all in black, Camilla Parker Bowles walked in and sat down in a pew close to the front. When Diana and Charles arrived, they could not fail to notice the woman who had haunted their marriage. Her name was not on the official guest list, but astonished reporters inside the Abbey soon learned that Mrs Parker Bowles had come to support her elderly father, Major Bruce Shand, who sat beside her proudly wearing one of the nation's highest honours, the Military Cross.

Princess Diana must have known the real reason Camilla had dared to show her face. It was the desperate act of a woman who had no other way to see her former lover.

In 1991, Prince Charles told Camilla Parker Bowles that their long-running love affair was over. He was making a last-ditch effort to save his crumbling marriage. His wife had threatened to walk out on him and he did not want his family to break up. But he found it very difficult to rid himself of the woman who had once meant so much to him. Distraught at losing the love of her life, Camilla tried repeatedly to revive his interest in her. She simply refused to be dumped.

Charles had no real wish to give Camilla up. No other woman had ever meant so much to him. But for once, the indecisive

Prince had made his mind up. Aware that his relationship with a married woman could ruin him if it became public, he refused to see her again.

It was only after months of silence from Charles that Camilla summoned up the courage to brave the stares and whispers of the assembled guests as she walked with head high down the nave of Westminster Abbey.

When the service ended, the Prince and Princess disappeared through a side door where their limousine was waiting to whisk them away. Camilla, by contrast, was left to the mercy of a crowd of photographers and reporters. They pursued her down the street, shouting questions as she searched for a taxi. When she finally found one an over-enthusiastic *Daily Mail* cameraman jumped into it with her. There was no police protection for a woman tossed aside by a Prince.

He had fallen for Camilla when he was twenty-three. She was dating one of his friends, Andrew Parker Bowles, an officer in the Blues and Royals. He found the witty, worldly blonde madly attractive and they struck up an instant rapport. She shared his love of hunting and the outdoor life. But the world's most eligible bachelor had a string of gorgeous girlfriends, and was not keen to get seriously involved with any of them. Even when his feelings for Camilla turned to love, he simply wouldn't propose. He felt he was far too young to settle down, and his career as a serving naval officer would take him away for long months at sea.

He used to say the right age to marry was around thirty, and that he did not want to let his heart rule his head. While he dithered, Camilla grew tired of waiting and soon announced her engagement to Andrew Parker Bowles. After her marriage, Camilla and the Prince continued to mix in the same circles, seeing each other at the polo and race meetings. Charles renewed his friendship with both Andrew and Camilla and was soon a regular visitor to their Wiltshire home.

When he was courting Lady Diana Spencer, she often stayed at Bolehyde Manor when Charles was camping out at Highgrove House, while the property was being renovated.

The Prince of Wales actually proposed to Diana in a cabbage patch on the Parker Bowleses' property. At the time there were rumours that Camilla had approved his choice before he popped the question. Even then, her influence over the Prince of Wales was widely recognized.

But an almost forgotten incident in 1980 suggests that he never quite broke the bond with Camilla. On a visit to the West Country, he spent the nights of 5 and 6 November aboard the royal train, parked in a siding near Holt in Wiltshire. The *Sunday Mirror* learned this, and published a story alleging that Lady Diana Spencer had driven down from London on 5 November to stay with Charles until the early hours. The story 'DI'S LOVE DATES ON ROYAL TRAIN' contained unmistakable innuendos. But both Buckingham Palace and Diana strenuously denied that she had ever been on the train.

The Queen's press officer Michael Shea wrote to the *Sunday Mirror* demanding a retraction. The letter said:

Prince Charles was on the royal train on the nights in question. On the first occasion he had three guests on board: the secretary of the Duchy of Cornwall, his successor and the local land steward, and they were discussing the Duchy of Cornwall estate.

On the other occasion the train stopped there between 2.00 and 5.00 in the morning and there was no question of anyone coming aboard. It was quite absurd to suggest that anyone be smuggled aboard.

This vehement denial from Buckingham Palace certainly convinced me that Lady Diana Spencer was not the Prince's visitor. But it did not convince the editor of the *Sunday Mirror*, Bob Edwards. He had a police source who had told him that a blonde woman did board the train on the night of 5–6 November.

Another possible solution to the mystery has been discussed by royal watchers for years. Camilla Parker Bowles then lived at Bolehyde Manor, near Chippenham, Wiltshire, less than

189

twenty miles from the siding where the royal train had stopped overnight. She could easily have driven over to see Charles and then spent several hours in his company. I have since learned that this is what Lady Diana Spencer suspected when she read the *Sunday Mirror* story. She knew that she had not been on the train, and realized that there was only one other woman who it could possibly have been: her arch-rival for the Prince's affections. This is the reason she angrily demanded that the Buckingham Palace press office should clear her name.

Two days before before Prince Charles married Diana in July 1981, he left his fiancee at Buckingham Palace, where she was lunching with her sisters, to visit Camilla. He had bought a gift specially for her. It was a gold chain bracelet with a blue enamel disc bearing the initials 'F' and 'G' intertwined.

When it arrived at the Palace, Diana opened the parcel meant for Camilla, thinking it was one of her wedding presents. She was outraged and ran sobbing from the room. Later, she told friends that the Prince had ordered it as a memento for the older woman. The initials 'F' and 'G' stood for Gladys and Fred, Diana claimed, and were the jokey endearments which Camilla and Charles used for each other. But a senior member of the Prince's staff denied this. He told writer Penny Junor that the Princess did indeed find a bracelet Prince Charles had bought for Camilla. But the initials on it represented Girl Friday, the Prince's favourite name for the woman he regarded as a special friend. Unfortunately, when this was made public in 1992 few people believed the glib explanation.

Charles and Diana's marriage was in trouble almost from the start. By the time the 'Dianagate' and 'Camillagate' tapes were recorded, it was over in all but name. And after Diana betrayed Charles by revealing every sordid detail to Andrew Morton through her friends, the Prince's supporters were desperate to defend him.

He begged them not to say a word. Charles believed his wife was mentally disturbed. He had consulted medical experts about her bulimia and felt she was not responsible for her actions.

Despite threats that he would never speak to them again, several members of the Highgrove Set could not resist speaking out when approached by journalists.

One woman, burning with outrage, spoke out in the strongest terms. 'The Princess of Wales is a megalomaniac,' she said. 'Her behaviour is endangering the future of her marriage, the monarchy and the country itself. She is clinically mad and I wouldn't be surprised if she did commit suicide because she really does need treatment.'

Still indignant, she added: 'People must question the Princess of Wales's motives and her actions. Why has she done this? Can she really claim to be a loving mother and caring person if she goes to these lengths to damage her husband?'

The woman's husband joined in the defence of the Prince. 'It is not in Prince Charles's nature to answer back. He has not been brought up like that. There was always a huge intellectual gap between the two of them and it will now never be healed.

'The Prince has worked hard at the relationship because he thought they could grow together, but that never happened. They grew apart. She wanted to take over. She wants to be the Princess of Wales without the Prince of Wales. She is convinced she is the one thing propping up the monarchy.'

He went on: 'It is no coincidence that we see lovely family photographs of the Princess with her boys at Alton Towers and Thorpe Park. How do the pictures happen to be taken? The answer is simple. It is common knowledge that many of the tip-offs to photographers come from those closest to the Princess herself. This is all part of her campaign to cultivate her image as a royal superstar in her own right. She wants to be the top of the pile. She wants to be seen as the greatest woman in the world.

'Prince Charles may take the children to school, but you won't see a picture of it because that is not his style, and never has been. She is a manipulative and scheming woman. He has tried hard to make their marriage work, but she has given up.'

Obsessed by Camilla Parker Bowles, the middle-aged woman she believed had stolen her husband, Diana's bitterness knew

191

no bounds. She was the most adored woman in the world, but her husband was in love with someone else. Feeling humiliated and rejected, she constantly exploded with rage.

Prince Charles's friends would listen for hours as he sadly related the latest hysterical scene his wife had staged. He also consulted Dr Allan McGlashan, one of London's top psychotherapists. Charles has visited his Sloane Street office for at least six years, arriving around six o'clock in the evening when other patients have long gone and his arrival is unlikely to be noticed.

When he visited the doctor Charles's mind was in turmoil. He did not want his marriage to end, but he could not live with his wife. Dr McGlashan helped him to cope. But it was to Camilla that the Prince of Wales turned when he wanted a woman's advice and comfort. They discussed how he should deal with the Princess's eating disorder, and her irrational behaviour.

In spring 1992, while covering the State Opening of Parliament, I bumped into an old friend and former employee of the Princess of Wales. We discussed the recent unhappy tour of India by Charles and Diana, and wondered how long their marriage could last.

My friend said sadly: 'The problem was Camilla. It was always Camilla. Forget all the others, Kanga and the rest; they didn't mean a thing. Camilla was the only woman he loved.'

He went on to explain that the Prince had ended the affair almost a year earlier. 'It's over now. They don't see each other any more,' he confided. Then he added: 'I should point out there is fault on both sides. The Princess has had her moments.'

Two months later, everyone knew the truth about the Waleses' marriage when Andrew Morton published *Diana, Her True Story*. Camilla disappeared from her Wiltshire home for many weeks, lending credibility to all the allegations. But in late summer, just when the scandal was dying down, an even bigger bombshell exploded. A newspaper came into possession of a tape-recording of a phonecall between the Prince of Wales and Mrs Parker Bowles. Although it didn't publish a full transcript, details of the intimate nature of their conversation did emerge. Once again, Camilla went to ground to escape the hot pursuit of the press. In January 1993, the 'Camillagate Tape' was finally published in all its explicit detail. Apart from its unambiguously sexual content, the tape was noteworthy for revealing that Charles and Camilla shared a very real and deep love. Just a snippet of their taped conversation indicates the strength of their feelings for each other.

CHARLES: I'm so proud of you.
CAMILLA: Don't be so silly. I've never achieved anything.
CHARLES: Yes, you have.
CAMILLA: No, I haven't.
CHARLES: Your great achievement is to love me.
CAMILLA: Oh darling, easier than falling off a chair.
CHARLES: You suffer all these indignities and tortures and calumnies.
CAMILLA: Oh, darling, don't be so silly. I'd suffer anything for you. That's love. It's the strength of love. Night, night.

The Prince was referring to recurring newspaper reports over many years linking him with Mrs Parker Bowles. When he shattered his right arm in a polo accident in 1990, she was a frequent visitor to Highgrove. And a former policeman who worked there told the *News of the World* that, while patrolling the grounds, he once looked through a window and saw Charles and Camilla canoodling on the floor behind a sofa.

Throughout this period, Camilla continued to deny that her relationship with Charles was anything other than friendship. When pressmen caught up with her, she once said: 'The allegations are a load of utter and complete nonsense. I obviously can't talk about my friendship with the Prince.'

Her loyalty to the man she loved for so long has cost her dear. If her name had been Smith, Jones or Brown it might have been easier to hide from the fierce glare of publicity the tape generated. But while she remains Mrs Parker Bowles she will forever be remembered as the Prince of Wales's mistress, in the same way that her great-grandmother Alice Keppel has gone down in history as King Edward VII's lover.

Charles's liaison with Camilla was undoubtedly the most ful-filling, but also the most damaging, of his life. It may still one day cost him his throne.

The Prince of Wales is cocooned in his privileged world, protected from the press and the curious public by an army of servants and police. He is also shielded from an unwanted lover.

Having no way to break through the wall of silence that developed between them after he ended the affair, Camilla went to Westminster Abbey. Her motive was undoubtedly a longing to see Charles again, and also to have him see her. It was unwise but understandable.

Soon after the 'Camillagate Tape' was published in full, the Queen summoned Andrew Parker Bowles to Sandringham, in Norfolk, where she was staying with Prince Philip and Prince Charles.

The meeting between the Prince of Wales and the wronged husband was hideously embarrassing for them both. But, trained to contain their emotions, both men tried to make the confron-tation as painless as possible in their anxiety to work out a damage-limitation plan.

Everyone in the room conceded that the revelations of the 'Camillagate Tape' had placed them all in a highly difficult and humiliating situation.

After some delicate discussion, they arrived at a gentlemen's agreement. The Prince of Wales would never see Camilla again, and the Parker Bowleses would say nothing and keep a low profile.

Brigadier Parker Bowles is director of the Royal Army Veterinary Corps, and his work brings him into occasional contact with members of the Royal Family. He is a professional soldier and an honourable man, who has kept a stiff upper lip and stood by his wife throughout the scandal. His loyalty to the Crown and devotion to his family mean he will continue to do the decent thing.

His wife's family agree that keeping quiet is the only way to deal with their problem. Her father, Major Bruce Shand, said: 'I think in the circumstances it is best that we keep our traps

194

shut. Silence is a lot more dignified, and I think that in this case, the old adage that silence is golden is the right course. I think most other real friends would agree.'

After her conversation with the Prince was published, Camilla received hundreds of hate letters, branding her a marriage-wrecker. But until that time she had toyed with the idea of speaking out to clear her name from what she described as 'a tissue of lies'.

She said: 'We are getting to the stage where the Sellotape is going to have to be taken off the mouths.' She patronizingly branded Diana 'a silly girl, who was not in the best of health'. After January 1993, Prince Charles acknowledged that to be seen with Camilla Parker Bowles once again would finally wreck any chance of his ascending the throne.

Even if it leaked out that he had written to, or telephoned her, he would be finished. The British people would not give him a second chance.

He became very much aware of this on one of the first public engagements he carried out in London after the 'Camillagate Tape' was general knowledge. On a walkabout in east London, an elderly ex-serviceman called out: 'Have you no shame, Charles!' I watched as the smile vanished from the Prince's face, and he hastily climbed into his car and left.

Communications experts reckoned that only a national-security organization like MI5 or Special Branch would have had the sophisticated technology capable of producing the 'Camillagate Tape'.

No one else, they claim, could have obtained such a clear recording of both ends of a phonecall. Later, backing up this theory, evidence emerged that the tape had been altered or rebroadcast after the phonecall was made. During it, Camilla referred to her son Tom's birthday party being held 'tomorrow'. His birthday is 18 December, the day the call was recorded. For this reason GCHQ, the Government's ultra-secret listening post near Cheltenham, was also suspected of involvement.

As soon as the 'Camillagate Tape' was widely distributed, calls for an enquiry began. Buckingham Palace refused to make any comment, hoping the furore would quickly die down. And for some days the Prince's personal staff wondered if an impersonator was the male voice on the tape. His valet, Michael Fawcett, is renowned for mimicking his boss perfectly. He sounds so grand that he has been nicknamed 'Prince Michael of Kensington' by his fellow workers. And Princess Diana has been known to comment: 'Michael has twice as many clothes as I have.'

If his valet could fool people into thinking he was the Prince of Wales, so could someone else. Both the Prince and the Royal Household thought there was no real evidence that Charles and Diana were the people recorded on the sensational tapes. But times, dates and names on each one convinced the world that the Royals had really been caught unawares.

The 'Dianagate Tape' not only blew the lid off the Princess's friendship with bachelor James Gilbey, it proved that someone had bugged her personal handset. Originally, most people believed that Cyril Reenan, a keen radio ham, had recorded the call accidentally with a scanner.

They accepted that while sweeping the airwaves he had come across James Gilbey using a mobile phone to talk to Princess Diana. This forced Cellnet, a mobile-phone company, to investigate. They found that the Princess was the victim of electronic eavesdropping on her landline phone, not on Gilbey's car phone. Their enquiry proved that no scanner could have obtained such a clear, balanced recording of her call. For the same reason, I now believe that Camilla Parker Bowles's home telephone was tapped, and not Prince Charles's mobile phone.

Adding to the confusion was a tape-recording of the Duke and Duchess of York. This was made within days of the other Charles and Diana tapes. The content was not as sensational as the others', but it clearly showed how unhappy the Duchess had become in her marriage. It uncovered her yearning to escape from the pressure of life at court and flee to her mother in Argentina. When this recording was made, the Duke of York was speaking to his wife using a mobile phone aboard his ship HMS *Campbelltown*.

The odds against accidentally recording three different royal telephone calls on three separate occasions are beyond calculation. The inevitable conclusion must be that someone was bugging the Royals.

Some top advisers to the Queen believe the buggers were attempting to destabilize the monarchy. They believe that a sinister right-wing group planned to discredit the Windsors. Their hope was that Britain would move closer to a Federal Europe if the monarchy lost its popularity. If a United States of Europe became a reality, its head of state would outrank the Queen and wield more influence on the world stage.

The security services were anxious to clear their name, and constantly asked Buckingham Palace if they wanted an official investigation into the royal phone taps. The answer was always no. A top Scotland Yard contact told me: 'Prince Charles knew that if he requested an enquiry it would confirm what the world already suspected. The tapes really were genuine.'

Later, a government investigation cleared the security services, so the plotters behind the tapes that rocked the throne have gone undetected. Investigators are positive that whoever recorded the Royals must have dozens of similar tapes of their private conversations. If so, where are they? And when will they suddenly surface?

Prince Charles has had his home swept by a surveillance team and scramblers have been fitted to all his phones. But all this caution has come far too late. The Royal Family may not be able to survive another major scandal.

CHAPTER SIXTEEN

The Fall and Rise of Fergie

The picture I cherish most of all is one taken not by me, but by Inspector Brian Ford of the Metropolitan Police. It is a snap of the Duchess of York dancing with me in an Alpine restaurant.

In January 1992, the Rat Pack was at Klosters, covering Sarah's first holiday in the Alps with both her little daughters, Beatrice and Eugenie. We had done a deal with the Duchess which involved three separate photo calls with the little girls, and our newspapers were all 'Fergied out'.

Princess Beatrice, then aged three, had arrived in the last stages of chicken pox, so we had stayed on in the resort just in case her sister, eighteenth-month-old Princess Eugenie, caught the illness.

Towards the end of the week we all went out to dinner in a restaurant called the Hohwald, which every Wednesday night has an oompah band. We were tucking in to our second course when in walked Fergie and her staff.

She was looking very glamorous in a flimsy black checked chiffon blouse and black trousers beneath a sheepskin coat. As she walked past my table I looked up and said: 'Are you harassing me?'

She laughed, and raised her hands to her eyes as though peering through a camera.

Half an hour later, the band began to play and the Duchess got up to dance with her ski guide Bruno Sprecher. It suddenly dawned on me that this could be a night to remember, and I turned to Ruki Sayeed, the *Sun* reporter accompanying me, who is a sharp little operator, and asked her to keep her eyes open.

199

By this time Sarah had finished her first dance, a sedate waltz, and was standing chatting to her pals. The band launched into a fast quickstep, so I got up and caught her eye. With a nod in the direction of the dancefloor she said: 'How about it, Arthur? Come on, let's boogie.'

Before I knew it, my arm was around her waist and we were twirling around the floor. I couldn't believe I was dancing with the Duchess of York. It was something I never dreamed would ever be possible. If my old mum Dolly had only lived to see this day, I thought. She would have bored everyone to death in every bingo hall in east London about it.

Sarah has a fantastic sense of rhythm and is a great little mover. I was really glad I had been forced to take ballroom-dancing lessons when I was a lad at school in Stepney. As the band speeded up, we danced faster and faster and everyone in the room was cheering us on.

Without stopping for a breather, the musicians went straight into another number at the same fast pace. All I can remember in the breathless bopping around the room was how slim Sarah had become. 'You're looking very fit, ma'am,' I said.

She laughed and replied: 'Yes, but you've tired me out.'

We must have been on our feet for fifteen minutes, and one of the numbers the band played was 'I Could Have Danced All Night'. It certainly summed up my feelings that evening. After I escorted Sarah back to her table, her policeman came over to me and said: 'The Duchess says if you ask her to dance again I can take a photograph of you both.'

Half an hour later, I went over to her and asked for the next dance. She jumped up and we were off again. Spinning around the room with such a good partner took me back to my youth at the Ilford Palais. I swear I dropped thirty years in three minutes each time I danced with the Duchess. It was a lot of fun. And, as he had promised, Brian Ford clicked away with a camera he had borrowed from royal nanny Alison Wardley.

When our dance ended, the Duchess and her friends said goodnight and headed off to the Walserhof Hotel, where they were staying. Fergie is no snob. That evening she danced not just with me, but with several other diners in the restaurant. When she joined in changing partners in a Paul Jones routine, she whirled around the room with a ski-lift attendant and a postman, among others.

I have always been extremely fond of Fergie. When people ask me to name my favourite member of the Royal Family I always reply without any hesitation: 'The Duchess of York!' My philosophy is 'speak as you find', and she has always been wonderful to me. She makes it so easy to get a great picture. But it's not just her kind heart and willingness to help cameramen that make me like her.

I believe the old guard at Buckingham Palace crucified Sarah when she would not conform to their way of doing things. She promised when she married into the Royal Family that it wouldn't change her, and it never did. Unfortunately, Sarah's independent spirit, which at first endeared her to the Queen and the Royal Household, finally made them turn against her. She is totally honest, but sometimes astonishingly naïve. To be so genuine is praiseworthy to some, but foolhardy to others. And it is fatal when pitted against the might of the monarchy.

Sarah is highly intelligent, too bright to endure the sexism and antiquated attitudes of palace disciplinarians, who often referred to her in the most patronizing terms. 'What does she know, she's only a gel,' a charity worker once overheard a private secretary observe. Such comments really infuriated Fergie when they were reported back to her. Instead of responding with a witty putdown, she would lose her temper like a typical redhead. This, of course, antagonized her opponents even more. And when she turned to her husband for support, he lacked the clout to defend her.

It may be hard to believe, but people like the Prince of Wales and the Duke of York have very limited power. They are locked into an outdated system which regards the survival of Britain's ruling family as paramount. The people who really pull the strings at the Palace are the Queen's top advisers. And they have no mercy when they believe the Crown is threatened.

Anyone who rocks the boat gets tossed overboard. And that is exactly what happened to Sarah. This point was rammed home when I heard the Duchess had been stripped of full-time protection by Scotland Yard after her separation. Prince Andrew was livid, and went to protest in person to the Royal Protection Squad. Their pathetic reply was that separated spouses don't qualify for protection. One senior police officer explained: 'The Princess Royal's ex-husband Mark Phillips doesn't have bodyguards, so we can't provide them for the Duchess.'

Andrew slammed his fist down on the table and shouted: 'Yes, but he was a bloody soldier, I'm talking about a defenceless woman!'

All his protests were in vain. The Duchess now gets police protection only when out with her children or when carrying out engagements which have been publicized in advance.

When told about the Duke's intervention on her behalf, Sarah was touched by his concern. But realizing where the real authority lay, she said sadly: 'I'm afraid the power to change things is on a level way above his head.'

As a Windsor wife, she was denied any control over her own life. She once graphically summed up her situation as totally Victorian. She was not allowed to make decisions for herself, and denied the freedom to go wherever she liked without first gaining permission. The Queen's aides hoped to force her into the background. Their long-term plan was that she would eventually resemble the sweet, silent Duchesses of Kent and Gloucester, rarely seen and even more rarely heard.

Extroverted Sarah just could not fit into that mould. During the last days of her marriage, she confided to a friend that she felt 'trapped in a Grimm brothers nightmare'. From my experience mixing with the Royal Household over many years I can sympathize with her plight. The knives really were out for Fergie, just as the BBC radio reporter Paul Reynolds revealed on the day her split from the Duke was announced. But she has fought to retain her own identity. And I respect the way she has refused to let the Palace machine crush her spirit.

The rest of the Rat Pack take the mickey out of me mercilessly because of my affection for her. They say: 'How is your lovely Duchess, today, Arthur?' and then they make disparaging remarks about her to wind me up. Often they succeed, and we all end up laughing together. I like the fact that Sarah has stayed loyal to her family through their troubled times. She realizes that her father, Major Ronald Ferguson, and her sister, Jane Makim, have suffered press invasions into their private lives only because she is the Queen's daughter-in-law.

If she had not married Prince Andrew, the Ferguson family scandals would not have hit the headlines. Although they basked in the reflected glory of her royal position, the price they have paid for it is extremely high.

The photographers who pursue her admit that Fergie never lets them down when it matters. On a tour of Australia in 1990, a scuffle broke out at the airport in Broken Hill, New South Wales, between British cameramen and the local police. Mike Lawn of the *Today* newspaper was arrested and hauled off in a police car to the local nick. As she boarded her plane to fly back to Sydney, Fergie spotted him being dragged away and called to me: 'Arthur, what's going on?'

When I told her, she sent her Scotland Yard bodyguard Inspector Brian Baston to intercede on Mike's behalf. It was unprecedented for the tough Aussie cops in this outback city to back down, but a few hours later Mike was released without charges thanks to Her Loveliness.

She stepped in again to help us on a private visit to Warsaw in 1992. When her over-zealous Polish minders blocked photographers taking pictures on her arrival, she later scolded them. 'Don't ever do that again,' she ordered. 'That's not the way I work.'

Sarah never walks out of a building with head down to foil the photographers the way the Princess of Wales sometimes does. No matter how unhappy she may feel, or how badly mauled she has been by the media, she never lets it show.

Even at the lowest point in her life, when topless pictures taken with her financial adviser in St Tropez appeared in the press, she held her head high as she arrived back in London.

No member of the Royal Family has ever been pilloried so cruelly for so long. From the day she married her Prince, up until the present, she has been continually attacked. Yet most of the editors and bitchy women columnists who pour vitriol about the Duchess down their readers' throats have never met her. Their comments are based only on what they have read in newspaper reports.

I know another Fergie, a much misunderstood woman who cries when she reads distorted stories about her in the press. On an official trip to France in 1990, she bumped into a reporter whose byline had been published with many stories viciously attacking Sarah over several months. She gamely tackled him about this.

'Why do you write these awful stories about me?' she asked.

'What I write and what appears in my paper are two totally different matters,' he explained. 'Everything I do is changed and there is nothing I can do about it.' This was the chief reason he left the newspaper soon afterwards.

The Duchess of York does a lot of work with people who are the most vulnerable in our society and don't always make pretty pictures for the newspapers. I have seen her make amazing contact with brain-injured children, and give dying men and women the will to live longer than any doctor expected. She even wrote to a friend of mine who was gravely ill with cancer. Her letter gave him a massive boost. It made him feel that he was still someone who mattered, and his will to live grew stronger.

But her work for motor neurone disease (MND) sufferers is now legendary. This horrific illness, known in the United States as Lou Gehrig's disease, paralyses the body but leaves the mind unaffected. Unable to move a muscle, victims of MND become prisoners in their own useless frames.

I'll never forget the day she visited a clinic for sufferers in Sydney, Australia. As she moved around the room chatting to patients and their families, one man of Italian origin burst into tears when she stopped beside him. His wife explained that he desperately wanted to talk to the Duchess, and was so frustrated at being robbed of his voice, that he couldn't stop crying.

Sarah sat down and held his hand. 'I know how you feel,' she said. 'Don't worry, I'll be your voice. I'll do your talking for you. And I'll go on shouting about motor neurone disease until we find a cure. So you mustn't give up. You've got to hang on.'

Her comforting words came straight from her heart. And every hard-bitten hack covering her visit was moved by the scene. A Sydney TV reporter, his eyes filling with tears, commented: 'That was amazing, but I can't possibly put these pictures out on the evening news. They are far too upsetting.'

The Director of the Motor Neurone Disease Association, Peter Cardy, has since told me that the Duchess has vowed to be the voice of all the silent sufferers of this wasting illness around the world. She is in every sense their spokeswoman. She speaks up for the people who can no longer speak for themselves.

I don't believe Sarah gets the credit she deserves for her fund-raising on their behalf. In one afternoon in Geneva I saw her generate more than £100,000 for the charity's coffers.

Sadly, her good deeds are always overshadowed by damaging stories for which she is often not to blame. A great example of this came in Florida while she was visiting Palm Beach in January 1992.

The Duchess attended a dinner in aid of motor neurone disease victims at the Everglades Club, an exclusive country club. British embassy officials, who checked out the venue, failed to discover that the Everglades did not admit Jews, Catholics or Blacks. American journalists pounced on this titbit of information with glee and used it to attack Sarah. They accused her of having a high old time at a place which discriminated against minorities. Although she had nothing to do with selecting the club, she carried the can.

Of course, Sarah has her faults. Her time-keeping used to be appalling. She would keep statesmen, bankers and friends waiting up to an hour for her arrival. She was once booed in a London theatre for walking in after the first act had started. And in October 1991 a British Airways jet was kept waiting for three hours at Los Angeles Airport while the Duchess went shopping in Rodeo Drive. Surprisingly, she has always managed to get her daughters to school on time. And since she no longer does royal duties, her punctuality has improved out of all recognition.

The number of holidays she takes also attracts unfavourable comment. Some of this is justified. But very rarely is there a good word to say about Prince Andrew's wife.

Press pundits called her heartless when she left her newborn baby Beatrice to accompany the Duke to the 1988 Bicentennial celebrations in Australia. And when she extended her stay for two more weeks, they screeched that she was a disgrace to motherhood. But her intentions were totally misconstrued. She simply felt her husband, who had been away at sea for six months, needed her more than her baby did at that point.

In fact, the Duke of York had insisted that she leave her baby behind because after months away from home he wanted his wife all to himself. And as Fergie told me later: 'My husband needs me just as much as my child. Beatrice doesn't know if I'm with her or over here. Of course, I miss her, but she is in safe hands and I'll be home soon.'

Time has proved that Princess Beatrice suffered no ill-effects whatsoever from the separation and could not be more devoted to her mother.

Worst of all were the attacks on Sarah's weight and her wardrobe. Inevitably, she was compared with her sister-in-law, Diana, everyone's idea of the perfect Princess, adored for her fashions and her model-girl figure. Sarah's father Ronald Ferguson was quick to jump to her defence when columnists dubbed his daughter 'Frumpy Fergie'. He once told me: 'She is not the same shape as Diana, so why do they compare them?'

The Duchess did not suffer from any eating disorder like bulimia to help keep her weight down. By sheer determination and a strict regime of exercise and dieting she whittled away the extra inches.

While this barrage of bad publicity continued, Sarah had absolutely no guidance or support from Buckingham Palace. She once told a friend: 'The only advice they have ever given me is to wave more slowly.'

Her husband was away at sea for long stretches, and when he came home he failed to understand her distress. As a blood Royal, he was shown far more respect by the Queen's aides.

One particular year, 1988, was so stressful that any normal person would have cracked up completely. Sarah was expecting her first baby when she underwent a series of personal traumas. A close friend died in a skiing accident while they were on holiday together in Switzerland. Her father attracted embarrassing publicity concerning his visits to a massage parlour. Her sister's marriage began to break up acrimoniously. She was in a traffic accident on the M4 motorway. And her figure ballooned as a result of her pregnancy until she was three stone heavier.

To add to her troubles, she was dispatched on a tour of California when she was still suffering from morning sickness. She put on a brave face and threw herself into making the trip a success. But the press found fault with her outrageous fashions and effusive manner.

The Duke of York did little to help her through these difficult months. He returned home from sea just days before their first child was born, and made some extraordinary demands on her. He was determined that press photographers camped outside Castlewood House, their rented home in Egham, Surrey, would not catch them when Sarah went to hospital, so only hours before the baby arrived, he smuggled her out in the most unregal manner. He insisted she should walk through a small wood and climb over a fence to a car waiting in Windsor Park. He forced his wife to undergo all this additional stress and effort just to avoid a few cameramen.

When Prince Andrew was in one of his foul tempers, his wife found it easier to give in than to argue with him. I remember asking them both to pose for me while they were visiting a vineyard near Bordeaux in 1987. The Duchess took one look at the scowl on her husband's face and said: 'I will, but he won't.'

Her readiness to do whatever Andrew asked indicates just how much she tried to make her marriage work. She even went along with his much-ridiculed design for their first real home, Sunninghill Park. The American-style red-brick mansion, described as a cross between a Tesco supermarket and a Little Chef restaurant, was immediately dubbed SouthYork. No other royal couple had ever built a brand-new home, and this one seemed more like 'Dallas' than a palace.

The whole project, estimated to have cost £5 million, was planned by Prince Andrew and that was fine by her. Covering her official engagements and tours, I got the distinct impression that Andrew set the agenda and she was happy to follow it. More than anything, she wanted his family to accept her. So she tried carriage-driving to impress her father-in-law, the Duke of Edinburgh. And she went out riding with the Queen at every opportunity, something Diana attempted only once or twice. Sarah threw herself into supporting Prince Edward at his 'It's a Royal Knockout' television show for charity at Alton Towers. Sadly, her exuberance and wholehearted determination to make the day a success attracted only criticism.

She is just as generous to Palace staff. When the Queen's press secretary Michael Shea left his job in 1987, the whole Royal Family was invited to his farewell party. Fergie was the only one who bothered to turn up.

She gained her pilot's wings so she could share her husband's love of flying, and dared to try any black run on ski trips with Prince Charles.

I remember a tour of Mauritius by Andrew and Sarah in 1987. When the official part of the visit was over, the Yorks stayed on for a short holiday at the luxurious Hotel La Tousseroc. The royal suite had its own private beach, jetskis, waterskis, snorkelling, windsurfing and even private his and hers loos were provided on the sand.

But the Duke of York just wanted to stay inside the hotel, watching videos and resting. His wife, who loves swimming, sunbathing and all sports, dutifully kept him company. It couldn't have been much fun for her, but Andrew was determined not to come out to play.

Frustrated by not having one picture published on the entire tour, I devised a plan to make my feelings known to the lovely Duchess. With a few colleagues, I wrote a message on a bedsheet and cruised past her hotel balcony holding it aloft. It read: 'OK, Sarah, you win.'

The Mauritian police quickly sped over to our boat and confiscated our statement of surrender. But at a press party later that year I asked Prince Andrew if he had seen it. He laughed. 'Yes, we got your message,' he said. 'In fact, we used it as a tablecloth for our barbecue that night.'

I forgave the Yorks for robbing me of a picture because I knew that they had taken Prince Charles's press officer Vic Chapman and his wife Cecile on the trip. Vic, a lifelong smoker, was then in the last stages of lung cancer and could barely breathe. Fergie asked them to come on the royal holiday and paid all their expenses. Soon afterwards Vic, the best press officer who ever worked at Buckingham Palace, returned to his native Canada and died a few months later. Whenever the Duchess visits Ottawa, she always makes certain that Cecile Chapman is invited to any receptions she attends.

I am convinced that Prince Andrew's moody character contributed to the break-up of his marriage to Sarah. From a very early age, the Duke has been a pompous fellow. A matelot serving aboard the royal yacht *Britannia* in the late sixties was once assigned to keep an eye on the Queen's younger sons, Andrew and Edward, as they played on an upper deck. Concerned that the older boy might topple overboard, the sailor warned: 'Don't go too near that rail, laddie!' Andrew turned around with a pained look and rebuked the older man: 'I'm not a laddie, I'm a Prince.'

His shipmates and fellow officers in the Royal Navy have often complained about his arrogance and unpredictable nature. One of the men serving alongside him while he was training told me: 'He wants to be one of the lads one minute, and a Prince the next. The trouble is, you never know which one he is at that particular time.'

He may be a Prince, but at times he can also be a pain in the neck. I have never forgotten the way he sprayed paint over a group of us in 1982 on a visit to Watts, the notorious crime-ridden suburb of Los Angeles. He was on a building site watching painters at work when he picked up a paint-sprayer, tested it on the ground, then swung around and aimed it straight at us.

Luckily, I was in the back row and escaped, but many of my colleagues had their clothes and camera equipment ruined. The British embassy – that is, UK taxpayers – had to pay the compensation.

Afterwards, walking away while cursing photographers and television crews were dripping with paint, I overheard Andrew say to his hosts: 'I enjoyed that.' He halfheartedly apologized two days later.

Prince Andrew can't cope with criticism of himself or his family. While on manoeuvres in the Mediterranean, the ship he was serving on called in at Cyprus, and the Duke of York was invited to lunch in the Officers' Mess at RAF Akrotiri. In a polite attempt to meet as many people as possible he decided to eat each course at a different table. As the dessert was served, he was chatting to a young officer who had been on the base for some time. 'How do you get on with the Cypriots?' Andrew asked. Without a moment's hesitation, the airman replied: 'The Turkish Cyriots are very nice, but I just can't stand those bloody Greeks.' The Duke's smile disappeared as he snatched up his plate and moved quickly to the next table. The embarrassed officer suddenly remembered that Andrew's father was a Greek Prince and that the Duke of York had been named after his grandfather, Prince Andrew of Greece.

Fergie would have laughed her socks off at that thoughtless remark. But to her husband, slighting comments about his family, however amusing, are no laughing matter. When journalists quizzed him about his mother's reaction to the big fire at Windsor he was quick to remind them about the proper way to refer to the Queen. 'Her Majesty is shocked,' he said stiffly.

He was once known as Randy Andy, the royal ladykiller. When he came home from the Falklands conflict a war hero, he had the world at his feet. Within a few weeks, he went on holiday in the Caribbean with soft-porn starlet Koo Stark and had the world at his throat. But his playboy image did not reflect the real Prince. Andrew got all the thrills he wanted from his job as a Royal Navy officer and just wanted to fall down and relax when he got home.

The Yorks' relationship lost its magic just at the time when the Duchess was most in need of support and comfort. The Duke used to send his wife dozens of red roses on even the most minor anniversaries. He thought that was all he had to do.

A short conversation the Duchess had with the Duke came into my hands, and it sheds a fascinating light on the problems of life inside the Royal Family.

ANDREW: Are you feeling any better?

FERGIE: Yah. I'm just sort of disenchanted, really. I just want to run away and stay with Mum in Argentina. Got to get away from everything. I just feel, I want to run away, preferably with you, but I can't do that. We're both chained to our stupid duties and ruining our lives together. But if that's what your family want, then that's what they want. I've lost my spirit today. If they want to have another unhappy marriage, they're going the right way about it.

ANDREW: (*pleading*) But darling, what have they done to make you unhappy?

SARAH: Well, you've done it, haven't you? You've told them that we've had a discussion, a heated discussion.

ANDREW: I didn't say heated discussion.

SARAH: Well, you did. You told them that we were in opposition about something. You thought it was a bad idea, and just tell me if I'm going mad or not. That's what you probably said to her. Anyway, never mind, forget about it. Speak to you later, OK, because it's now ten to nine. I've got to get on and you have too.

ANDREW: All right, darling.

SARAH: OK?

ANDREW: Yes, darling.

SARAH: OK.

ANDREW: I love you.

SARAH: All right, be good today.
ANDREW: I love you, darling.
SARAH: I love you too.

This intimate, early-morning conversation could be that of any married couple, except that the four-letter word duty hangs like a menacing shadow over every royal marriage.

Andrew, the Queen's favourite son, saw everything he ever desired in a bride in Sarah Ferguson. But their relationship still failed because of the pressures on her.

All Sarah ever wanted was to be part of her own loving family. And no matter how much her husband implored her to 'keep trying', the mountain was truly unconquerable. The dilemma even tortured Andrew himself. For the first time, he could see the strange world that he was part of, and sided with his wife against his own family.

Never was his torment clearer than on the day he stood with his estranged wife at Ascot Gate in Windsor Great Park. He stood at Sarah's side, waving a white handkerchief as other members of his family rode in their carriages towards Royal Ascot. She had pleaded with him to accompany her, because the day before when she took her daughters to see the carriage procession a member of the royal entourage had openly insulted her. Sarah was terribly upset and when she told Andrew about the incident he vowed it would not happen again. That was the reason he briefly joined his wife as an outsider, looking at his family through her eyes.

His symbolic gesture did not go unnoticed, and to this day he would dearly love to win his wife back. But Fergie, although fond of Andrew, whom she calls 'my best friend', could never re-enter the world of the Windsors. She prefers life in the real world. As she said, when I sympathized after the break-up of her marriage: 'I'm just too much of a free spirit.'

The Duke is now slowly coming to terms with the end of his marriage, and is starting to date other women. The great Windsor fire sparked his romance with Cazzy Neville, the twenty-nine-year-old blonde who works as a loans officer for the royal collection of paintings. She was due to go to the Duke's home to change several paintings from the collection the day the fire broke out.

The Duke had politely invited her to stay for lunch, and her colleagues had teased her before she set off about the glint in Andrew's eye. But halfway through the morning, Andrew took a call from Windsor about the castle being on fire, and they both drove at high speed to Windsor.

They then spent the rest of the day helping with the massive clearing-up operation, turning a business relationship into a romantic one.

Late in the day, Prince Charles arrived to help and the two Princes invited a stunned Caroline back to Sunninghill Park for dinner. She was embarrassed about her scruffy appearance, but Prince Charles reassured her, and the cosy threesome spent the entire evening sitting and chatting.

Andrew then sent Cazzy a glass paperweight for her birthday with a letter saying how much he had enjoyed her company, and thanking her for her help in the clean-up operation.

Ironically, almost a year before, Cazzy had been invited to the house when Fergie had lived there, to help the couple select paintings from the collection for their bedroom. The Queen had given special permission for the paintings to be loaned.

It was not another man who broke up the Yorks' union, it was a lot of men, all the Queen's men, who drove her away from her husband.

When she showed too much thigh getting out of a car in New Jersey, there was a lot of tut-tutting inside the Royal Household. Her nervous smoking on occasion in public prompted even further criticism. But more damaging were the claims that she was using her position as a member of the Royal Family to make vast sums of money from books, TV appearances and magazine interviews.

Although she was a member of one of the world's richest families, throughout her marriage Sarah was constantly short of cash. Of the £250,000 the Yorks received from the Civil List, more than 80 per cent was eaten up by staff salaries, according to a House of Commons report. Other running costs sharply reduced what was left. Unfortunately, the public believed the whole amount went straight into Fergie's pocket. She was expected to look like a royal duchess on almost a pauper's budget. As a result she got steadily deeper and deeper in debt.

Desperate to have some money of her own, she wrote a series of children's books about Budgie the Little Helicopter, and a historical work called *Victoria and Albert, Life at Osborne House*. When she refused to donate all the royalties from these books to charity, she was called greedy and grasping. Royal aides reminded her that Prince Charles had been more generous. He had given all the proceeds from his children's storybook, *The Old Man of Lochna'gar*, and his best-selling book on architecture, *A Vision of Britain*, to worthy causes.

Sarah pointed out that her brother-in-law had an annual income of £3 million from the Duchy of Cornwall, while she herself was receiving demanding letters from her bank manager. This made no difference to the public, who were by then convinced that the Duchess of York was a royal gold-digger.

In the last year of her marriage, one newspaper calculated that the Yorks had spent only forty-seven days together. When Andrew did return home, he spent many of his off-duty hours playing golf. His other favourite way of relaxing was slumping down on a sofa to watch videos. Throughout 1991, Sarah became increasingly desperate to find a way out. At a dinner party in October of that year, she asked a friend who had just legally freed himself from his wife: 'I want a divorce too. How do you get one?'

As Fergie's follies got more and more flak from the media, the Queen's top advisers turned against her. By January 1992, almost ten weeks before the Yorks announced their separation, members of the Queen's staff were openly stating that the Duchess had become a liability.

Surrounded by character assassins on all sides, she realized she could not go on. The constant criticism and life in a goldfish bowl far outweighed the privileges of Palace life. The signs were there the night I danced with the Duchess. Even though her tormentors from the tabloids were sitting yards from her table, she lit up a cigarette. It was as if she was saying to them: 'Write whatever you like. I don't care any more.'

A few days later, I flew with her to Florida, where she was raising funds for motor neurone disease in West Palm Beach. This trip was reported as 'another freebie for Fergie' by her enemies in the press. Back in London, photographs had been found in a flat rented by her friend Steve Wyatt, a wealthy Texan, which showed them relaxing together. In retrospect, the pictures of them out riding and another of Wyatt with Princess Beatrice by a swimming pool look tame. Most of these snaps, which caused a sensation when published, were actually taken by the Duke of York, who knew all about his wife's friendship with the Wyatt family.

I have since learned that Steve Wyatt did not carelessly leave the pictures in his London flat. They were planted there to embarrass the Duchess and damage the Wyatts. But throughout the Florida trip, Sarah was plagued by pressmen scouring the bushes around her Palm Beach hideaway, hoping to spot her Texan friend. The strain clearly showed on her flight home from Florida. Sarah behaved very erratically and at one stage, under the beady gaze of the *Daily Express* royal reporter Ashley Walton, she defiantly covered her head with a paper bag.

A few days later, the Queen and Prince Philip summoned Sarah to Sandringham and coldly accused her of bringing the family into disrepute. One man who was at the estate that day said later: 'Here was a woman who was clearly falling apart in front of their eyes, but they showed no mercy. They were absolutely vicious, and didn't seem to care that she was on the verge of a breakdown.'

The Queen and her husband told their daughter-in-law that they wanted her to withdraw from the spotlight for a few years and re-emerge when the public had forgotten about her indiscretions.

Sarah interpreted this as a prison sentence. She would be locked away from the real world with no way out. She knew she could not carry on with this tortured existence, and so she decided to walk out on the Royal Family.

When she left Prince Andrew she was overdrawn at Coutts Bank by almost £1 million. In an effort to sort out her money worries she and the Duke called in American financial adviser John Bryan, who immediately worked out a way to cut costs and eliminate the overdraft completely. It wasn't surprising that she was impressed by his business acumen.

He understood that emergency action had to be taken to save her from cracking up completely. He quickly became her rock, as she knew of no other man who was willing to fight her corner and take on all comers.

When Fergie did a flit to Thailand and Bali with her children, carefully evading the press, I should have realized she was hiding something. For the first time in her royal life she didn't want to be photographed. The reason was that John Bryan was with her, and she didn't want the world to know how close she had become to the balding businessman from Delaware.

John Bryan has not managed to win many friends in Britain. His brash American manners did not impress snooty courtiers and cynical journalists. But he definitely endeared himself to the Duchess. He has a great sense of humour, and he could always make the Duchess forget her troubles with a joke. More importantly, when she was attacked, he fought back on her behalf. He continually berated editors who published inaccurate stories. And, in a French court, he successfully sued the photographer Daniel Angeli, whose damning pictures of the Duchess in the arms of Bryan did more to destroy her reputation than anything else.

Sarah has now created a new life for herself which revolves around her children. Any visitor to Romenda Lodge will testify that providing a secure and happy home for them is her top priority. The house is awash with photographs of the little Princesses. Snaps of them as babies in silver teddy-bear-shaped frames adorn her sitting room, huge pastel portraits of them hang on the walls above the sofa. And their laughing faces in large and small pictures cover the top of her desk, as well as every other flat surface.

Whenever she is invited to appear anywhere Sarah says: 'I only have Mondays to Fridays free. My weekends are sacrosanct. I save them for the girls.' It is then that she and her daughters get a taste of ordinary family life. The staff are off-duty, so Sarah cooks, vacuums the floors and goes shopping.

On a Saturday in spring 1993, she was spotted dashing into a supermarket near her Sunningdale home. She whirled around the cabinets with her trolley, grabbing – among other things – a packet mix for a chocolate fudge cake. 'It's for Beatrice,' she explained to a check-out girl. 'She wants to cook a Mother's Day cake for me, so we're going to spend the afternoon making a lovely mess in the kitchen.'

Her elder daughter has an outgoing personality, just like her mother's. A very confident and happy little girl, Beatrice has reddish hair like her mother and the same energetic manner.

Although it is a bit early to spot any ability she may have, Bea shows signs of being a talented artist. She loves painting and drawing. Her artistic creations are stuck up all over her home.

Her little sister, Eugenie, is a very affectionate and sweet-natured kid, utterly adored by the staff at Romenda Lodge. She is also a dead ringer for her dad. It is eerie to see Prince Andrew's features reproduced so clearly on his little daughter's face. When I visited Romenda Lodge I met the children's puppies, two West Highland terriers. These dogs have taken the place of the much-loved hound Bendicks, who stayed with the Duke at Sunninghill Park when the Yorks separated.

Romenda Lodge has floors covered with fitted cream wool carpet and beautiful pale rugs, which the puppies are doing their best to turn a shade of acid yellow. As a result, they are often banished to the garden. 'They are called Cutie and Deena, names that the girls dreamed up, not me,' Sarah said, rolling her eyes heavenwards.

Most of the money from her financial settlement, reported to be only £1.5 million, is earmarked for her children, leaving her very little to live on. This means she must pay her own bills in future. Spurred on by necessity, the Duchess is producing more books on various subjects and the cartoon version of *Budgie the Little Helicopter* is set to be televised in at least fifty different markets around the world.

This deal should enable her to live quite comfortably, and provide a certain amount of backing for her charity projects.

Disturbed by the plight of sick children whom she met in 1992 on a visit to an area of Poland known as the most polluted in Europe, Sarah decided to found her own charity. Children in Crisis was set up in spring 1993 specifically to care for the youngsters of 'yesterday's headlines'. Sarah has vowed not to let us forget the children who live in misery long after the disaster which wrecked their lives has disappeared from the front pages.

To cynics who claim she is using her charity work to restore her damaged reputation, she says simply: 'I can't sit around worrying about my image when children are dying.' Her quiet dedication to worthwhile organizations is slowly winning her recognition which is long overdue.

Despite her hard-won independence, Sarah will always live in the long shadow of the Crown. She will never really be free from the royal straitjacket. As the mother of two little Princesses, who are fifth and sixth in line of succession to the throne, she must seek the Queen's approval for almost every move she makes.

Whenever she wants to travel overseas, with or without her children, she must gain permission. Often it is not forthcoming. She was not allowed to visit hospitals and refugee camps in Bosnia and Croatia at the height of the former Yugoslavia's civil war. 'I cannot go; my hands are tied,' the Duchess me. The reason for this, I suspect, was that the Prince of Wales was scheduled to visit this war-torn country at the same time and Palace advisers did not want any publicity stolen from him.

In February 1993, Sarah was on holiday with her daughters at the Imperial Hotel in Torquay. Heavy rain had lashed the area for days, so she decided to return home earlier than planned. As she looked out at the grey skies one morning, Sarah began chatting to another guest at the hotel. 'I was planning to go to the West Indies this week, but the powers that be wouldn't let me,' she revealed. 'They said: "We don't want you flaunting yourself on a beach in a bikini like the Princess of Wales."'

The Duchess went on to explain she had already rented a holiday home and paid the deposit when Palace officials wrecked her plans. 'It didn't make any difference, they still wouldn't let me go,' she said sadly.

Such humiliations and restrictions will last as long as she has custody of two of the Queen's grandchildren. But Sarah believes that keeping her daughters with her is worth any sacrifice.

CHAPTER SEVENTEEN

Taxing Times

In all the years I have worked for newspapers, I never thought I would ever be the subject of a front-page story myself. But that is exactly what happened for the first time on Christmas Eve 1992. The double-decker headline on the *Sun* splash screamed out: 'QUEEN BANS OUR ARTHUR: Revenge for Royal speech story'.

This referred to the fact that I had been refused permission to photograph the Royal Family going to church on Christmas Day. Buckingham Palace had banned me in revenge for the *Sun*'s scoop in publishing her annual Christmas address to the nation two days earlier than scheduled.

John Kay, the newspaper's brilliant chief reporter, had got his hands on a copy of the speech the Queen was due to broadcast on television and radio on 25 December. Naturally, the editor published it immediately. It contained the Queen's thoughts on a year of turmoil, ending with the great fire at Windsor Castle, and made a great news story. Unfortunately, Buckingham Palace retaliated by taking away the rota pass I had been given to go to the royal church service on Christmas morning.

I was gutted when this occurred, because I had covered the previous ten Christmases with the Royal Family without any problems or complaints. But I was comforted by the fact that the ban was not personal, just a petty attempt to hit back at the *Sun*.

Instead of driving up to the Queen's estate, I headed for Northamptonshire, where Princess Diana was spending Christmas with her brother Earl Spencer and his family at their stately home Althorp. A week later, I went to cover another church service at Sandringham and met an ardent royal fan called Mary Relph. In a broad Norfolk accent she said: 'I don't know who was more missed up here on Christmas Day – you or the Princess of Wales.'

So many of my best brushes with the Royals have happened at Sandringham that you never know what surprises are in store when you get there. The Duke of Edinburgh, who is very keen on carriage-driving, was exercising his team of ponies one New Year's Day when snow was thick on the ground. I chanced my luck and as he drove by, and I yelled out: 'Happy New Year.'

He turned, looked down with a scowl from his lofty seat on his carriage, and said simply: 'Bollocks!'

His lack of festive spirit was not reserved just for me. Some hapless French hacks who turned up later and approached him got the same treatment in their own language. *'Vous êtes fous! Restez chez vous,'* he barked at them. Instead of being upset, they praised his Parisian accent.

Sandringham is the Queen's favourite home. She loves its seclusion and its glorious location, surrounded by pine woods and rolling farmlands bordering the Wash. She feels she can retreat there and not be on show. It is her own property, unlike Buckingham Palace and Windsor Castle, and she enjoys the peace and privacy of the estate.

So, when she sees her Scotland Yard bodyguards or the local Norfolk constabulary on patrol, it reminds her of the ever-present dangers she would rather forget.

As a result, at Sandringham she breaks one of the strictest security rules: she orders the police to stay out of her sight. In fact, they have been instructed to remain a quarter of a mile away from her when she goes out riding or strolls around the grounds. Risking her wrath, they ignore her demands and quietly stay on watch without her realizing it. They know that the Queen and her family must be safeguarded twenty-four hours a day whether she likes it or not.

But they were caught on the hop in January 1991, when a Range Rover driven by the Princess of Wales roared out of the

Jubilee Gates and disappeared in the direction of Snettisham. After a row with her husband, Diana had dashed out of Sandringham House to cool off by the sea. She managed to elude her police minders and walked for an hour on a deserted beach before returning home.

The Queen Mother also loves strolling along the sands when on holiday in Norfolk. She likes picnicking with her friends on Holkham Beach on even the most miserable afternoons. In her old felt hat and hooded blue raincoat, no one would imagine she was the Queen's mother. Wrapped up warmly against the wind, she reminds royal staff of a famous cuddly toy bear, and they have nicknamed her Paddington.

The Queen is a kind-hearted boss, but if you work for her you must love dogs. Her famous corgis are the real loves of her life, and accompany her wherever she goes, off-duty. Palace staff use them as an early-warning system as they scamper ahead of her, signalling her imminent approach.

When the Queen arrives at Windsor for the weekend, her car always stops just inside the gates. Then she gets out to exercise her dogs by walking the quarter of a mile to the state apartments. One afternoon, she got out of the car with four of her dogs, leaving three others still locked in the back seat. Just then the four in her charge started fighting furiously. This set off a battle between the other dogs, who began snapping and snarling inside the car.

As the Queen desperately tried to separate the first lot of corgis, she shouted at her chauffeur for help. 'Can you sort out the other dogs in the back?' she asked.

The man took one look at the vicious bites the dogs behind him were inflicting on each other, then he turned to his boss and declared: 'They're your bleedin' dogs, you sort 'em out yourself!'

He never drove the Queen again, but he wasn't sacked. He retired early to a grace-and-favour cottage he was given on the Windsor estate.

Although she looks after her staff wonderfully well, the Queen is rather standoffish with them. She calls them all by their surnames and issues orders to below-stairs servants through members of the Royal Household. In contrast, the Prince and Princess of Wales and the Duke and Duchess of York address all their employees by their Christian names.

The Queen and her sister still refer to each other by the names they used in the nursery. Elizabeth is 'Lilibet', and the Princess is 'Margo'. Courtiers who overhear them chatting often wonder if two children are standing nearby, not two ageing women.

For obvious reasons, the Queen tries not to let anyone know that she sacks people. If she is dissatisfied with someone she just freezes them out. A few months of cool treatment usually make people realize that they have fallen from favour. Quite often, they take the hint and resign. This diplomatic form of dismissal prevents a lot of unpleasantness.

The Queen's more than forty years on the throne have seen dramatic changes in the social and ethnic composition of Great Britain. Yet there have been few changes behind Palace walls. There are no black or disabled people and no women in top positions in the Royal Household. In a 1990 survey, it was revealed that out of 891 employees only nine were non-whites. But the Queen is not bound by the laws against racism and sex discrimination that the rest of her subjects must obey.

Many people believe that Her Majesty is ill-served by her staff, who today appear to be still 'a tweedy, tight little enclave of English ladies and gentlemen' just as the critic Lord Altrincham described them in the fifties.

There are no distinguished civil servants on her payroll. Most of her advisers appear to have very little experience of ordinary life, and sycophancy seems to be the main qualification for gaining a job at the Palace. Royal staff almost always succumb to the fatal disease known as 'red-carpet Fever', for which there is no known cure. The symptoms are blind loyalty, bowing and scraping, and tightly zipped lips.

One man who briefly worked for the Prince of Wales told me: 'You have no idea what a load of yes men they are. It's not just that their jobs depend on being toadies, their whole lives are locked into royal service. Their friends, their families, and their social standing are all dependent on where they work.'

The Duke of Edinburgh computerized all the archaic workings of the royal palaces in the early eighties. Until he did so, a lot of money and time was wasted. No proper accounting or checks were made of what came in and what went out. This sloppy management was especially prevalent in the kitchens. Whole hams and legs of lamb used to walk out the door and the cellars were regularly raided by staff.

This no longer happens. Every tiny biscuit that the pastry chefs bake, every pound of sugar and every piece of fruit is logged. This modernization has saved the Queen thousands of pounds.

According to her employees, the Queen is careful with her money. When she goes off to Balmoral for the summer, her staff take the opportunity to ask her if any redecoration should be done. They may point out a tattered carpet which has fallen victim to the marauding corgis – or the worn covers on chairs and sofas, but the Queen will usually suggest a compromise. 'Move the furniture around to cover up the worn bits,' she advises, and recommends sending the covers to the cleaners. 'She is a very frugal lady,' one senior aide reveals.

The Queen also has a forgiving nature. Her long-term personal bodgyard Commander Michael Trestrail, who was forced to resign after a homosexual affair with a male prostitute, has been completely rehabilitated. He is now a regular at the various leaving parties at the Palace.

After his resignation, he wrote a long personal letter to the Queen, explaining what had happend and thanking her for the opportunity of serving her. His reward was an invitation to the resignation party of Sir Philip Moore, the Queen's former private secretary, held in the picture gallery at Buckingham Palace. His arrival was almost greeted with euphoria, with both the Queen and the Duke of Edinburgh rushing towards him to welcome him. It was the most important day of Trestrail's life and he felt happy that he would not forever be known as the man who 'let down' the Queen.

According to one member of the Royal Household, Trestrail was almost regarded as a gay martyr when he resigned. He found himself on the invitation list for all the top homosexual parties in London and saw a side of life he had never witnessed before. He has also become a father-figure to the gays at the Palace, who frequently turn to him for advice and guidance. Since he left, Trestrail has taken two degree courses and works in a bookshop in Richmond, Surrey. He is a familiar figure in the area, riding his bicycle through nearby Teddington wearing his deerstalker hat with a rucksack on his back.

Anyone who falls from grace gets sympathy and understanding, but there is often less charity for the staff who try to appear infallible. The man who wields most power inside the Palace is the Queen's private secretary, Sir Robert Fellowes. In 1992, his position as the Queen's most trusted aide seemed shaky after the public outcry about her non-payment of tax.

In fact, she made her revolutionary decision to start being taxed on her personal income in June 1992, months before the government announced this. She brought up the subject at one of her regular Tuesday-night meetings at Buckingham Palace with Prime Minister John Major.

These meetings are always held in private. No minutes are taken, and if there is any follow-up action it is carried out by the respective private secretaries. In this case there was an exchange of notes between Sir Robert Fellowes and his counterpart at No. 10 Downing Street. The Queen had hoped matters would move swiftly and that legislation could be introduced before Parliament broke for the summer recess. In reality, Sir Robert, say Palace insiders, dragged his feet because he did not agree that the Queen should pay tax and actively urged her to reconsider. He considered it an 'insult' to her position. His delaying tactics meant that the announcement was made only in February 1993, after the Queen and the Royal Family had been considerably embarrassed by various scandals and the Windsor fire.

As one in royal circles told me: 'If the decision had been made and the Queen had not been put off last summer, it would have taken the sting out of so much of the criticism that came later in the year. When the question arose about who would pay for the fire damage at Windsor the government could have said the Queen would be paying like every other taxpayer.'

According to my informant, the Queen was 'furious' with Sir Robert: 'The fact was, that she was more in touch with public opinion than her private secretary and that showed a terrible lack of judgement on behalf of someone so senior. She had her finger very much on the button. She is a truly extraordinary woman, both wise and naïve at the same time.'

CHAPTER EIGHTEEN

Crown Duels

The Queen Mother was not well in the summer of 1992. Depressed by the sad state of her favourite grandson's marriage, she seemed suddenly to become dangerously frail. Unable to shake off a persistent cold she arrived at the Castle of Mey, her home near John o'Groats, looking weak and tired.

When the royal yacht *Britannia*, bringing the Queen and her family on their annual Western Isles cruise, stopped at Scrabster, she forced herself to go out in damp weather to meet them. After they left she retreated from the chill winds that whip in across the Pentland Firth, and for the rest of her stay at Caithness she rarely left the castle.

At the end of August when she moved on to stay at Birkhall near the Queen's Balmoral estate, a serious chest infection had developed and Prince Charles became seriously worried about her health. He knew that his grandmother's sight was failing and that she had had several nasty falls in recent months.

He decided to move out of Balmoral and into Birkhall so that he could take care of her. She had been so unwell for so long that it was touch and go whether she would attend the Highland Games at Braemar on the first Saturday in September. It turned out to be such a beautiful, warm day that against her family's advice she decided to go after all. Prince Charles and the Queen agreed on condition that the local GP Doctor Douglas Glass went along to keep an eye on her.

Unfortunately, just when she was on the mend, a number of house guests, one or two suffering from summer colds, arrived at Birkhall and reinfected the delicate old lady.

As her condition deteriorated Prince Charles became more and more concerned. At one point she sank so low that he was afraid he might lose the woman who was as dear to him as his mother. Although he pleaded with her to go down to London for treatment, she refused, as if determined to end her days in the land where she had grown up.

Her illness seemed to make her despondent and she told Prince Charles that she blamed herself for his unhappiness. 'It's all my fault, it's all my fault,' she kept repeating.

The Queen Mother had been delighted when her much-loved grandson married the granddaughter of her best friend Ruth, Lady Fermoy. But when the young couple became estranged she had not wanted to hear about their problems. Renowned in the Royal Family for staying aloof from any unpleasantness, she had been sure they would come to their senses and sort out their difficulties somehow.

Now she regretted not offering more support to Diana, and begged Charles to give his marriage one more try. If he didn't, she warned, he might never be King. To please his ailing grandmother, the Prince reluctantly agreed.

When he returned to London he tried to find out everything about bulimia, its causes and effects. He overcame his natural reluctance to examine a subject that revolted him in a last-ditch effort to hold his family together. But his new-found consideration did not impress his wife. She told him that his interest in her eating disorder came years too late. She poured scorn on his eleventh-hour concern, and was so hostile towards him that Charles soon gave up.

Although worried that his grandmother would be disappointed he confided to a woman friend: 'I don't care if it costs me the throne, I'll never go back to Diana. I couldn't bear it.'

The Prince of Wales was desperately confused. He had fully expected that after the 'Dianagate Tape' was published the disillusioned British public would turn against his wife. Instead, they had blamed him for the whole mess. The general view was his neglect had forced her to find comfort with another man.

He soon realized that he had become an even blacker villain in the eyes of the world, and his bitterness increased.

This was the start of the final chapter of Charles and Diana's marriage.

One autumn day in 1992, a clothes rack was unceremoniously dumped in the reception area of the Prince and Princess of Wales's office at St James's Palace. It was a metal rail on wheels of the type used by major department stores all over Britain, and it was crammed full of Prince Charles's uniforms covered in black plastic bags.

To the staff who saw it standing there it seemed a poignant sign that the royal marriage had irretrievably broken down. They interpreted it as evidence that the Princess of Wales had thrown her husband out of the family home at Kensington Palace.

One Palace worker who saw the uniforms said: 'It was the final straw for me. It was like seeing the Prince of Wales being thrown out on to the street, a very sad sight indeed.'

The scale of the war between the Prince and Princess of Wales during the dying days of their marriage had to be seen to be believed. Terrible shouting matches and long, long silences created an atmosphere that left most Royal Household staff in no doubt where events would lead.

Diana has a fiery temper and would start yelling at her husband, calling him names or hurling insults at him like: 'You miserable old sod', or 'Can you buck your bloody ideas up?' Sometimes the couple would simply clash over their engagement diary when other Royal Household staff were present.

During the worst battles, Diana threw furniture across the private sitting rooms of Kensington Palace and Highgrove. Vases were snatched from mantelpieces and thrown through the air in no particular direction before smashing to the ground.

The Prince of Wales's former butler, Harold Brown, who now works for Princess Diana, witnessed several showdowns. He would always try to withdraw discreetly when the shouting started, but Charles would bark at him: 'You stay here! This is business!'

When the big split came in December 1992, staff were given a choice as to whom they wanted to work for. Harold chose the Princess. A member of the household said: 'It became hideously embarrassing for us all. Gradually the tension got to everyone and the Palace turned into a very gloomy place. The rows were so frequent that the staff often ended up being caught in the middle of a real humdinger.

'The Princess of Wales seemed to enjoy goading the Prince until he cracked or walked away. He also had a short temper and is quite capable of going off the rails over something quite trivial.' The Prince had often experienced spontaneous outbursts of madness from his wife, but he never got used to them. He just could not cope with these scenes. Neither his mother nor his grandmother had ever behaved in this manner with him. He had never had any previous experience of anyone so irrational and could not deal with his wife. This infuriated her even more.

His answer was to run away to the sanctuaries he loved, like Balmoral, or Wood Farm at Sandringham. He would retreat there to escape from the problem, and leave his wife to calm down and sort herself out.

The member of their household went on: 'In all the Prince's friendships and relationships he had never seen such behaviour as his wife demonstrated in these clashes. They could barely look at each other or talk to each other. Their tour of Korea was a disaster, with the Princess more distressed than ever.'

The crunch came in the last week of November at St James's Palace, when the warring couple met with their respective private secretaries, Commander Richard Aylard for the Prince, and Patrick Jephson for the Princess. With other advisers, they sat down to plan their next six months of official engagements. The meeting was stormy and aides found it impossible to agree to a long-term programme acceptable to both Charles and Diana.

The duties had to slot in with the movements of the children Prince William and Prince Harry, who were both away at Ludgrove School. This included where the young Princes would spend Christmas and New Year.

After considerable debate and no agreement in this unofficial tug of love, it was decided that the whole issue could be resolved much more simply if it was made formal. There seemed no other option for the couple and Palace but to accept that the marriage was over. This turned out to be the course taken when the Prime Minister John Major made the announcement in the House of Commons on 9 December 1992.

Despite the enormity of the step, the news made everything easier, although still painful. It was decided it was better to make the statement while the children were safely tucked up at school, and not at the mercy of the media. Afterwards, the way was clear to plan the next six months of separate duties. And they equally divided the time which William and Harry would spend with their mother and father.

Theirs was the third failed marriage of the Queen's four children, a poor record of personal disasters, even by modern British standards, where one in three marriages ends in divorce. The Queen's youngest son, Prince Edward, is yet to marry, but may not be strongly attracted to an institution that has taken such a devastating toll on his family and six of the Queen's grandchildren.

The Prime Minister's statement, which ended years of speculation, condemned Diana to her worst ever Christmas, because she had to allow her boys to celebrate with their father at Sandringham. She went instead to Althorp to spend the festive season with her brother Earl Spencer and his family. I went up to the estate on Christmas morning to see if the Princess would attend the local parish church.

A hundred miles away, Prince Charles was smiling as he proudly escorted their sons past a cheering crowd into St Mary Magdalen church on the Sandringham estate.

Diana did not venture out into the cold, damp day. No doubt she felt the price of her freedom was very high as she endured the Christmas festivities.

A senior member of the Royal Household said: 'The end of the marriage was not a very neat or tidy way of doing things, but at least the announcement allowed life to go on in some way, to allow both the Prince and Princess of Wales to make plans for the future and for their sons, which they were most concerned about.'

Everyone in their household had been living in agony for almost a year.

An undercurrent of suspicion and conspiracy about the marriage swept through the royal palaces early in 1992, well before the momentous events that were to follow. One woman who worked in the Prince of Wales's office told her colleagues: 'We have reason to believe that our phones are tapped.'

It is not clear whether Buckingham Palace itself was monitoring and eavesdropping on calls, but the effect was to put every employee on such a high alert that they were reluctant even to preface their calls with the most innocent of pleasantries like: 'How are you?'

Those staff closest to the couple, as well as senior members of the Royal Family, knew the marriage had been dead for several years. But everyone, including the couple themselves, was happy to act out the charade of togetherness, because of their overwhelming sense of duty. As time wore on and Diana's frustrations with her predicament grew, she became less enthusiastic about her role in this farce.

One royal relative said: 'Everyone thought they should make a go of it for two reasons: the children and the country. They had succeeded up until last year and there is no doubt that without Andrew Morton's book, and the tapes, the sham would have continued, as it has done with so many royal marriages before.'

Because of Diana's pivotal role in Morton's book, senior Royal Family members believe she used it as a springboard for her exit from the family, and for the destruction of her marriage.

After the publication the Princess felt she was almost invincible. In one fell swoop she had dealt a fatal blow to her husband, portraying him as a cold, uncaring father and husband, and worst of all, a man who loved another woman ten years her senior.

This all seemed a far cry from the sweet, demure Diana who had joined the protective custody of Buckingham Palace before her marriage and endeared herself to the staff, calmly walking the plush red-carpeted corridors of the Palace wearing only her swimming costume and a towel wrapped around her dripping hair after an early-morning swim, or a stunning skin-tight leotard after dancing in the music room.

Her refreshing naïveté prompted heads to pop out of doors when she was due to pass. But the Master of the Household felt compelled to run to the Queen and complain of Diana's immodest attire. The Queen took Diana aside and told her the rules of the house.

One courtier said: 'The Princess was doing what anyone would do in their new home. But Buckingham Palace is not really a home – it is an office block with a few bedrooms.' That early experience probably taught Diana more about her artificial new life than anything else.

In Morton's book, Diana emerged as almost saint-like, an inspirational figure to children, women, the elderly and the sick alike. The book was a triumph for the Princess of Wales, albeit a short-lived one. Although not gifted academically, she was shrewd and clever enough to sense she had drawn blood.

She was not even ashamed of it, and later confronted Prince Charles, about two weeks after the book's publication. She stood in front of him, their noses almost touching, and yelled at him: 'Now try and get rid of me!'

The future King's top aides swiftly saw through the book as a superb public-relations exercise, aimed at the continual promotion of Diana, as a self-proclaimed Princess of the people. Her other aim, some believe, was to destroy the Prince of Wales and damage the Royal Family as an institution, previously much loved and respected throughout the world.

Astonishingly, Buckingham Palace did not react, or even recognize the possible effects of such a devastating book. They did not make use of their many resources to vet the book before publication. Then they compounded their failure by refusing to

235

develop any strategy to counteract the revelations and protect the image of the heir to the throne.

Their arrogance and contempt were amazing. They even proudly boasted about their intention to do nothing. A senior aide told me: 'We are not going to dignify it by making any comment at all.' This was the standard Buckingham Palace line on every embarrassing incident. They had no contingency plan to contain the damage.

The Prince's closest aides now openly but reluctantly accept that he had an affair with married mother of two Camilla Parker Bowles early on in the marriage and on and off later in the marriage. One senior aide to the Prince, who even now expresses surprise that people were shocked by the affair, which was confirmed by the 'Camillagate Tape', says: 'Do people really care that the Prince of Wales has had an affair?' This again shows how out of touch the Palace is with public opinion.

The overwhelming verdict of the British people is 'yes'. And even other members of the Royal Family believe his affair was the single most damaging revelation to hit the monarchy during the Queen's Annus Horribilis.

The aide continued: 'Why does any man have an affair? It is usually because he is unhappy in his marriage and looks for comfort or love or sex elsewhere. And the Prince of Wales was no different from other men in that way.

'Camilla had been a friend for years and a girlfriend for a long period of time. No one knows what really triggered off the affair in the marriage again, but it would be fair to say that his marriage was empty, even in the early years. Eventually, like other couples, they grew further and further apart. The age-difference was a big problem. Bigger than the intellectual gap. Diana is very knowledgeable about opera and classical music.

'The Prince now feels an enormous burden has been lifted from him with the end of the marriage. It cast a shadow over his daily life and now, quite simply, he wants to get on with the rest of his life. He is quite clear about his future.

'He sees no barriers or reason why he should not become King. He is in many ways a man without a role until he becomes the monarch. And he regards that as his ultimate destiny, and the real reason for his life.

'He clearly regrets what happened with Camilla, but does not think it will in any way influence the people's view on him becoming King.'

Prince Charles suffers from the same problem today as he has suffered all his life. 'He is a lonely little boy,' said a senior royal courtier who works at Buckingham Palace. 'His upbringing left him deprived of affection, not because of anyone's deliberate neglect, just as an innocent victim of circumstances beyond his control.

'He was just four years old when his mother learned she was to be the new Queen. It was not his fault but from that day on he never had a conventional upbringing and he finds it difficult to show affection naturally,' the courtier added. 'Charles, although distressed over the attention his wife received in the early days of their marriage, tried to understand it.'

Palace officials say that now the couple have formally separated they both have a better life. 'The Prince and the Princess have their own separate interests and they can pursue them independently without fear of upsetting or upstaging each other.

'There is no animosity between them, but if the Prince goes to a hospice and sits around talking to people it does not appear in the newspapers. If Diana goes, it gets maximum publicity and quite naturally he finds that very frustrating because it adds to the myth that he is in some way uncaring or cold, which could not be further from the truth.

'He relates to children and the elderly in exactly the same way. He can get down on his knee to cheer someone up, but the Princess appears to have captured the market in compassion.'

The courtier ended: 'The Prince still does not find it easy, even to this day, to walk into a room of strangers and start a conversation. He has read the potted biographies about people he is going to meet, but that doesn't really help to strike up a conversation. It is something he still finds hard and the Princess finds perfectly natural.'

Buckingham Palace's attitude to any unpleasant story has always been a lofty 'No comment!' This a policy that is slowly beginning to change, not before time. But it is difficult to persuade the Palace old guard to change their ways overnight.

Another aide said: 'It will all blow over. Just sit on the banks of the river and watch the water flow by.' By December 1992, the banks had burst and the Royal Family was in mortal peril, as one disaster followed another. Fergie's frolics with her financial adviser, the 'Dianagate Tape' and 'Camillagate Tape' all came hard on the heels of Morton's book. Then the great fire of Windsor erupted after prolonged pressure on the Queen to pay tax.

It all came as a huge letdown for the public after the high expectations surrounding Princess Diana's arrival in the Royal Firm. Demure Diana, the fairy-tale Princess who blushed easily and developed a love affair with the camera, had promised so much. As a royal relative confided: 'I greeted the entry of Diana Spencer into the family with a degree of excitement and enthusiasm. She was a breath of fresh air, and I told her so. She brought a new vigour to the Royal Family and the monarchy.

'It is true and fair to say that the Princess of Wales has propped up the Royal Family for over ten years, so when the fall came it was always going to be monumental. Because of the great height her popularity had reached, she had a very long way to fall.'

He added: 'Diana is the type of woman who can make a difference. She has an enormous heart, and finds it easy to be demonstrably affectionate, which the Prince of Wales finds hard because he has never known it himself.

'The Princess totally overshadowed her husband in an amazingly short time, and he found it almost impossible to take or understand.'

Today the Princess of Wales is a new woman. She oozes confidence and she has a clear-cut vision of her role in life and within the Royal Family. She is perfectly happy to endure an existence in the monarchy. But she has laid down her terms to the Queen and senior courtiers. They have little choice but to accept the new-born Diana because they realize she is a vote-winner with the public and is still a rare shining light in the shop-soiled monarchy.

Her image is a cross between American supermodel Cindy Crawford and the world's most compassionate woman, Mother Teresa. It is a formidable combination, even for the Palace to confront. When we see her today we see a different woman from the one who suffered a nightmarish marriage to Prince Charles, in which she was both unloved and almost unnoticed by her husband.

She lives for her sons, Princes William and Harry, and she wants to be like other mums, doing ordinary things with her children. This is well illustrated by the procession of outings she has organized for them during school holidays. She takes them to theme parks, the cinema, historical monuments like the Tower of London, and even to High Street burger joints.

Her closest friends do not live on big country estates where they spend weekends huntin', shootin' and fishin'. They are people she trusts implicitly, like her personal protection officer Inspector Ken Wharfe, whose duties go far beyond that of a policeman.

He is her adviser, her friend and protector, and a valuable buffer between the Princess and those she wishes to keep at arm's length. Others include her girlfriends Kate Menzies, a wealthy heiress who runs a catering company; and Catherine Soames, the former wife of Nicholas Soames, the Conservative Member of Parliament for Crawley, Sussex. Another woman who acts as both confidante and mentor is Lucia Flecha de Lima, the wife of Brazil's Ambassador to the Court of St James. The elegant South American was her guide on a private week-end in Paris, and they regularly lunch together.

Although determined to remain part of the Royal Family, Diana will not allow it to swallow up her life again as it did throughout her marriage.

She remains driven by compassion in her public life, and part of her private life. The Princess feels she has a talent for helping others and derives her greatest pleasure from it. She carries on her good works quietly and even at long distance. When she was in Korea with the Prince of Wales she was heartbroken when she learned that her lady-in-waiting Laura Lonsdale had lost her eleven-month-old baby son Louis, a victim of cot death.

She later attended the funeral and spent hours comforting Laura, both in person and on the phone. A close friend of Laura said: 'The Princess of Wales is the nearest thing to an angel on earth. She has a unique quality of being able to comfort someone without being pushy or over the top. She has a magic touch all of her own.'

During her 1991 summer holiday in the Mediterranean with her family, Lord and Lady Romsey, and Sir Angus Ogilvy and his wife Princess Alexandra, her thoughts often drifted away from the sunshine to Adrian Ward-Jackson, who was dying of AIDS.

She used the satellite phone on the yacht *Alexander* to call his family, and even had a helicopter on stand-by in case she had to dash back to Britain. Diana was at his bedside, clutching his hand, in the last few days of his life. And she was called from her bed at one in the morning when he was on the point of death. She flung on the first clothes she could find and raced to the hospital, knowing she looked a mess. Sadly, she arrived just half an hour too late.

Noticing a photographer waiting outside, the tearful Princess begged: 'Please, please, don't take my picture.' Two hours later, when she left, she had composed herself and had changed into a more appropriate outfit.

From now on Diana would be happy to cultivate a new image of herself, still as caring and compassionate as ever, but also as a stronger woman. But she cannot forget she is at the centre of a tug of love over her two Princes with their father. Since the break-up of their marriage the Prince of Wales's children have become much more precious to him.

For several years he had felt excluded from his own family, denied the right to introduce the boys to his pleasures and passions, mostly in the countryside. He had bitter experience of his wife keeping his children from him.

In 1991 he cancelled his skiing holiday in Switzerland because he felt it would be inappropriate to go abroad during the Gulf War. Looking for something to do instead, he decided to join his wife on an official visit to Wales. He was astounded to discover that she was taking their son William, the next Prince of Wales, with her. It would be the young Prince's first visit to the Principality, and he had planned to introduce his heir to the Welsh people himself. A member of the Highgrove Set told me: 'He only found out what his wife had secretly organized at the last minute, and managed to join them.'

The woman added: 'I raise my glass and say: "Thank God for Saddam Hussein." If it had not been for him the Prince of Wales would have been upstaged by his wife.'

There were other occasions when the Princess did not allow him to share adventures with his sons. During their 1991 summer cruise of the Mediterranean, Charles wanted to teach William to sail. His wife went into a tantrum and refused to allow the child to go with his father.

The old chum added: 'It is true to say that like many people who live through an unhappy marriage and then finally break free, he feels that a massive burden has been lifted from his shoulders. His personality has started shining through again. His smile and his natural eccentricity have returned.

'He no longer looks as if he is carrying the world's problems on his back with a furrowed brow and intense expression. He is once again learning how good life can be.'

He knew the marriage was a mistake years ago, but felt so guilty that he forced himself to make it work. Royal Household staff were amazed when on the second stage of his honeymoon at Balmoral he left his bride alone for hours to go off and paint. An estate worker told me: 'We all thought it would be such a romantic gesture to wander off together into the hills and teach her how to paint. But he just went off all alone. I remember thinking how odd it was.'

Headstrong Charles loves Balmoral, and even when criticism over the long separations reached a crescendo he would deliberately resist the pleadings of his friends to join Diana and his sons in London, saying he would not 'pander' to the press. His stubbornness did nothing to endear him to his family and reinforced the view of everyone around him that he had given up totally on the union. That stand-off situation continued until the sham could no longer be tenable, as growing evidence of both his and his wife's extra-marital interests slowly emerged.

Prince Charles sought the opinion of his friends and their counsel before he made the biggest decision of his life. At least two of his close circle urged him to think again. They felt the age-difference was unbridgeable and expressed concern about the intellectual gulf between them.

Those same friends often witnessed at first hand the traumas of the marriage. Because they regarded themselves as friends of the future King, they blamed Diana for wrecking his life. They claimed she was a cunning woman who had deliberately set out to steal the show, to become the superstar of the Royal Family.

One friend said: 'Charles really did his best to make the marriage work, but Diana became too hot to handle. She made it clear she resented the style of life in the Royal Family. She hated being ignored so she set out to change it all, and came damn' near to wrecking it all in the process.'

The Prince's oldest friends shrugged off Diana's illnesses and her various suicide attempts as nothing more than the pathetic attention-seeking 'cries for help' of an unbalanced woman. They were equally aware that Charles was more comfortable in the company of his old flame Camilla Parker Bowles, who lived just fifteen miles from the front door of his Highgrove home near Tetbury, Gloucestershire.

But they never believed it had reached the stage of a fully-fledged affair within his loveless marriage.

A friend of the Prince explained: 'We always believed Camilla was the sort of friend that everyone would love to have. She made it clear she was there for him any time he needed her. Twenty-four hours a day, any time of the day, she would be available.'

As well as the Highgrove Set, his closest friend during the marriage deterioration was his private secretary Commander

Richard Aylard, who quietly orchestrated a positive propaganda campaign on behalf of the Prince following the Morton book. His camp became aware what the author was planning in spring 1992, and the atmosphere in the Royal Family was at its iciest during the traditional Buckingham Palace balcony appearance after the annual Trooping the Colour ceremony.

One person present said later: 'It was a terrible experience; nobody knew what to say to each other or where to look, whether to smile or look sympathetic. It was most uncomfortable for all concerned. You could have cut the atmosphere with a knife.'

When speculation reached its peak in the summer of 1992, with a daily bombardment of news stories about the marriage, Charles ordered his friends to maintain a 'dignified silence'. This policy did his image enormous harm and allowed his wife to emerge unscathed. Several friends were so outraged at the ferocity of the attack on Charles as a man, a husband and a father that they launched their own defence plan, aimed at discrediting Diana and her motives.

This was a war of the coldest kind; the Queen despaired of it, and senior aides failed miserably to quell it.

The Princess had been summoned soon after the publication of Morton's opus to the offices of the Queen's private secretary and her own brother-in-law, Sir Robert Fellowes. There she was ordered to sign a pre-typed document confirming that she had had nothing to do with Morton's book, in effect disowning its publication and its devastating contents.

Diana had no choice but to refuse. To sign would have been a terrible betrayal of the handful of friends, like James Gilbey and Carolyn Bartholomew, whom she had personally given permission to speak to Morton. Diana wanted the book to be the launching pad for her new life, either inside the Royal Family or outside it. She was prepared for both.

Charles was both 'hurt and betrayed' by the venom of the attack and furious when he was finally convinced that his own wife was part of the conspiracy against him. One friend said soon afterwards: 'From that moment he could never forgive her, whatever happened.'

At this time, the couple were so hostile towards each other that if they happened to be in the same home, they would arrive and leave by separate entrances and exits to eliminate the possibility of seeing each other. When under the same roof, they even dined in separate rooms.

In the summer of 1992, after the Morton bombshell hit the monarchy, the same friends who had implored the Prince of Wales not to marry Lady Diana Spencer twelve years previously were not celebrating their sad prophecy with a resounding chorus of 'We told you so'; they were simply repeating their advice to him to 'dump' Diana there and then, and begin a new life.

Today, the two opposing camps continue to exist within St James's Palace, their London office. But Charles and Diana seem almost like strangers.

How does all this upheaval affect the future of the monarchy?

A relative of a senior member of the Royal Family recently told me candidly what he thought would happen. He also gave a fascinating assessment of what had happened.

I feel sorry for the Queen personally, and I think a large number of people feel the same. The year 1992 was supposed to be a celebration, the fortieth year of her reign, yet it will only be remembered for the royal disasters. Everyone had looked at the Royal Family as perfect mortals and now they have turned out to be nothing more than human beings with the same failings as the rest of us.

Whether the monarchy will survive I don't know. The crucial question is that it depends on how long the Queen lives, and whether the Prince of Wales is acceptable to the public with his unfair image of being uncaring and unfeeling.

Whatever people may say or feel about the monarchy, I think the one thing everyone agrees on is that we have a marvellous Queen and that is standing us in good stead in these times.

She may well be seen to be out of touch or out of date, but that is not necessarily a bad thing. It helps to maintain a little of the mystique where so much has been torn away.

We have had one terrible disaster after another, which, to be honest, was terribly bad luck by anyone's standards, but now we have to look to the future. The Prince of Wales is determined to be King but there are even problems there. If, for instance, he wanted to marry again, it would be very difficult for him and the country, as he is head of the Church of England. If he does not marry again, I do not believe there will be any problem to his eventual accession to the throne.

We have to accept that over the last year the monarchy and the Royal Family have come under the closest possible examination, and that an increasing number of young people regard the whole institution as being old-fashioned, a waste of money, and of no use at all, which, of course, is a dangerous trend.

People may say why have a lady-in-waiting, for instance, but if you start attacking the very fabric of the monarchy then the whole thing goes. They have to maintain their own importance in terms of tourism and state visits and all the positive benefits of the monarchy rather than let their personal lives and behaviour deflect from the advantages of having the Royal Family.

The Queen's decision to pay tax has, I believe, gone a long way to helping matters. It has taken too long to come, but that was not necessarily all to do with the Queen herself. Over the years, civil servants have resisted the move, saying it is ridiculous for the Queen to pay tax to herself. But it was being discussed more and more in Buckingham Palace.

There is no doubt in my mind that enormous damage has been done to the institution of the monarchy. I think most of it has been caused by the separation of the Prince and Princess of Wales. If a marriage does not work, then the view certainly in the Royal Family is that you should work at it, so that it *does* work. This is not just for the sake of the couple or their children, but for the good of the

245

country. I now believe that the Prince and Princess married for the wrong reasons. The Prince felt under a great pressure to marry out of duty and he felt it had to be the right sort of girl, regardless of whether he loved her.

My feelings today are that he never really loved her in the way that most people would regard love. The chemistry did not work at the beginning and was never going to work. In earlier days, Kings would have mistresses if relationships were unhappy, but in these days of more accountability and a lively media that is impossible.

The Princess herself was at fault for her role in manipulating the press, and I don't think there is any doubt that when she realized what a predicament she had found herself in, she set out to destroy him and almost succeeded. She is a lot more manipulative than we realize, and she is a natural PR girl. She has a natural gift for public relations.

Throughout all this it is the Queen who has come shining through. It should have been a year of celebration and instead she has had to exercise the most amazing self-control in the most difficult of circumstances.

She has carried on smiling and working. I have never seen her cry or say despairingly: 'My God, have you heard what has happened now?' And you might expect that of anyone else in the same situation. This is all down to her training, her enormous sense of duty, that she never shows her emotions. You may hear her talk about another member of the family, but she will never shout someone down, face to face. She does not like rows or confrontations. She is a very reserved person.

Her speech at the Mansion House which used the words 'Annus Horribilis' was a terrible mistake. It was the only time she has put a foot wrong throughout the whole unbelievable mess. It is difficult to believe that someone would advise her to use those words. They will hang around the Queen for ever like a millstone around her neck. While giving a small insight into the emotional turmoil of her year, she inadvertently gave the headline writers a field day and even more ammunition with which to mock the monarchy.

Since the break-up of the marriage there is no doubt that both the Prince and Princess are much happier. I know that the Princess of Wales was deeply wounded by her husband's affair with Camilla but I genuinely feel if it had not been for Morton's book and the tapes they would have carried on, keeping up the front, for the sake of the country and out of duty, as long as everyone kept their mouths shut. Since the controversy over the Queen's tax, several of the more peripheral members of the Royal Family have openly offered to withdraw from official duties, but the Queen would not even entertain the idea. She was very much of the opinion: 'I need all the troops I can get.' It was a reflection that she had lost the Duchess of York, and to an extent the Princess of Wales, because she only pursued her own interests and duties which she felt drawn to.

The Royal Family is fabulously rich and its members enjoy extraordinary privileges, but they are, I have discovered, rather ordinary and undistinguished people. The exception is undoubtedly Diana, who really is a magical human being.

Overall, the Mountbatten-Windsors are pretty average. Not one is a likely candidate for MENSA, the club for the super-intelligent. They have few accomplishments and are not remarkable in any way, except for what they are, an accident of birth. They achieve nothing through their own efforts, and this is why they appear as living relics as we enter the next millennium. To survive they must do more to earn their pre-eminent place in society, just as the Princess of Wales now does.

Diana's position within the system is now precarious. On her tour of Nepal in March 1993 I asked one of her closest confidants how she was coping with her solo role. 'It's going OK so far,' I was told. 'But she doesn't know how long it will last.'

On past performance, I would predict that I will be taking pictures of the Princess of Wales, and hopefully swapping more jokes with her, for a very long time.

CHAPTER NINETEEN

The Royal Tapes

Here are the transcripts of the notorious tapes that shook the monarchy. What was the reason for releasing these private conversations? Could there be a sinister plot to discredit the monarchy? Read them and make up your own mind.

CAMILLAGATE

CHARLES: He was a bit anxious actually.

CAMILLA: Was he?

CHARLES: He thought he might have gone a bit far.

CAMILLA: Ah well.

CHARLES: Anyway you know, that's the sort of thing one has to beware of. And sort of feel one's way along with, if you know what I mean.

CAMILLA: Mm. You're awfully good at feeling your way along.

CHARLES: Oh stop! I want to feel my way along you, all over you and up and down you and in and out...

CAMILLA: Oh.

CHARLES: Particularly in and out.

CAMILLA: Oh, that's just what I need at the moment.

CHARLES: Is it?

(Scanner enthusiast who recorded conversation speaks over couple to record date – 18 December.)

CAMILLA: I know it would revive me. I can't bear a Sunday night without you.

CHARLES: Oh God.

CAMILLA: It's like that programme 'Start the Week'. I can't start the week without you.

CHARLES: I fill up your tank!

CAMILLA: Yes you do!

CHARLES: Then you can cope.

CAMILLA: Then I'm all right.

CHARLES: What about me? The trouble is I need you several times a week.

CAMILLA: Mmm. So do I. I need you all the week. All the time.

CHARLES: Oh, God. I'll just live inside your trousers or something. It would be much easier!

CAMILLA: (*laughs*) What are going to turn into, a pair of knickers? (*both laugh*) Oh you're going to come back as a pair of knickers.

CHARLES: Or, God forbid, a Tampax. Just my luck. (*laughs*)

CAMILLA: You are a complete idiot! (*laughs*) Oh what a wonderful idea.

CHARLES: My luck to be chucked down a lavatory and go on and on forever swirling round on the top, never going down!

CAMILLA: (*laughing*) Oh darling!

CHARLES: Until the next one comes through.

CAMILLA: Oh, perhaps you could just come back as a box.

CHARLES: What sort of box?

CAMILLA: A box of Tampax so you could just keep going.

CHARLES: That's true.

CAMILLA: Repeating yourself. (*laughing*) Oh darling. Oh I just want you now.

CHARLES: Do you?

CAMILLA: Mmmm.

CHARLES: So do I.

CAMILLA: Desperately, desperately, desperately. Oh, I thought of you so much at Garrowby.

CHARLES: Did you?

CAMILLA: Simply mean we couldn't be there together.

CHARLES: Desperate. If you could be here – I long to ask Nancy sometimes.

CAMILLA: Why don't you?

CHARLES: I daren't.

CAMILLA: Because I think she's so in love with you.

CHARLES: Mmmm.

CAMILLA: She'd do anything you asked.

CHARLES: She'd tell all sorts of people.

CAMILLA: No she wouldn't, because she'd be much too frightened of what you might say to her. I think you've got, I'm afraid it's a terrible thing to say, but I think, you know, those sort of people do feel very strongly about you. You've got such a great hold over her.

CHARLES: Really?

CAMILLA: And you're... I think as usual you're under-estimating yourself.

CHARLES: But she might be terribly jealous of something.

CAMILLA: Oh! (*laughs*) Now that is a point! I wonder, she might be, I suppose.

CHARLES: You never know, do you.

CAMILLA: No. The little green-eyed monster might be lurking inside her. No, but I mean, the thing is you're so good when people are so flattered to be taken into your confidence, but I don't know they'd betray you. You know, real friends.

CHARLES: Really?

CAMILLA: Darling, listen, I talked to David tonight again. It might not be any good.

CHARLES: Oh no!

CAMILLA: I'll tell you why. He's got these children of one of those Crawley girls and their nanny staying. He's going, I'm going to ring him again tomorrow. He's going to try and put them off till Friday. But I thought as an alternative perhaps I might ring up Charlie.

CHARLES: Yes.

CAMILLA: And see if we could do it there. I know he's back on Thursday.

CHARLES: It's quite a lot further away.

CAMILLA: Oh is it?

CHARLES: Well, I'm just trying to think. Coming from Newmarket.

CAMILLA: Coming from Newmarket to me at that time of night, you could probably do it in two-and-three-quarters. It takes me three.

CHARLES: What, to go to, um, Bowood?

CAMILLA: To go to Bowood would be the same as me really, wouldn't it.

CHARLES: I mean to say, you would suggest going to Bowood, uh?

CAMILLA: No, not at all.

CHARLES: Which Charlie then?

CAMILLA: What Charlie do you think I was talking about?

CHARLES: I didn't know, because I thought you meant...

CAMILLA: I've got lots...

CHARLES: Somebody else.

CAMILLA: I've got lots of friends called Charlie.

CHARLES: The other one, Patty's.

CAMILLA: Oh! Oh there! Oh that is further away. They're not...

CHARLES: They've gone...

CAMILLA: I don't know, it's just, you know, just a thought I had, if it fell through, the other place.

CHARLES: Oh right. What do you do, go on the M25 then down the M4 is it?

CAMILLA: Yes, you go, um, and sort of Royston, or M11, at that time of night.

CHARLES: Yes. Well that'll be just after, it will be after shooting anyway.

CAMILLA: So it would be, um, you'd miss the worst of the traffic. Because I'll, er, you see the problem is I've got to be in London tomorrow night.

CHARLES: Yes.

CAMILLA: And Tuesday night A's coming home.

CHARLES: No...

CAMILLA: Would you believe it? Because, I don't know what

he is doing, he's shooting down here or something. but darling, you wouldn't be able to ring me anyway, would you?

CHARLES: I might just. I mean, tomorrow night I could have done.

CAMILLA: Oh darling, I can't bear it. How could you have done tomorrow night?

CHARLES: Because I'll be (*yawns*) working on the next speech.

CAMILLA: Oh no, what's the next one.

CHARLES: A Business in the Community one, rebuilding communities.

CAMILLA: Oh no, when's that for?

CHARLES: A rather important one for Wednesday.

CAMILLA: Well at least I'll be behind you.

CHARLES: I know.

CAMILLA: Can I have a copy of the one you've just done?

CHARLES: Yes. Can I? I would like it.

CAMILLA: Can I? Um, I would like it.

CHARLES: OK, I'll try and organize it...

CAMILLA: Darling...

CHARLES: But I, oh God, when am I going to speak to you?

CAMILLA: I can't bear it. Um...

CHARLES: Wednesday night?

CAMILLA: Oh, certainly Wednesday night. I'll be alone, um, Wednesday, you know, the evening. Or Tuesday. While you're rushing around doing things I'll be, you know, alone until it reappears. And early Wednesday morning. I mean, he'll be leaving at half-past eight, quarter-past eight. He won't be here Thursday, pray God. Um, that ambulance strike, it's a terrible thing to say this, I suppose it won't have to come to an end by Thursday.

CHARLES: It will have done?

CAMILLA: Well, I mean, I hope for everybody's sake it will have done, but I hope for our sakes it's still going on.

CHARLES: Why?

CAMILLA: Well, because if it stops he'll come down here on Thursday night.

CHARLES: Oh no.

CAMILLA: Yes, but I don't think it will stop, do you?

CHARLES: No, neither do I. Just our luck.

CAMILLA: It would be our luck. I know.

CHARLES: Then it's bound to.

CAMILLA: No it won't. You musn't think like that. You must think positive.

CHARLES: I'm not very good at that.

CAMILLA: Well I am going to. Because if I don't, I'd despair. (*pause*) Hm – gone to sleep?

CHARLES: No. How maddening.

CAMILLA: I know. Anyway, I mean, he's doing his best to change it, David, but I thought, but I just thought, you know, I might just ask Charlie.

CHARLES: Did he say anything?

CAMILLA: No I haven't talked to him.

CHARLES: You haven't?

CAMILLA: Well, I talked to him briefly, but you know, I just thought I – I just don't know whether he's got any children at home, that's the worry.

CHARLES: Right.

CAMILLA: Oh...darling, I think I'll...

CHARLES: Pray, just pray.

CAMILLA: It would be so wonderful to just have one night to set us on our way, wouldn't it?

CHARLES: Wouldn't it? To wish you a happy Christmas.

CAMILLA: (*indistinct*) happy. Oh, don't let's think about Christmas, I can't bear it. (*pause*) Going to go to sleep? I think you'd better, don't you? Darling?

CHARLES: (*sleepy*) Yes, darling?

CAMILLA: Will you ring me when you wake up?

CHARLES: Yes I will.

CAMILLA: Before I have these rampaging children around. It's Tom's birthday tomorrow. (*pause*) You all right?

CHARLES: Mm. I'm all right.

CAMILLA: Can I talk to you, I hope before those rampaging children.

CHARLES: What time do they come in?

CAMILLA: Well, usually Tom never wakes up at all, but as it's his birthday tomorrow he might just stagger out of bed. It won't be before half-past eight. (*pause*) Night, my darling.

CHARLES: Darling...

CAMILLA: I do love you.

CHARLES: Love you too. I don't want to say goodbye.

CAMILLA: Well done for doing that. You're a clever old thing. An awfully good brain lurking there, isn't there? Oh darling, I think you ought to give the brain a rest now. Night-night.

CHARLES: Night, darling. God bless.

CAMILLA: I do love you and I'm so proud of you.

CHARLES: Oh, I'm so proud of you.

CAMILLA: Don't be silly, I've never achieved anything.

CHARLES: Yes you have.

CAMILLA: No I haven't.

CHARLES: Your great achievement is to love me.

CAMILLA: Oh, darling. Easier than falling off a chair.

CHARLES: You suffer all these indignities and tortures and calumnies.

CAMILLA: Oh, darling, don't be so silly. I'd suffer anything for you. That's love. It's the strength of love. Night-night.

CHARLES: Night, darling. Sounds as though you're dragging an enormous piece of string behind you, with hundreds of tin pots and cans attached to it. I think it must be your telephone. Night-night, before the battery goes. (*blows kiss*) Night.

CAMILLA: Love you.

CHARLES: Bye.

CAMILLA: Hopefully talk to you in the morning.

CHARLES: Please.

CAMILLA: Bye, I do love you.

CHARLES: Night.

CAMILLA: Night.

CHARLES: Night.

CAMILLA: Love you forever.

CHARLES: Night.

CAMILLA: G'bye. Bye, my darling.

CHARLES: Night.

CAMILLA: Night-night.

CHARLES: Night.
CAMILLA: Bye bye.
CHARLES: Going.
CAMILLA: Bye.
CHARLES: Going.
CAMILLA: Gone.
CHARLES: Night.
CAMILLA: Bye. Press the button.
CHARLES: Going to press the tit.
CAMILLA: All right, darling, I wish you were pressing mine.
CHARLES: God, I wish I was. Harder and harder.
CAMILLA: Oh darling.
CHARLES: Night.
CAMILLA: Night.
CHARLES: Love you.
CAMILLA: (*yawning*) Love you. Press the tit.
CHARLES: Adore you. Night.
CAMILLA: Night.
CHARLES: Night.
CAMILLA: (*blows a kiss*)
CHARLES: Night.
CAMILLA: G'night, my darling. Love you...

Charles hangs up.

DIANAGATE

HIM: And so, darling, what other lows today?
HER: So that was it, I was very bad at lunch. And he really started blubbing. I just felt really sad and empty, and I thought: 'Bloody hell, after all I've done for this fucking family.'
HIM: You don't need to. Cos there are people out there, and I've said this before, who will replace emptiness. With all sorts of things.

HER: I needn't ask horoscopes, but it is just so desperate. Always being innuendo, the fact that I'm going to do something dramatic because I can't stand the confines of this marriage.
HIM: I know.
HER: But I know much more than they because...
HIM: Well, interestingly enough, that thing in the *People* didn't imply either one of you.
HER: No.
HIM: So I wouldn't worry about that. I wouldn't worry about that, I think it's common knowledge, darling, and amongst most people, that you obviously don't have...
HER: A rapport?
HIM: Yeh, I think that comes through loud and clear. Darling, just forgetting that for a moment, how is Mara?
HER: She's all right, no, she's fine, she can't wait to get back.
HIM: Can't she? When's she coming back?
HER: Saturday.
HIM: Is she?
HER: Mmmm.
HIM: I thought it was next Saturday.
HER: No, Saturday.
HIM: Not quite as soon as you thought it was.
HER: No.
HIM: Is she having a nice time?
HER: Very nice.
HIM: Is she?
HER: I think so. She's out of London. It gives her a bit of a rest.
HIM: Yeh. Can't imagine what she does the whole time.
HER: No.
HIM: The restaurant. If you have a restaurant, it's so much a part of your life, isn't it?
HER: I know, people around you all the time.
HIM: That's right. The constant bossing and constant ordering and constant sort of fussing. And she hasn't got that. She's probably been twiddling her fingers wondering what to do.
HER: Hmmm.
HIM: Going to church every day.

HER: I know.

HIM: Did you go to church today?

HER: Yes I did.

HIM: Did you, Squidge?

HER: Yes.

HIM: Did you say lots of prayers?

HER: Of course.

HIM: Did you? Kiss me, darling. (*sound of kisses being blown down the phone*)

HER: (*sound of laughter and returns kiss*)

HIM: I can't tell what a smile that has put on my face. I can't tell you. I was like a sort of caged rat and Tony said to me 'you are in a terrible hurry to go.' And I said: 'Yeh, well I've got some things to do when I get there.' Oh God (*sighs*), I am not going to leave the phone in the car any more, darling.

HER: No, please don't.

HIM: No, I won't. And if it rings and someone says: 'What on earth is your telephone ringing for?' I will say: 'Oh, someone's got a wrong number or something.'

HER: No, say one of your relations is not very well and your mother is just ringing in to give you progress.

HIM: All right, so I will keep it near me, quite near to me tomorow, because father hates phones out shooting.

HER: Oh, you are out shooting tomorrow, are you?

HIM: Yeh. And, darling, I will be back in London tomorrow night.

HER: Good.

HIM: All right?

HER: Yes.

HIM: Back on home territory, so no more awful breaks.

HER: No.

HIM: I don't know what I'd do. Do you know, darling, I couldn't sort of face the thought of not speaking to you every moment. It fills me with real horror, you know.

HER: It's purely mutual.

HIM: Is it? I really hate the idea of it, you know. It makes me really sort of scared.

HER: There was something really strange. I was leaning over the fence yesterday, looking into Park House and I thought, 'Oh what shall I do?' and I thought, 'Well my friend would say go in and do it.' I thought, 'No cos I am a bit shy' and there were hundreds of people in there. So I thought, 'Bugger that.' So I went round to the front door and walked straight in.

HIM: Did you?

HER: It was just so exciting.

HIM: How long were you there for?

HER: An hour and a half.

HIM: Were you?

HER: Mmm. And they were so sweet. They wanted their photographs taken with me and they kept hugging me. They were very ill, some of them. Some no legs and all sorts of things.

HIM: Amazing, Leonard Cheshire.

HER: Isn't he.

HIM: Yeh, amazing, quite extraordinary. He devoted himself to setting up those homes. To achieve everything, I think it's amazing. Sort of devotion to a cause.

HER: I know.

HIM: Darling, no sort of awful feelings of guilt or . . .

HER: None at all.

HIM: Remorse?

HER: None. None at all.

HIM: Good.

HER: No, none at all. All's well.

HIM: OK then, Squidgy. I am sorry you have had low times . . . Try, darling, when you get these urges, you must try to replace them with anger like you did on Friday night, you know.

HER: I know. But do you know what's really quite un . . . whatever the word is? His grandmother is always looking at me with a strange look in her eyes. It's not hatred, it's sort of interest and pity mixed in one. I am not quite sure. I don't understand it. Every time I look up, she's looking at me and then looks away and smiles.

HIM: Does she?

HER: Yes. I don't know what's going on.

HIM: I should say to her one day: 'I can't help but ask you. You are always looking at me. What is it? What are you thinking?' You must, darling. And interestingly enough, one of the things said to me today is that you are going to start standing up for yourself.

HER: Yes.

HIM: Mmm. We all know that you are very capable of that, old Bossy Boots.

HER: I know, yes.

HIM: What have you had on today? What have you been wearing?

HER: A pair of black jodhpur things on at the moment and a pink polo neck.

HIM: Really. Looking good?

HER: Yes.

HIM: Are you?

HER: Yes.

HIM: Dead good?

HER: I think it's good.

HIM: You do?

HER: Yes.

HIM: And what on your feet?

HER: A pair of flat black pumps.

HIM: Very chic.

HER: Yes. (*pause in tape*) The redhead is being actually quite supportive.

HIM: Is she?

HER: Yes, she has. I don't know why.

HIM: Don't let the . . . down.

HER: No, I won't. I just talk to her about that side of things.

HIM: You do? That's all I worry about. I just worry that you know she's sort of . . . she's desperately trying to get back in.

HER: She keeps telling me.

HIM: She's trying to tag on to your . . . She knows that your PR is so good, she's trying to tag on to that.

260

HER: Jimmy Savile rang me up yesterday and he said: 'I'm just ringing up, my girl, to tell you that his nibs has asked me to come and help out the redhead, and I'm just letting you know so that you don't find out through her or him. And I hope it's all right by you.' And I said: 'Jimmy, you do what you like.'

HIM: What do you mean, help out the redhead, darling?

HER: With her publicity.

HIM: Oh, has he?

HER: Sort her out. He said: 'You can't change a lame duck or something but I've got to talk to her cos that's the boss's orders and I've got to carry them out. But I want you to know that you're my number-one girl and I'm not...'

HIM: Oh darling, that's not fair, you're *my* number-one girl.

HER: Well, he's sort of heterosexual and everything else I think.

HIM: Heterosexual?

HER: Yes.

HIM: Is he, what do you mean heterosexual?

HER: Everything.

HIM: Oh he's everything. That's not heterosexual, darling. (*starts laughing*) Oh, Squidge you're so, (*laughs*) do you know what heterosexual is?

HER: No.

HIM: You and me.

HER: Oh right.

HIM: That's hetero.

HER: Oh.

HIM: The other is sort of alternating current, I never know how you, what is it bi? Is he bi?

HER: (*voice much quieter in the background*) 'Harry, it might be in my bathroom.' What did you say about babies?

HIM: Is he bi?

HER: You didn't say anything about babies did you?

HIM: No.

HER: No.

HIM: Why, darling?

HER: (*laughing*) I thought you did.

261

HIM: Did you?

HER: Yes.

HIM: Did you, darling, you have got them on the brain.

HER: Well yeh, maybe I . . . well actually I don't think I am going to be able to for ages.

HIM: I think you've got bored with the idea actually.

HER: I'm going to . . .

HIM: You are aren't you, it was a sort of hot flush you went through.

HER: A very hot flush.

HIM: Darling, when he says his nibs rang him up, does he mean your other half or PA rang him up?

HER: Eh? My other half.

HIM: Your other half.

HER: Yes.

HIM: Does he get on well with him?

HER: Sort of mentor. Talk in the mouthpiece, you moved away.

HIM: Sorry, darling, I'm resting it on my chin, on my chinless. Oh (*sighs*) I get so sort of possessive when I see all those pictures of you. I get so possessive, that's the least attractive aspect of me really. I just see them and think: 'Oh God, if only . . .'

HER: There aren't that many pictures, are there? There haven't been that many.

HIM: Four or five today.

HER: Oh.

HIM: Various magazines. So, darling, I . . .

HER: I'm always smiling, aren't I?

HIM: Always.

HER: I thought that today.

HIM: I always told you that. It's the old, what I call the PR package, isn't it? As soon as you sense a camera – I think you can sense a camera at a thousand yards.

HER: Yes.

HIM: That smile comes on. And the charm comes out and it stays there all the time, and then it goes away again. But darling, tell me, how was your tea party?

HER: It was all right. Nicholas was there and his girlfriend Charlotte Hambro. Do you know Charlotte?

HIM: Yes. She was there, was she? How was that?

HER: It was all right. I went in in terrific form.

HIM: Where are they staying then? Nicholas?

HER: They are all staying with her sister down the other side of Fakenham.

HIM: Oh, Jeremy?

HER: Yes.

HIM: Was he there?

HER: Yes. Difficult man.

HIM: Very difficult man. Saw him at the ballet the other night.

HER: Oh, he's always there.

HIM: Yes, always. So quite a long drive, then?

HER: Yes. But the great thing is, I went in and made a lot of noise and came out.

HIM: Were they all very chatty?

HER: Yes. Very very very.

HIM: Very kowtowing?

HER: Oh yes.

HIM: Were they?

HER: Yes, all that.

HIM: Darling, you said all your yeses and noes, pleases and thankyous. You stared at the floor and there were moments of silence . . .

HER: No, no, no, no. I kept the conversation going.

HIM: Did you?

HER: Yes.

HIM: What about?

HER: Oh God, anything.

HIM: What's she like? His wife looks quite tough.

HER: Suzanne? I think she's quite tough. I think she's given quite a tough time.

HIM: Is she?

HER: Yes.

HIM: So there with Charlotte and Willy Teale.

HER: Yep.

HIM: I don't know him at all.

HER: She's a very sexy number.

HIM: Quite. Bit worn out I reckon.

HER: (*laughs*)

HIM: Bit worn out, I reckon, darling. I wish we were going to be together tonight.

HER: I know. I want you to think of me after midnight. Are you staying up to see the New Year in?

HIM: You don't need to encourage me to think about you. I have done nothing else for the last three months. Hello.

HER: Debbie says you are going to go through a transformation soon.

HIM: That I am?

HER: Yes. She says you are going to go through bits and pieces and I've got to help you through them. All Libra men, yeh. I said great. I can do something back for him. He's done so much for me.

HIM: She doesn't know my name does she?

HER: No, no. But we are quite keen to know when you were born. (*laughs*)

HIM: Are you? Squidgy, laugh some more. I love it when I hear you laughing. It makes me really happy when you laugh. Do you know I am happy when you are happy?

HER: I know you are.

HIM: And I cry when you cry.

HER: I know. So sweet. The rate we are going we won't need any dinner on Tuesday.

HIM: No I won't need any dinner actually. Just seeing you will be all I need. I can't wait for Ken to ring. And of course I will be thinking of you after 12 o'clock. I don't need any reasons to even think about you. Mark Davis kept saying to me yesterday: 'Of course you haven't had a girlfriend for ages.' 'What's the transfer list looking like?' He said: 'What about that woman in Berkshire.'

HER: Oh God.

HIM: And I said: 'No, Mark, I haven't been there for months.' He said: 'Have you got any other transferees in mind?' I said

'No.' We then went off on a walk and we started talking about Guy Morrison and was telling me how extraordinarily Guy had behaved towards me at Julia's party. And he said: 'Oh well. The only reason he probably didn't want to speak to you was because you had been speaking to you-know-who for a long time.' And so I just didn't sort of say anything. And I said: 'I suppose that is my fatal mistake really.' And Mark said: 'You spend too much time with her' and that was that. And then he said: 'I wonder whom she's going to end up with.' And I said: 'What do you mean?' And he said: 'Well she must be long, long overdue for an affair.' And I said: 'I've no idea. I don't talk to her about it. And I have only spoken to her twice since I saw her anyway.' And that was it, I just kill every conversation stone dead now. It's much the best way. Darling, how did I get on to that. Oh, the transfer list? So I said: 'No there was no list drawn up at the moment. And even less likely there was anybody on it.' I tell you, darling, I couldn't. I was just thinking again about you going all jellybags, and you mustn't.

HER: I haven't for a day.

HIM: You haven't?

HER: For a day.

HIM: For a day. Why? Because you have no other people in the room. There were only three of us there last night. Four, actually. Mark, Antonia, their nanny and myself, and that was it. And I definitely didn't fancy the nanny, who was a 23-year-old overweight German.

HER: Did you just get my hint about Tuesday night. I think you just missed it. Think what I said.

HIM: No.

HER: I think you have missed it.

HIM: No, you said: 'At this rate, we won't want anything to eat.'

HER: Yes.

HIM: Yes I know. I got there.

HER: Oh well, you didn't exactly put the flag out.

HIM: What, the surrender flag?

HER: Oh.

HIM: Squidge, I was just going over it. I didn't think I had made too much reference to it.

HER: Oh bugger.

HIM: I don't think I made too much reference to it. Because the more you think about it, the more you worry about it.

HER: All right. I haven't been thinking about a lot else.

HIM: Haven't you?

HER: No.

HIM: Well, I can tell you, that makes two... I went to this agonizing tea party last night. You know, all I want to do is get in my car and drive around the country talking to you.

HER: Thanks. (*laughter*)

HIM: That's all I want to do, darling. I just want to see you and be with you. That's what's going to be such bliss, being back in London.

HER: I know.

HIM: I mean, it can't be a regular future, darling, and I understand that but it would be nice if you are at least next door, within knocking distance.

HER: Yes.

HIM: What's that noise?

HER: The television, drowning my conversation.

HIM: Can you turn it down?

HER: No.

HIM: Why?

HER: Because it's covering my conversation.

HIM: All right ... I got there Tuesday night, don't worry. I got there. I can tell you the feeling's entirely mutual. Ummmm, Squidgy.... what else? It's just like unwinding now. I am just letting my heartbeat come down again now. I had the most amazing dream about us last night. Not physical, nothing to do with that.

HER: That makes a change.

HIM: Darling. It's just that we were together an awful lot of time and we were having dinner with some people. It was the most extraordinary dream, very vivid, because I woke up in the morning and I remembered all aspects of it. All bits of it.

I remembered sort of what you were wearing and what you had said. It was so strange, very strange and very lovely too.

HER: I don't want to get pregnant.

HIM: Darling, it's not going to happen.

HER: (*half laugh*)

HIM: All right.

HER: Yah.

HIM: Don't look at it like that. It's not going to happen. You won't get pregnant.

HER: I watched 'EastEnders' today and one of the main characters had a baby. They thought it was her husband's but it was by another man. (*burst of laughter*)

HIM: (*moaning*) Squidgy...kiss me. (*sounds of kisses by him and her*) Oh God! It's wonderful, isn't it? This sort of feeling. Don't you like it?

HER: I love it.

HIM: Um.

HER: I love it.

HIM: Isn't it absolutely wonderful? I haven't had it for years. I feel about 21 again.

HER: Well you're not. You're 33.

HIM: I know.

HER: Pushing up the daisies soon, right?

HIM: No more remarks like that. It was an agonizing tea yesterday with, er, do you know Simon Prior-Palmer?

HER: I know who you mean, yes.

HIM: And his wife Julia. Julia Lloyd-Jordan, you must remember her?

HER: Yes, I dooo.

HIM: Do you?

HER: God, yes ... who was she after – Eddie?

HIM: I can't remember. She lived in that flat in Cadogan Gardens, didn't she, with Lucy Manners?

HER: Yes, she did.

HIM: She lost weight. You lived there for a while, didn't you?

HER: No, it's the wrong place. (*could be saying an address like Feine or Alleyn Place*)

HIM: Oh! But the umm ... Honestly, I loved going to [?]. I mean, they've got quite a nice house and things. And there was quite a nice Australian/Polish friend of theirs who was staying. And God! Simon. He's 38 years old, but honestly he behaves older than my father. I cannot believe it. I find it so exhausting when there's people that age. They behave as if they're 50.

HER: I know.

HIM: Anyway, we did time there. And that was it. We got back. A very quiet dinner. Mark was sort of exhausted from last night. And that was it really. He was talking about ... hunting gets you gripped, doesn't it?

HER: It does.

HIM: I mean, he drove six hours yesterday.

HER: (*laughter*) My drive was two-and-a-half to three.

HIM: He's now talking about both ways. He drives three hours from Hungerford. He was hunting with – can't remember who he was with – oh yes – the Belvoir yesterday.

HER: The Belvoir, umm.

HIM: That was three hours there and three hours back.

HER: God.

HIM: And he'd done the same on Wednesday to the Quorn.

HER: How wonderful.

HIM: I know. Darling. Um! More. It's just like sort of ... um ...

HER: (*interrupts*) Playing with yourself ...

HIM: What?

HER: (*giggling*) Nothing.

HIM: No I'm not actually.

HER: (*giggles*) I said, it's just LIKE ... Just like ...

HIM: Playing with yourself.

HER: Yes.

HIM: Not quite as nice. Not quite as nice. I haven't played with myself actually. Not for a full 48 hours.

HER: (*giggles*)

HIM: Not for a full 48 hours. (*funny voice*) Pause. Umm. Tell me some more. How was your lunch?

268

HER: It wasn't great.

HIM: Wasn't it?...When are the Waterhouses turning up?

HER: Next Thursday, I think.

HIM: Oh I thought they were coming today.

HER: No, Thursday.

HIM: To hold on to you, I've gone back to another point about your mother-in-law, no grandmother-in-law, great-grandmother-in-law, no your grandmother-in-law. I think next time you just want to either outstare her and that's easy.

HER: No, no.

HIM: It's not staring...

HER: No, no, listen, wait a minute. It's affection, affection, it's definitely affection. It's sort of...it's not hostile any way.

HIM: Oh is it?

HER: So...She's sort of fascinated by me but doesn't quite know how to unravel it, no.

HIM: How interesting. I'm sorry. I thought, darling, when you told me about her you meant hostile.

HER: No, I'm all right.

HIM: I miss you, Squidgy.

HER: So do it.

HIM: I haven't spoken to you for 28 hours. I've thought of nothing else.

HER: I know, I know.

HIM: Oh, that's all right. If it's friendly, then it doesn't matter.

HER: It's all right, I can deal with that.

HIM: My stars said nothing about 1990 – it was all very sort of terribly general.

HER: Fine...but it's definitely him WITHIN the marriage.

HIM: Right.

HER: It's not ...

HIM: (*interrupting*) Did you see the *News of the World*?

HER: No.

HIM: He's got to start loving you.

HER: Yes, I saw that. Yeh. She...

HIM: Did you? I thought: 'Well there's not much chance of that.'

HER: No. I know. I know. But, um, definitely she said I am doing nothing. I am just having a wonderful, successful, well-awaiting year.

HIM: A sort of matriarchal figure.

HER: I know. She said anything you want, you can get next year.

HIM: You should read the *People*, darling. There's a very good picture of you.

HER: Arr.

HIM: Oh no, it's ... where is there a good picture? In the *Express*, was there? I think there's a ... wearing that pink, very smart pink top. That excellent pink top.

HER: Oh, I know, I know.

HIM: Do you know the one I mean?

HER: I know.

HIM: Very good. Shit hot, actually.

HER: Shit hot. (*laughs*)

HIM: Shit hot.

HER: Umm. Fergie said to me today that she had lunch with Nigel Havers the other day and all he could talk about was you. And I said: 'Fergie, oh how awful for you.' And she said: 'Don't worry, it's the admiration club.' A lot of people talk to her about me, which she can't help...her at all.

HIM: I tell you, darling, she is desperate to tag on to your coat tails.

HER: Well, she can't.

HIM: No, she absolutely can't. Now you have to make that quite clear ...

HER: If you want to be like me, you have got to suffer.

HIM: Oh! Squidgy.

HER: Yah. You have to. And then you get what you ...

HIM: Get what you want.

HER: No. Get what you deserve, perhaps.

HIM: Yes. Such as a second-hand-car dealer. (*laughs*)

HER: Yes, I know. (*laughs*)

HIM: (*laughs*)...Do you know, as we go into 1990, honey, I can't imagine, you know, what it was that brought us two together on that night.

270

HER: No, I know.

HIM: And let's make full use of it.

HER: I know.

HIM: Full use of it. Funnily enough, it doesn't hold any sort of terror, any fright for me at all.

HER: (*interuption: knock at the door*) Hang on. It's OK, come in, please. Yes, it's OK – come in. What is it?... 'Ah. I'd love some salad, just some salad with yoghurt, like when I was ill in bed. That would be wonderful. About 8 o'clock. Then everybody can go, can't they?'

MALE VOICE: 'Bring it up on a tray?'

HER: 'That would be gr... Eddie, Edward will come down and get it.'

MALE VOICE. 'We'll bring it up.'

HER: 'All right, bring it up. That'll be great, Paul. No, just salad will be great, Paul. Thanks, Paul.'

HIM: How much weight have you lost?

HER: Why?

HIM: Darling, I am sure lettuce leaves aren't going to keep you strong. You'll run out of energy driving to London.

HER: I am nine-and-a-half.

HIM: Are you? Are you? Nine-and-a-half. So are you staying in tonight?

HER: I am, because I am babysitting. I don't want to go out.

HIM: Oh, I see. So is he going?

HER: Yes. He doesn't know that I'm not yet. I haven't told him that yet.

HIM: I was going to say, darling. That was shitty. You can't face another night like last Friday, absolutely right. But you are there, darling.

HER: I know.

HIM: 1990 is going to be fine.

HER: Yes, but isn't it exciting.

HIM: Really exciting.

HER: Debbie said, I'm so excited for you. It's going to be lovely to watch ...

HIM: I don't know, I've been feeling sick all day.

HER: Why?

HIM: I don't know. I just feel sick about the whole thing. I mean wonderful. I mean straight-through real passion and love and all the good things.

HER: Becky said it would be all OK, didn't she? The most fulfilling year yet.

HIM: You don't need to worry, do you?

HER: She's never questioned someone's mental state, or anything like that.

HIM: What, his?

HER: Yes. Nobody has ever thought about his mind. They've always thought about other things.

HIM: ... something very interesting which said that serious astrologers don't think that he will ever make it.

HER: Yah.

HIM: And becomes a [?].

HER: And Becky also said this person is married to someone in great power who will never make the ultima ... or whatever the word is.

HIM: Absolutely. Oh Squidgy, I love you, love you, love you, love you.

HER: You are the nicest person in the whole wide world.

HIM: Pardon?

HER: Nicest person in the whole wide world.

HIM: Well darling, you are are to me too. Sometimes.

HER: (laughs) What do you mean, sometimes?

HIM: Sometimes. Umm. I haven't really got anything else. I got up quite late, went for a walk this morning, went for a walk this afternoon. Had lunch. I only got angry because Mark gave the nanny too much wine and she was incapable of helping at lunch.

HER: I love it.

HIM: He's a rogue, Mark David [?].

HER: Oh, Wills is coming. Sorry.

HIM: Are you going?

HER: No, no.

HIM: He's such a rogue, darling. He's the man you met [?]. I remember. I know. but I didn't recognize him.

HIM: He's incorrigible. He's really lovely.

HER: Would I like him?

HIM: He's a sort of social gossiper in a way. He loves all that, Mark. He's got a very comfortable life, you know. He hunts a lot . . . He's very, very successful.

HER: He's got the pennies?

HIM: He's got lots of pennies. He calls all his horses Business or The Office. Because when people ring up and he's hunting midweek, his secretary says: 'I'm terribly sorry, he's away on business.'

HER. Oh! (*laughter*) It's great to hear it. It's wonderful.

HIM: But, umm . . . an incredible, sort of argument last night about subservient women in marriage.

HER: Well, you're an expert. You know about them.

HIM: Umm?

HER: You know about them.

HIM: I kept very very low, very quiet actually. I could think, darling, of nothing but you. Nothing. I thought, well I should be talking to her now. You know, it's five past 11.

HER: I know.

HIM: It's our normal talking hour.

HER: I know.

HIM: You don't mind it, darling, when I want to talk to you so much?

HER: No. I LOVE it. (*enthusiastically*) Never had it before. I've never had it before.

HIM: Darling, it's so nice being able to help you.

HER: You do. You'll never know how much. You'll never know how much.

HIM: Oh, I will, darling. I just feel so close to you, so wrapped up in you. I'm wrapping you up, protecting.

HER: Yes please. Yes please . . . Do you know. That bloody Bishop. Do you know, that bloody Bishop. I said to him . . . I know . . .

273

HIM: What's he called? Is he called...

HER: The Bishop of Norwich...

HIM: What's his name...

HER: Err. I don't know. He said I want you to tell me how you talk to people who are ill or dying. What's the er...how how do you cope?

HIM: He wanted to learn. He was so hopeless at it himself.

HER: I began to wonder after I'd spoken to him. I said: 'I'm just myself.'

HIM: They can't get to grips that, underneath, there is such a beautiful person in you. They can't think that it isn't cluttered up by this idea of untold riches.

HER: I know. He kept wittering about one must never think how good one is at one's job. There's always something you can learn around the next corner. I said: 'Well, if people know me, they know I'm not like that.'

HIM: Yes. Absolutely. Absolutely right. So did you give him a hard time?

HER: I did, actually. In the end I said: I know this sounds crazy, but I've lived before. He said, how do you know that? I said I know because I'm a wise old thing.

HIM: Oh! Darling Squidge, did you? Very brave thing to say to him, actually. Very.

HER: It was, wasn't it?

HIM: Very. Full marks. 99 out of a hundred.

HER: I said: 'Also I'm aware that people I have loved and have died and are in the spirit world look after me.' He looked horrified. I thought: 'If he's the Bishop, he should say that sort of thing.'

HIM: One of those horoscopes referred to your, to Cancerians turning to less materialistic and more spiritual things. Did you see that?

HER: No I didn't. No.

HIM: That's rather sad, actually. Umm, I don't really like many of those bishops especially.

HER: Well, I felt very uncomfortable.

HIM: They are a funny old lot.

HER: Well, I wore my heart on my sleeve.

HIM: They are the ones, when they've got a five-year-old sitting between them, their hands meet. Don't you remember that wonderful story? Do you remember that.

HER: Yes, yes.

HIM: Gosh, it made my father laugh so much. Go on, darling. When you wear your heart on your sleeve ...

HER: No, with that Bishop, I said: 'I understand people's suffering, people's pain, more than you will ever know yourself and he said, well, that's obvious by what you are doing for the AIDs. I said, it's not only AIDs. It's anyone who suffers. I can smell them a mile away.

HIM: What did he say?

HER: Nothing. He just went quiet. He changed on to the subject about toys. And I thought: Ah! Defeated you.

HIM: Did you? Marvellous, darling. Did you chalk up a little victory?

HER: Yes, I did.

HIM: Did you, darling? Waving a little flag in your head.

HER: Yes.

HIM: How marvellous. You ought to do that more often. That flag ought to get bigger.

HER: Yes, my surrender flag. (*cackle*)

HIM: No, not quite.

HIM: Oh God.

HIM: You haven't got one, have you?

HER: Yes.

HIM: What, a big one?

HER: Well, medium sized.

HIM: Is it? Oh, darling. Well, don't wave it too much...

HER: No.

HIM: Squidge. Sitting in this layby, you know, you can understand how frightened people feel when they break down in the dark.

HER: I'm sure.

HIM: I suddenly thought someone could have shot at me from the undergrowth. Or someone suddenly tried to get into the car. I always lock the door when I stop for that reason.

275

HER: Gosh! That's very thoughtful. That's very good of you.

HIM: Umm. Darling, how are the boys?

HER: They are very well.

HIM: Are they? Having a good time?

HER: Yes, very happy. Yah. Seem to be.

HIM: That's nice. Have you been looking after them today?

HER: Well, I've been with them a lot, yes.

HIM: Has he been looking after them?

HER: Oh no, not really. My God, you know ...

HIM: Have you seen him at all today, apart from lunch?

HER: I have. We went out to tea together. It's just so difficult, so complicated. He makes my life real, real torture, I've decided.

HIM: Tell me more.

HER: But the distancing will be because I go out and – I hate the word – conquer the world. I don't mean that, I mean I'll go out and do my bit in the way I know how and I leave him behind. That's what I see happening.

HIM: Yah! Did you talk in the car on the way back?

HER: Yes, but nothing in particular. He said he didn't want to go out tonight. You know, that sort of thing.

HIM: Did you have the kids with you?

HER: No.

HIM: What, you just went by yourselves?

HER: No, they were behind us.

HIM: Oh, were they? Ummm. How did he enjoy it?

HER: I don't know. He didn't really pass comment.

HIM: No. Oh, Squidgy.

HER: Mmm.

HIM: Kiss me please. (*sound of kisses*) Do you know what I'm going to be imagining I'm doing tonight, at about 12 o'clock. Just holding you so close to me. It'll have to be delayed action for 48 hours.

HER: (*giggles*)

HIM: Fast forward.

HER: Fast forward.

HIM: Gosh! I hope Ken doesn't say no.

276

HER: I doubt he will.

HIM: Do you?

HER: He's coming down early on Tuesday and I'm going to tell him I've got to go back on Tuesday night. And I've got to leave and be back for lunch on Wednesday. But I can do that.

HIM: You can?

HER: And I shall tell people I'm going for acupuncture and my back being done.

HIM: (*hysterical laugh*) Squidge, cover them footsteps.

HER: I surely will do.

HIM: I think it's all right. I think those footsteps are doing all right.

HER: Yes.

HIM: Actually, from both points of view. Umm. I'm going to set off actually. Hold on. God. It's hot in here. It's like an oven.

HER: Well, I've got to kiss my small ones.

HIM: Oh! No, darling, No...

HER: I've got to.

HIM: No, Squidgy, I don't want you to go. Can you bear with me for five minutes more?

HER: Yes.

HIM: Just five.

HER: What have you got on?

HIM: I've got the new jeans I bought yesterday.

HER: Good.

HIM: Green socks. White and pink striped shirt.

HER: How very nice.

HIM: A dark apple-green V-neck jersey.

HER: Yes.

HIM: I'm afraid I'm going to be let down by the shoes.

HER: Go on, then. (*giggles*)

HIM: You can guess.

HER: Your brown ones.

HIM: What?

HER: Your brown ones...(*shrieks*) No...those black ones.

HIM: No, I haven't got the black ones, darling. The black ones I would not be wearing. I only wear the black ones with my suit.

277

HER: Good. Well, get rid of them.

HIM: I have got those brown suede ones on.

HER: Brown suede ones?

HIM: Those brown suede Guccis. (*laughs*)

HER: I know, I know.

HIM: The ones you hate.

HER: I just don't like the fact it's so obvious where they came from.

HIM: Di, nobody wears them any more.

(Cut off. Conversation reappears.)

HIM: I like those ordinary Italian things that last a couple of years, then I chuck them out. It was a sort of devotion to duty. I was seeking an identity when I bought my first pair of Guccis 12 years ago.

HER: Golly.

HIM: And I've still got them. Still doing me proud like.

HER: Good.

HIM: I'm going to take you up on that, darling. I will give you some money. You can go off and spend it for me.

HER: I WILL, yeh.

HIM: Will you? (*laughter*)

HER: I'm a connoisseur in that department.

HIM: Are you?

HER: Yes.

HIM: Well, you think you are.

HER: Well, I've decked people out in my time.

HIM: Who did you deck out? Not too many, I hope.

HER: James Hewitt. Entirely dressed him from head to foot, that man. Cost me a lot, that man. Cost me quite a bit.

HIM: I bet he did...At your expense?

HER: Yeh.

HIM: What, he didn't even pay you to do it?

HER: No.

HIM: God! What an ext...very extravagant, darling.

HER: Well, I am, aren't I? Anything that will make people happy.

HIM: No, you mustn't do it for that, darling, because YOU make people happy. It's what you give them ...

(Call breaks again, then returns)

HER: No, don't. You'll know, you'll know.
HIM: All right. But you always say that with an air of inevitability. (*giggles*) It will happen in six months' time. I'll suddenly get: 'Yes, James Who? (*giggles*) I don't think we've spoken before.'
HER: No.
HIM: I hope not. (*inaudible name*) Ummm. Well, darling, you can't imagine what pleasures I've got in store this evening.
HER: It's a big house, is it?
HIM: It's a nice house. Thirty people for dinner or something.
DI: God.
HIM: I know. Do you want me to leave the phone on?
HER: No, better not.
HIM: Why not?
HER: No, tomorrow morning.
HIM: I can't, I can't ... all right, tomorrow morning. Shall I give you a time to call me?
HER: Yes, well. I won't be around from 9.30 to 11.
HIM: You WON'T be?
HER: No.
HIM: From 9.30?
HER: Yes.
HIM: Why not?
HER: I'm going swimming with Fergie.
HIM: Are you? Are you taking the kiddies?
HER: Might well do.
HIM: You should do. It's good for you. Get them out. It gives you enormous sort of strength, doesn't it? Have the lovebugs around you.
HER: I know, I know.
HIM: Beautiful things pampering their mother.
HER: Quite right.

HIM: That's what she wants. I think you should take them, darling. At least you are not battling with the rest.
HER: No, I'm not.
HIM: Are you.

(Call breaks again, then resumes)

HER: I'd better, I'd better. All the love in the world and I'll speak to you tomorrow.
HIM: All right. If you can't get me in the morning ... you're impatient to go now.
HER: Well, I just feel guilty because I haven't done my other business.
HIM: Don't feel guilty. They'll be quite all ...

(Call breaks again, then resumes)

HIM: Just that I'll have to wait till Tuesday. All right.
HER: All right.
HIM: I'll buzz off and simply behave. I'll approach the evening with such enormous confidence now.
HER: Good.
HIM: And you, darling. Don't let it get you down.
HER: I won't, I won't.
HIM: All right.

FERGIEGATE

HER: ... and I'll be, erm, tonight I'll be here.
HIM: All right. Well I'll ring you later on when we get in.
HER: OK.
HIM: What time are you finishing this afternoon?
HER: No idea. Oh, I dunno. I'll be back here by five I should think.

HIM: All right. Well, I'll give you a ring later on.
HER: OK.
HIM: All right darling.
HER: All right. Well I hope it goes well today.
HIM: So do I.
HER: OK.
HIM: You [?] be good.
HER: Yah.
HIM: All right.
HER: OK.
HIM: Are you feeling any better?
HER: Yah. I'm just sort of disenchanted, really, I just want to run away and stay with mum in Argentina. Got to get away from everything. I just feel, I just want to run away. Preferably with you. but I can't do that. We're both chained to our stupid duties and ruining our lives together. But if that's what your family want then that's what they want. I've lost my spirit today. If they want to have another unhappy marriage they're going the right way about it.
HIM: (*pleading*) But darling, what have they done to make it unhappy?
HER: Well you've done it haven't you? You've told them that we've had a discussion, a heated discussion.
HIM: I didn't say we had a heated discussion.
HER: Well you did. You told them that we were in opposition about something. You thought it was a bad idea and just tell me if I'm going mad or not, that's what you probably said to her. Anyway, never mind, forget about it. Speak to you later OK, because it's now 10 to nine, I've got to get on and you have too.
HIM: All right darling.
HER: OK?
HIM: Yes darling.
HER: OK.
HIM: I love you.
HER: All right. Be good today.
HIM: I love you, darling.
HER: I love you too, Bunt [?].
HIM: OK, darling.